CAPTAIN JOHN SMITH

Captain John Smith

A SELECT EDITION OF HIS WRITINGS

EDITED BY KAREN ORDAHL KUPPERMAN

PUBLISHED FOR THE INSTITUTE OF

EARLY AMERICAN HISTORY AND CULTURE,

WILLIAMSBURG, VIRGINIA, BY THE

UNIVERSITY OF NORTH CAROLINA PRESS,

CHAPEL HILL & LONDON

The Institute of Early American History and Culture

is sponsored jointly by the College of William and Mary

and the Colonial Williamsburg Foundation.

Library of Congress Cataloging-in-Publication Data

Smith, John, 1580–1631.

[Selections. 1988]

Captain John Smith: a select edition of his writings / edited by
Karen Ordahl Kupperman.

p. cm.

Includes index.

ISBN 0-8078-1778-3 (alk. paper)

ISBN 0-8078-4208-7 (pbk.: alk. paper)

1. Virginia—History—Colonial period, ca. 1600–1775—Collected
works. 2. New England—History—Colonial period, ca. 1600–1775—
Collected works. 3. America—Discovery and exploration—English—
Collected works. I. Kupperman, Karen Ordahl, 1939–   .
II. Institute of Early American History and Culture
(Williamsburg, Va.) III. Title.

F229.S592   1988   87-21485

975.5′02—dc19   CIP

The paper in this book meets the guidelines for

permanence and durability of the Committee on

Production Guidelines for Book Longevity of the

Council on Library Resources.

92   91   5   4   3   2

PREFACE

JOHN SMITH deserves to be read. All those familiar with early American history think we know what Smith thought; his life has been reduced to a series of familiar catchphrases. His work is therefore slighted in favor of that of his reputedly more thoughtful contemporaries. A pleasant surprise is in store for anyone who picks up Captain Smith and reads him in some depth. His treatment of Virginia's founding and the process of settling among the Indians in an alien land is the best we have. He alone attempted to portray the complexity of Indian life and of the many-layered relationship between Americans and colonists, even looking beyond the confluence of short-range goals on both sides that led to initial trading relationships.

Smith has often been seen as a braggart, who wrote to magnify his own role in colonial affairs beyond all recognition. He dared to compare himself to Julius Caesar, who "wrote his owne Commentaries, holding it no lesse honour to write, than fight" (*Sea Grammar*, sig. A2^r; Barbour edition, III, 47). It is true that Smith reworked the same material in several books, and he became more insistent on the importance of his own role with each retelling, but each new work was also a milestone in Smith's continuing effort to work out a consistent philosophy of colonization. His final book, *Advertisements for the Unexperienced Planters of New England, or Any Where* (1631), presented a thoughtful and coherent picture of the future British Empire, the only such plan written at the time by an actor. John Smith richly repays time spent reading his works; his writing illuminates the history of New England as well as Virginia.

One of the personal benefits of preparing this edition of John Smith's writings has been the opportunity to work with the Institute of Early American History and Culture. Nicholas Canny, Philip Morgan, Thad Tate, and Alden Vaughan all gave me the benefit of their knowledge of Smith and the context in which he worked. Cynthia Carter Ayres has strengthened the manuscript in many ways. I was always conscious of following in the footsteps of great scholars. The text for this edition is taken from Philip L. Barbour's three-volume edition, *The Complete Works of Captain John Smith (1580–1631)*, published for the Institute by the University of North Carolina Press in 1986. Barbour knew Smith and his life better than anyone else. The edition was completed after his death by Alison and David Quinn, who command the field of early exploration and colonization, and who are the models for all editors of historical documents.

CONTENTS

ILLUSTRATIONS

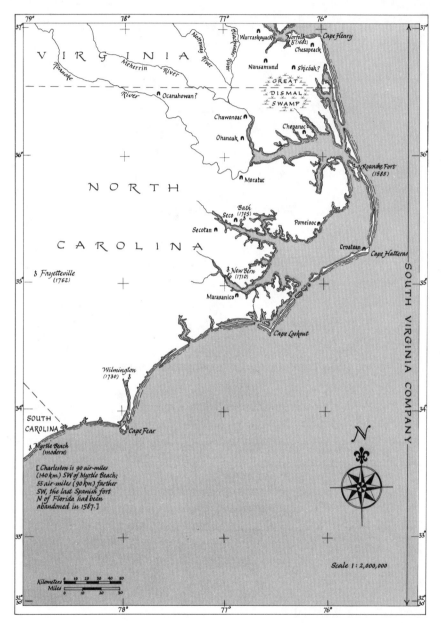

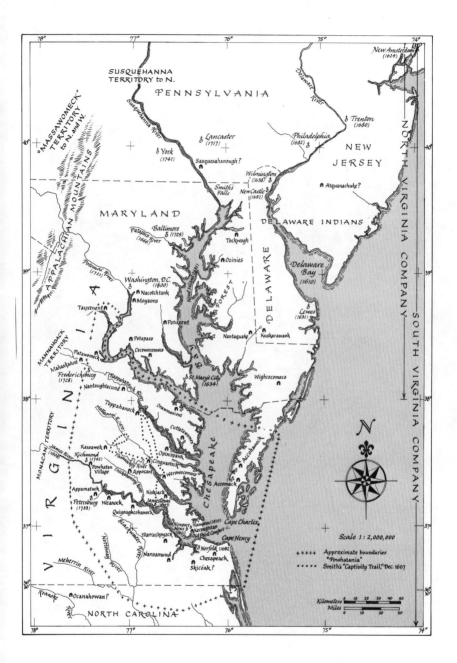

SUSQUEHANNA
TERRITORY to N.

P E N N S Y L V A N I A

New Amsterdam
(1624)

"MASSAWOMECK"
TERRITORY
to N. and W.

Delaware River

Trenton
(1680)

Lancaster
(1717)

Philadelphia
(1682)

NEW
JERSEY

York
(1741)

Sasquesahanough?

Atquanachuke?

Wilmington
(1638)

Smith's
Falls

New Castle
(1651)

MARYLAND

DELAWARE INDIANS

Patapso
River

Baltimore
(1729)

Tockwogh

A P P A L A C H I A N   M O U N T A I N S

Potomac River
(1721)

Ozinies

Delaware
Bay
(1610)

Washington, D.C.
(1800)

Nacotchtank

F O R E S T

Tauxenent

Moyaons

Lewes
(1631)

Patuxent

Nantaquake

Kiskarawaok

Wighcocomoco

MANNAHOACK
TERRITORY

Potapaco

Cecowocomoco

Patawomeck

Mahaskoad

Fredericksburg
(1728)

Rappahannock River

St. Mary's City
(1634)

Nantaughtacund

Toppahanock

Orawnament

Mattapony River

Cuttatawoman

D E L A W A R E

C H E S A P E A K E

Accohanock

V I R G I N I A

MONACAN TERRITORY

Rassawek
(1608)

James River

Richmond
(1742)

Powhatan
Village

Pamunkey River

Opiscapan

Cinquoateck

Accomack

N

Appocant

Werowocomoco

Appamatuck

Chickahominy River

Kiskiack

Petersburg
(1733)

Weanock

Jamestown
(1607)

Quiyoughcohanock

Blackwater River

Warrashoyack

Newport
News

Hampton (1610)

Kecoughtan

Old Point Comfort

Cape Charles

Scale 1:2,000,000

Nansamund

Nottoway River

Norfolk
(1682)

Cape Henry

++++ Approximate boundaries
"Powhatania"

Meherrin River

Chesapeack

Skicoak?

• • • • Smith's "Captivity Trail," Dec. 1607

Roanoke
River

Ocanahowan?

N O R T H   C A R O L I N A

Kilometers 0 10 20 30 40 50
Miles 0 10 20 30

NORTH VIRGINIA COMPANY

SOUTH VIRGINIA COMPANY

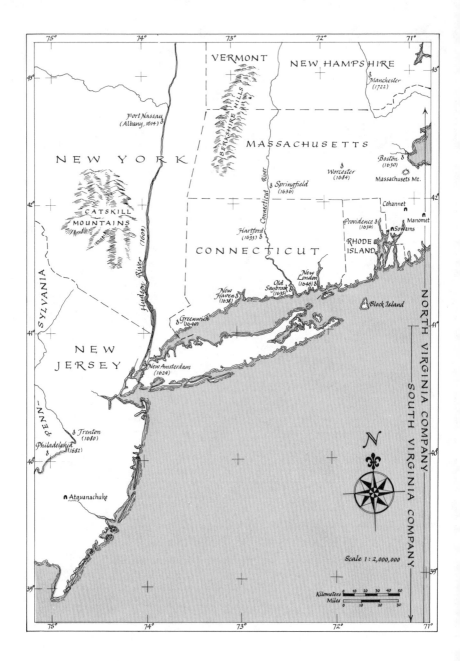

VERMONT

NEW HAMPSHIRE

Manchester
(1722)

Fort Nassau
(Albany, 1614)

NEW YORK

BERKSHIRE HILLS

MASSACHUSETTS

Boston
(1630)

Worcester
(1684)

Massachusets Mt.

Springfield
(1636)

Cohannet

CATSKILL
MOUNTAINS

Connecticut River

Providence
(1636)

Manomet

Sowams

Hartford
(1633)

CONNECTICUT

RHODE
ISLAND

Hudson River (1609)

New
London
(1646)

Old
Saybrook
(1635)

New
Haven
(1638)

Block Island

PENN
SYLVANIA

Greenwich
(1640)

NEW
JERSEY

New Amsterdam
(1624)

NORTH VIRGINIA COMPANY

SOUTH VIRGINIA COMPANY

Trenton
(1680)

Philadelphia
(1682)

N

Atquanachuke

Scale 1 : 2,000,000

Kilometers 0 10 20 30 40 50
Miles 0 10 20 30

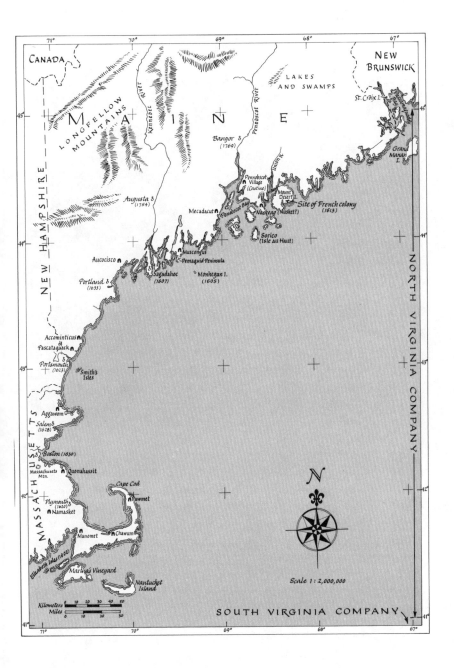

THE PORTRAICTUER OF CAPTAYNE IOHN SMITH / ADMIRALL OF NEW ENGLAND .

Æta 37
A° 1616

These are the Lines that shew thy Face; but those
That shew thy Grace and Glory, brighter bee :
Thy Faire-Discoueries and Fowle-Overthrowes
Of Salvages, much Civilliz'd by thee
Best shew thy Spirit; and to it Glory Wyn;
So, thou art Brasse without, but Golde within .

Capt. John Smith. Courtesy of the Houghton Library, Harvard University.

INTRODUCTION

No one can read Capt. John Smith and remain neutral about the man. Most historical characters lose over the centuries their capacity to inspire outrage or loyalty, and historians can calmly debate the wisdom of their policies and the motives behind them. Smith's case is different; he continues to live not only as an actor and a writer, but also as a *personality*. Historians hotly debate whether he was right about what the Virginia Company should or should not have been doing; but behind the heated academic debate, scholars also clearly like or scorn Smith. After reading his work, we feel we know him as a human being. Though most seventeenth-century people seem foreign, the 350 years that separate us from Smith seem to evaporate. He is a man one can understand; his many disappointments come across the page as fresh wounds. Despite his boastful and aggressive manner, he constantly revealed his vulnerability to slights and reverses. Almost against our will, we may find ourselves cheering his successes and feeling his pain.

John Smith's life was filled with irony and contradiction. He was a self-made man, but he always depended on the patronage of noble men and women. He claimed to have made his own fate, yet nothing would have been possible for him without that patronage. His ability to attract the eye of those with money and favors to bestow began early in his life. Born in 1580 in Lincolnshire, the son of a substantial farmer, he received a grammar school education, partly because the local leading man, Peregrine Bertie, Lord Willoughby, thought he showed promise. This education, along with the habits of reading that it instilled, was an important precondition for the life John Smith was to lead.

Most English families, even those who could afford servants of their own, sent their children off to work as servants or apprentices at about the age of fourteen or fifteen. This form of education ensured that children were still under family government but avoided the parent-child tensions of adolescence. Smith was apprenticed to a merchant in the nearby seaport of King's Lynn when he was fifteen. He found the life of a merchant too dull and left it after a few months to seek adventure; the recent deaths of his parents had released him from parental control.

He was soon in the Low Countries. Like many Englishmen, he fought to help the Protestant Dutch free themselves from the tyranny of the Roman Catholic Philip II of Spain. This warfare was a brutal education shared by many who later went to the colonies. After three years, Smith left the temporarily lulled fighting and traveled through France, sought work in Scotland, and spent time back home in England. Soon he returned to Europe, but professing his dislike for wars in which Christians slaughtered one another, he decided to take on the conflict at the frontiers of Europe, where Christians met the infidel. He entered service in the Austrian army fighting against the Turks in Hungary.

Smith describes himself as having been an invaluable aide, filled with ingenious schemes that time and again helped the Christian forces to turn back the Turks; his advice and courage led to rapid promotion and eventually his own coat of arms, an accomplishment of which the yeoman's son was very proud. Ultimately, though, his army was defeated and Smith captured to be taken into slavery in Turkey. Here again, a highborn patron stepped in. Smith became the property of a noblewoman, whose name he rendered as Charatza Tragabigzanda, and they became friends through their shared knowledge of Italian. She sent him to her brother, possibly to be trained for the Turkish imperial service; Smith, misunderstanding, saw his treatment as sadism and seized the opportunity to kill Charatza's brother and escape. From there he traveled to Russia and then through Europe and North Africa before returning to London. At the age of twenty-six, he was a seasoned veteran at survival in alien lands when the Virginia Company, forming its first colonization venture, was looking for apt men to lead it.

John Smith's experience of colonization was shared by no one else; his perspective on it is unique. Colonization offered Smith a chance to rise to the top through sheer energy and ability; publishing gave him access to public attention and lasting fame. Smith was one of the first to see the possibilities for self-promotion in the explosion of book and pamphlet literature designed to interest people in colonies; he virtually invented the autobiographical form in order to present his own version of events. Many people at the time and since have felt that he wrote too much about himself, but Smith knew no one else would tell his story or hammer home his points.

Smith has often been the subject of ridicule because his work frequently sounds like the effusions of the barroom braggart. Not only did his writing center on himself and his exploits, but also his stories grew as they were told and retold in his later books, always in the direction of making his role more important and the stakes for which he was contending higher. Until recently, his work has been dismissed, except for passages that could be corroborated by the work of others. Such skepticism has been overturned, and from an unexpected source. Careful checking of his narrative of the wars against the Turks has demonstrated that Smith was a reliable witness; many of the places and characters, once adjustment is made for Smith's spellings, can be identified. Moreover, work by ethnohistorians on the Algonquians of eastern North America has made many of his descriptions of Indian life and culture seem more realistic; he is now considered an important source on those cultures. Geographers also recognize his contribution; his are the earliest well-defined maps of Chesapeake Bay and New England. In a sense, then, the scholars have caught up with Smith.

Smith wrote within a recognized literary tradition, amending it to make it his own. In order to encourage colonization and exploration, several men had written compilations, usually running to many volumes, of letters, diaries, and books about foreign voyages. Richard Hakluyt's *The Principall Navigations, Voiages and Discoveries of the English Nation*, published in 1589 and, in a new and larger edition, in 1598–1600, was one of the earliest and best. Hakluyt devoted his life to gathering information and to interesting important people in possible ventures. The man who thought of himself as Hakluyt's successor was John Smith's friend Samuel Purchas, who published several multivolume collections, including *Hakluytus Posthumus or Purchas His Pilgrimes* in 1625. This work runs to twenty volumes in its modern edition.

Smith was writing in the same tradition as these men, but with one major difference: he had been on the ground and could speak more authoritatively than any mere scholar. Smith wove together his own experiences and the writings of others to create his great book, *The Generall Historie of Virginia, New-England, and the Summer Isles*,[1] pub-

---

1. The Summer Isles was a contemporary name for Bermuda, in honor of Sir George Somers, commander of a Virginia-bound fleet that was shipwrecked there in 1609. Since Bermuda, unlike the mainland colonies, was frost free, the name involved one of the puns that the English loved.

lished in 1624. Though he borrowed freely from the writings of others, the careful reader can see him intervening on every page to correct, augment, or admonish his sources. He shaped all the material to be his own; the constant voice is his. Judging by the list of people who wrote congratulatory verses for his works, he moved in London literary circles once his chief occupation became writing. Apparently he enjoyed a degree of acceptance in that world that he never achieved among the backers of colonization. Smith's later inclusion of stirring adventures such as his rescue by Pocahontas may have been in response to the stimulus of fellow writers who led him away from the goal of the plain unvarnished tale toward that of literary success.

Smith wrote to "save" the colonies from those who had mishandled them; his *Generall Historie* was written as the royal government was investigating the Virginia Company's actions preparatory to revoking the company's charter. He also wrote to establish his own reputation. He compared himself to Julius Caesar, another military leader who wrote commentaries on his own exploits. Much of what Smith wrote is extremely confusing, particularly his accounts of daily life while he was in America. When he was being self-consciously literary, his prose often became very effective, for example when he presented his dialogue with Powhatan about what the coming of the Europeans would mean. In his writings as in his actions, Smith never just followed the conventions. He created words or invented imaginative new uses for old words to convey a lively sense of reality. The *Oxford English Dictionary*, which chronicles the changing English language, often cites John Smith as the first user of a word, or as one who adapted or changed usage. His pride in his work can be seen in the final sentence appended to many of his books: "John Smith writ this with his owne hand."

C OLONIZATION MEANT great opportunities for new men, because no one in early seventeenth-century England knew how it was to be done. No one even knew for sure what colonies might accomplish. Such confusion offered Smith, a man uniquely experienced at surviving in strange cultures, his chance to command. As he never tired of pointing out, he was the sole figure in the early colonies who held office because of what he knew rather than who he was. In 1606, when the Virginia Company was composing the council for its projected colony, John Smith, recently returned from his adventures in Turkey, eastern Europe, and North Africa, was selected for the experience he would bring to that body. All others were "natural" leaders of high social rank.

Captain Smith's first book, *A True Relation of Such Occurrences and Accidents of Noate as Hath Hapned in Virginia*, was actually a long letter he wrote after the Jamestown colony's disastrous first winter, which saw the population fall from over one hundred to thirty-eight. The first Roanoke colony, planted two decades before by Sir Walter Ralegh, had been abandoned after a much less disappointing record, so it was essential to explain such dramatic failure and, more important, to convince the Virginia Company in London that the colony could succeed. In order to accomplish both tasks, Smith had to formulate a theory of colonization, including a model of how a settlement should be staffed and governed, an estimate of how much support should be necessary before it began to pay its way, and a set of reasonable expectations for returns from America. This is the task he assumed as he reworked his Virginia experiences in two books published in 1612, four years after the *True Relation*, which are collectively known as *A Map of Virginia*, Parts I and II; he continued to work at his model of colonization throughout the rest of his life. Other men developed theories of colonization, but as Smith constantly reminded his readers, none had his experience.

The most basic problem was management of the colonists, most of whom Smith considered unfit for the task of building a settlement in the wilderness. This problem was closely related to the general lack of consensus in England about what a colony should be expected to do. The Virginia Company sent large numbers of gentlemen with the retainers they considered necessary to life, perfumers and jewelers to develop the luxury products the company assumed, or at least hoped, would quickly be forthcoming, and to fill the colony's needs for manual labor, "the scum of the earth." As Smith saw it, the first two groups made their presence felt mainly by getting in the way and demanding more than their fair share of the colony's scanty resources, and the manual laborers presented constant problems of control. Smith relied on the few solid, experienced men. He contrasted their contribution, through which "the labour of twentie or thirtie of the best onely preserved in Christianitie by their industry, the idle livers of neare two hundred of the rest" (p. 74), with the whining of the inexperienced who fell into despair when they found no gold for the picking and no taverns or feather beds for their comfort. As Smith saw it, founding settlements in America offered enormous opportunities to men of "great spirit," but only terror and misery for the weak. Since most of the colonists were weak, they had to be forced to do what was necessary.

The Virginia Company tried a bold experiment in designing a government for the new colony. Rather than impose a hierarchy entirely in London, they permitted the settlers some flexibility. The company designated a council whose names were in a sealed box to be opened at sea. Those selected were then to choose a president from among themselves. When the box was opened, the gentlemen colonists found that the company had taken the unprecedented step of naming a man of modest family, John Smith. Their chagrin was compounded by the fact that Smith was already under sentence of death for mutiny; he had begun early his habit of speaking his mind regardless of whom he offended. The chains had now to be removed and Smith made one of the governors. But he was not to get his chance to assume the presidency until all his "betters" were either dead or disabled. In the months before he assumed control, he watched the colony destroy itself through mismanagement. He resolved that everything would be different once he took over.

Capt. John Smith is famous for his "he who does not work shall not eat" policy; he wrote with relish of how he put even the gentlemen to work felling trees. During his presidency, snug houses and secure fortifications were built, wells of fresh water were dug, and the colonists, who had been dying at an alarming rate, actually survived. He wrote that many found they enjoyed the work, though the soft hands of the gentlemen initially were so blistered that he had to institute an evening discipline of a mug of cold water poured down the sleeve for every oath uttered that day. Smith had discovered what psychologists now know: that enforced activity, and the sense of purpose it engenders, renders people healthier, especially in disorienting situations such as America, three thousand miles from home, must have been for the inexperienced colonists.

The colonists' sense of disorientation was accentuated by the enormous gap between the presumed superiority of European technology and their own inability, using that technology, to accomplish much. They quickly discovered that even men skilled in husbandry or mineralogy were quite helpless in this strange environment, whose demands and opportunities differed so drastically from England's. The Virginia Company had promised to supply the colony from home, but given the uncertainties of ocean voyages and English domestic concerns, only fools would have counted on that source alone. The lesson of the final Roanoke colony, abandoned for three years when England faced the threat of Spanish invasion, was in everyone's mind. Therefore, the colonists had to learn to cope for themselves. Their natural tendency was to huddle together in the fort at Jamestown, but Smith knew that this would be self-defeating in the long run and that in the short run such behavior produced the strange apathy and despair that, combined with disease and malnutrition, sapped the colonists' will to live.[2]

Smith made the kind of bold stroke possible only for him. He built forts along the James River, which had the effect of getting the colonists away from the disease-ridden environment of Jamestown. He dispersed many of the men to live among the true experts, the Indians, to learn as much as they could about the resources, particularly foods, of the region. He later boasted that, while he was president, his settlers lived for ten months solely on what the country provided.

Smith is interesting partly because he was not frozen into one point of view; he fervently believed in the superiority of English culture, yet he acknowledged Indian command of the American environment and sought to learn from them. He included long descriptions of Indian foods, both gathered and raised, and their uses and warned that some deceptively attractive plants could be dangerous if not processed under Indian guidance. Like many colonists, he was particularly impressed by the tremendous yield and versatility of Indian corn, far superior to any English grain. The colonists grew it by preference, but to do so required attentive study of Indian women, whose province was agriculture. Smith's long description of corn culture stresses their laborious care.

John Smith realized that relations with the Indians held the key to English survival in America. Not only must the colonists learn from the Americans, but they must also establish a relationship that would allow settlers to move freely about the country if the plantation was to develop the economic base necessary to its continued support from England. Smith was not really interested in the ethics of colonization;

2. See Carville V. Earle, "Environment, Disease, and Mortality in Early Virginia," in Thad W. Tate and David L. Ammerman, eds., *The Chesapeake in the Seventeenth Century: Essays on Anglo-American Society* (Chapel Hill, N.C., 1979), 96–125, and Karen Ordahl Kupperman, "Apathy and Death in Early Jamestown," *Journal of American History*, LXVI (1979), 24–40.

for him survival was an absolute value, self-evidently justified. Like most of his contemporaries, he believed that in human relationships one side always dominated; that was simply a fact of nature. He was determined that, however unequal the odds, the English must dominate the Algonquians of Chesapeake Bay. Here is Smith at his most controversial; he viewed the Indians much as he viewed his own men. They must be disciplined and controlled or they would bring ruin on the English settlements. He ridiculed the Virginia Company's call for tender treatment of the Indians, believing that it would be interpreted as weakness, which could only lead to contempt.

The first step, Smith believed, was to learn enough of the Indians' language to carry on trade and diplomacy. Nothing so clearly demonstrates the seventeenth-century English view of human relations, particularly the treatment of the "lower orders" (whether English or Indian), than the way this was accomplished. Smith followed standard practice in leaving English boys, sent to Virginia as servants, with various Indian communities to learn native languages and customs. These boys, often exchanged as pawns for Indians who went to live with the English on similar grounds, were retrieved as and if it became convenient. Everyone was expected to serve the primary goal of establishing a thriving English plantation; that the Indians had not elected to be part of the experiment was irrelevant in Smith's view.

Smith explored the regions around Jamestown, partly to gather corn for the starving colonists. Despite his realization that the settlement was utterly dependent on the Indians for food, Smith aimed always to intimidate his hosts with shows of force and determination. He maintained to the end of his life that his policy of firmness had not been cruel; rather he believed that, because it was thoroughly rational, it was superior to the random or vengeful cruelty of weaker actors. When he said that Powhatan's friendship would turn to "treachery" if the English relaxed their policy of overawing the Indians, Smith was acknowledging that the English were intruders whose presence would ultimately be unwelcome.

Smith's writing was most self-conscious in the passages where he reproduced his dialogues with Powhatan. He believed that Powhatan, as a great military leader himself, respected Smith and his policies and that he scorned those who took the path of appeasement, especially in giving the Indians too much in English trade goods for their corn. When dealing with other English leaders, Powhatan "valued his corne at such a rate, that I thinke it better cheape in Spaine" (p. 164). The two leaders could understand each other in a way denied those who held high position merely through social rank in English society. One of the most interesting threads running through Smith's accounts of his encounters with Powhatan is the constant struggle between the two men, conducted in the language of diplomacy, over whether the English should come armed into Powhatan's presence. Powhatan maintained that true friends did not need weapons; Smith responded that demands for disarmament were unfriendly. The sparring over this question suggests that Powhatan, referred to frequently as a "politician," was, like Smith, constantly probing for points of vulnerability.

Smith functioned as an ethnographer as well as an explorer and leader of men. His reports constitute one of the major sources for our understanding of the Algonquians of coastal North America in the period of first European settlement. During his captivity and in his other contacts with Indians, he constantly added to his fund of information and understanding; such knowledge would lead to more effective control. He did his best to conceal English weakness, as when he broke the cock on his pistol rather than allow his Indian captors to see how erratic such weapons were, and he noted everything he thought might be useful about Indian culture and society.

As we now know, Captain Smith was a perceptive observer. The Jamestown colonists had intruded on a culture in the process of change. The "Great Emperor" Powhatan, as the settlers called him, was consolidating control over many tribes in the Chesapeake region; about thirty had become clients under his patronage. This extension of control may have been facilitated by the devastating European diseases brought by travelers before Jamestown's founding; in the absence of natural immunity, Indian villages were devastated by epidemics and native leadership was in disarray.

Some scholars postulate that, had the process of empire building not been interrupted by European intrusion, relationships such as Powhatan was establishing might have developed over the next several centuries into state systems similar to those of Central America. Certainly all the colonists, like Smith, described their great awe on entering Powhatan's presence because of his immense dignity and the state in which he appeared before his subjects. The effect was often compared to an audience in the finest courts of Europe. Powhatan cautiously welcomed the English and the valuable trade goods they brought, especially the metal tools that made Indian tasks much easier. He could greatly enhance his own position by acting as middleman between the English and other tribes.

John Smith accurately located the center of power in the region; he was also able to identify the tribes that resisted Powhatan. He corrected those in England who had written that Indians lacked the attributes of organized society: law, inheritance, religion, and agriculture. We know that tribal leadership drew its authority from its redistributive function. That is, the chief assumed control of the tribe's assets, but his or her power came from the process of redistributing resources among those who needed them. Therefore, when Smith wrote that everything that was stolen from Jamestown ended up in Powhatan's hands, he was both telling his readers something important and demonstrating that his observations were carefully made.

The Virginia Company in London, whose knowledge of the situation in the colony, drawn largely from disgruntled men who had returned to England, was always very imperfect, remained unimpressed with Smith's accomplishments. The company had expected much more substantial results. In 1609 they decided to reorganize the colony and its government, reasoning that the poor showing could be improved by sending a large population under grander leadership. The Virginia Company, like Smith, was striving to evolve a model of colonization that would work. Not all of the great fleet sent in 1609 arrived in Jamestown; the flagship containing all the leading men was wrecked on Bermuda in a storm and these voyagers did not arrive until much later.[3] A struggle ensued between Smith, who considered himself the legal president until the new governor and the new charter arrived, and his former sparring partner, Capt. Gabriel Archer, who returned to the colony in one of the ships that had escaped the storm. Archer insisted that the company intended to remove Smith. In the end an accident in which Smith was badly burned by the explosion of his gunpowder bag ended the dispute; the incapacitated president had no choice but to return to England. When the shipwrecked remnant ar-

3. The wreck of the great fleet on Bermuda provided inspiration for Shakespeare's play *The Tempest*. In Frank Kermode's introduction to the Arden Edition (London, 1964), section 3, "The New World," he demonstrates both that Shakespeare was familiar with the documents that described the great storm and the salvation of its victims, and that he borrowed images from them.

rived in the colony six months later, the several hundred colonists had been reduced to sixty starving skeletons.

Smith was never to see Virginia again, and the Virginia Company seemed little interested in what he had to tell them. In the next decade, he turned his attention to New England, which he considered a better location for future development. But while the Virginia Company attracted hundreds of investors, and thus the capacity to sustain colonies over a long period, New England was the focus of only a few backers. In 1614 Smith sailed in a tiny fleet sharing command with an unscrupulous ship captain named Thomas Hunt. This voyage was inconclusive from the investors' point of view. A second expedition, in which Smith and a handful of men aimed to establish a settlement, never reached its destination. A third attempt, which ended in his captivity by French pirates for several months, was his last.

Captain Smith, despite the meager resources available and the untrustworthiness of Hunt, produced a survey of the New England coastline that led to a more accurate map and an ethnographic survey that correctly charted the fur trade and its participants. He coined the name New England and tried to give names to all the prominent features of the territory, including a short-lived attempt to call Cape Ann after his patron Tragabigzanda. Despite the brevity of his time in New England, he decided that this country, with its plentiful supply of fish, held the key to England's imperial future. His further writings stressed constantly that development of the resources he had found would serve England better than any mines.

Meanwhile Captain Smith continued to follow events in Virginia closely. He watched the colony limp along as a small military settlement for the next several years. By the end of its first decade, the Virginia Company began to make drastic changes. John Rolfe's marriage to Pocahontas in 1614 had signaled the beginning of a guarded peace with the Indians; his experiments in tobacco culture had finally provided the settlers with a valuable commodity. After 1618, the Virginia Company began pouring large numbers of colonists into the plantation. Poor emigrants paid their way by signing contracts that required them to work as servants for a stated number of years, and they were promised fifty acres of land when their terms were up. As tobacco culture flourished, and in the absence of overt Indian resistance, settlers swarmed over the land. Powhatan died in 1618; in 1622 his brother Opechancanough determined to stop the inroads of the

English on Indian land by staging a massive attack simultaneously on all the settlements up and down the James River. Though some colonists were forewarned, many were surprised. About 350 English were killed, ushering in a decade of warfare.

John Smith, watching events unfold from England, was supremely frustrated. He pointed out that the colonists had been lulled into a false sense of security by the apparent peace and had allowed Indians free access to the settlements. In short, the breakdown of his policy of overawing the Indians had invited the attack. Smith never acknowledged, probably never saw, the more important reason: the planters' expropriation of the agricultural lands of the Algonquians, which pushed them against other, sometimes hostile, tribes to the west.

Smith's comments on Indian relations as he grew older and his actual experience of America receded become increasingly painful to read. In his comments after 1622 all the subtlety and sensitivity in his understanding of the Indian side of the equation are gone; his later writings refer only to "savages" and suggest the harshest kind of military actions against them. Smith now envisaged harnessing Indian labor to maintain the plantations. As his views hardened and simplified, Smith provided what amounted to a caricature of his earlier views; the respect he had formerly shown for Indian culture and technology had evaporated. He was out of touch with American realities.

NATURAL HISTORY also attracted John Smith's attention; his appreciation of the American environment was a crucial part of his campaign for English colonization. Many people, after the disastrous starving times in early Jamestown, had reached the conclusion that the climate was deadly to English people and that southern colonies were untenable. The very rapid failure of a colony planted in Maine at the same time as Jamestown had convinced investors that New England was too cold and barren to be worth developing. If Smith was to keep interest in colonization alive, he had to prove that English men and women could survive in America and that, even though gold was not readily available, colonists could develop valuable products for export.

European scientists were interested in America. The beginnings of modern science were rooted in a drive to acquire and classify all knowledge; God, it was thought, had concealed the existence of America until Christendom was prepared to make use of the information it would reveal. John Smith may have had this audience partly in mind when he wrote about the New World environment. He had read some of the science of his day, particularly the *Briefe and True Report of the New Found Land of Virginia* published by Thomas Harriot in 1588, passages of which John Smith reprinted in his own *Generall Historie*. Harriot, one of the most interesting and least known actors on the early colonial scene, was a young mathematician just out of Oxford when Sir Walter Ralegh sent him and a painter named John White to describe the environment of the North Carolina Outer Banks where the colony of Roanoke was founded in 1585. Their report, written by Harriot and illustrated with woodcuts from White's paintings, was the most accurate representation of the American Indians and environment of the entire colonial period. Together they also produced a truly remarkable map of the Carolina coastal region.

White's portrayals of the coastal Algonquians, though his beautiful watercolors were not published until this century, were extremely influential as woodcuts. John Smith followed White and Harriot in the excellent maps he made of the Chesapeake and New England, and he began a long-lived tradition by adapting some of the woodcut figures to adorn his maps and illustrations.

The *Briefe and True Report* was an excellent natural history model for John Smith. Harriot strictly distinguished information that came through his own experience from that acquired by hearsay. If he was not sure about his information's accuracy, he always said so. Though he was young, he had a scientist's eye. He tested every food or mineral he found, either through his own devices or by questioning the Indians. There was no puffery in Harriot's book; he acknowledged that hard work would be required to make colonies succeed and that such success would come from an economy built on development of the humble commodities of America, not on easily acquired gold. Like Smith he scorned the weak colonists who hindered the work: "Because there were not to bee found any English cities, nor such faire houses, nor at their owne wish any of their olde accustomed daintie food, nor any soft beds of downe or fethers; the countrey was to them miserable, & their reports thereof according."[4]

John Smith, like Harriot but less systematically, set out to describe the environment and resources of America. This effort grew in impor-

4. Thomas Harriot, *A Briefe and True Report of the New Found Land of Virginia* (London, 1588), sig. A4–A4v. Harriot published only this book during his lifetime. His scientific papers have been recovered in this century and reveal him to have been a major scientist ranking with his contemporaries Kepler and Galileo.

tance in Smith's later books. He used two basic approaches: he reasoned from analogy, comparing American flora and fauna to those his audience knew; and he reasoned from a model of the world that assumed God had created a symmetrical globe in which experience of one region revealed the qualities of others in the same latitude. Smith did not invent either of these techniques. They were used by everyone who attempted to describe this new environment to people who had never seen it.

Where Smith did depart from most other writers was in his attempt to be absolutely truthful. Many promoters were cavalier in their discussions of the American environment, and the English public was justifiably skeptical about reports of the colonies. Robert Gordon of Lochinvar, for example, lifted sections from Harriot's description of the Carolina environment for a book urging colonization of Newfoundland, apparently assuming that the two environments would not differ much.[5] John Smith certainly was not always correct in his judgments, but he clearly tried; he believed great harm had been done by those who had exaggerated the possibilities of America, leading investors to underestimate the needs of the colonies and to send inappropriate men to develop them. Among the most striking aspects of Smith's writing are his refusal to hold out hopes of easy wealth and his stress on the amount of hard work necessary to develop the humble products on which an American empire would eventually be built.

The most urgent task was to demonstrate that English people could survive in the south. News of the high death rate in Jamestown had spread rapidly among potential investors. A certain number of deaths had been expected as colonists experienced the process known as "seasoning." Moving from one environment to another was seen as a major cause of disease in this period. The danger was assumed to be at its worst when one went from a moderate climate like England's to an intemperately hot one. As English promoters looked at the map of the Atlantic and saw that Virginia was opposite southern Spain and North Africa, they anticipated that all colonists would sicken during the seasoning process and that many would not survive it.

They did *not* anticipate deaths on the scale seen in Jamestown's first few years. Smith faced this problem squarely in his early books. He

---

5. Robert Gordon of Lochinvar, *Encouragements. For Such as Shall Have Intention to Bee Under-takers in the New Plantation of Cape Briton* (Edinburgh, 1625). Compare his discussion, sig. C4–C4v, with Harriot's, sig. C–C2v.

argued that English people could live comfortably in Virginia once they were seasoned, and that the seasoning process could be made easier as physicians found remedies native to the area. Using drugs suitable to England's sluggish climate in the speeded-up bodies of Virginians could be very dangerous. Colonists could tap Indian lore for native medicines that would make survival possible.

Meanwhile, a disciplined life was the best way to ensure reasonably good health. Smith's argument never strayed far from this point: it was the dissolute and aimless lives of the poorly led colonists that had produced such high death rates. Mortality had plunged almost to zero while Smith was president because activity and purposefulness had engendered the will to live. Smith hammered this message home throughout his work because the alternative explanation for death and failure could only be "the barrennesse and defect of the Countrie, as is generally supposed" (p. 130).

Much about the American environment was disturbing. The hot summers in Virginia and New England were expected for those latitudes, but the cold winters that brought frost to all areas in continental North America were a shock. Since countries in the same latitudes in the Old World did not have such great extremes of temperature, many wondered whether the American environment was defective. The year of Jamestown's founding, 1607–1608, was one of the worst winters of the century and a half known as the Little Ice Age. Smith pointed out that the suffering of the settlers was greatly compounded by the extreme cold, but he was anxious to remind readers that the winter was severe everywhere that year. Though Jamestown did pull through, the cold helped kill its companion settlement in Maine and left New England with the reputation of "a cold, barren, mountainous, rocky Desart" (p. 220).

John Smith wrote against this background of disappointed expectations. North America was cold, much of it looked extremely forbidding, the Indians seemed to have no precious minerals but copper, and tropical crops were out of the question. Smith, undaunted, set out to teach his readers about American reality. He began by looking on the bright side. Winter cold in America meant that expectations for "merchantable commodities" would have to be scaled down, but also that the land would be more healthful, and even more pleasant.

The English were profoundly ambivalent about heat, because they believed in a direct relationship between heat and riches: very hot areas produced richer and more abundant crops as well as precious minerals and gems. The English, locked in their perpetually cool island, set their colonies in the south to gain a share of the great wealth that flowed into the Spanish empire. On the other hand, to do so was to gamble with the colonists' health, even their lives. Virginia's mix of heat and cold seemed about right. Hot summer weather proved debilitating, but was offset by the break of winter with its cleansing winds and frosts. Smith wanted to present this trade-off in the best possible light. His lists of hoped-for products, unlike those of many writers with less experience, eschewed unrealistic tropical commodities and instead stressed items England was forced to buy from northern countries. While disappointing to some, this more realistic assessment suggested that English people could live comfortably in America and could transplant their own culture with some hope of success. In Smith's view, nature, throughout English America, was more benign and familiar than many thought possible.

Smith's second major line of reasoning was that the American environment would be better in the future. Nature, he argued, may cloak a particularly fine and rich interior with a rough exterior meant to protect and discourage violation. Just as one would not estimate the quality of wood in a tree by its bark, America should not be judged by its coast. He affirmed that the interior of the continent would be much more fruitful than the forbidding coast, especially in New England, where, he admitted, the rocky shoreline served "rather to affright then delight one." His experienced eye could see tokens of richness within, even in the "spectacle of desolation" (p. 234) offered by New England.

Not only would productivity improve as settlement moved inland, but also the environment would actually change as Europeans cultivated it. The land as it stood gave only a shadowy promise of its future productivity, because it had to be developed and improved. John Smith, inventor of the term *technological*, believed in the efficacy of European methods. He implied that, once English agricultural practices began to dominate the land, all the old expectations might indeed be fulfilled; American lands might bear the products of comparable latitudes in the Old World.

Smith, like most people of his time, thought that God created the world as pure potential; it had to be tended and tamed to be brought to its greatest fruitfulness. Adam and Eve began this important work in theirs, the first plantation. Human beings were not separate from and above nature, but were an essential part of it. God could have created nature in a perfect state, but instead he created humankind as his agents. Our role was absolutely essential; without human agency, nature would not just remain unfulfilled, but would actually degenerate.

Smith, and others who did not understand Indian agricultural and hunting techniques, argued that America was inadequate because the Indians had shirked, or not understood, their duty. Here was the reason why America's climate differed so radically from that of Europe in the same latitudes. Old World environments were mature, having been subdued by long cultivation, and were therefore moderate. The extreme shifts from great heat to deep cold, the violent coastal storms that Smith said were seldom or never seen in Europe, the prolonged droughts alternating with periods of heavy rains—all these were symptomatic of an adolescent climate, subject to the wild swings of emotion characteristic of that stage of life. Once the environment matured through the application of European technology, the discrepancy between it and Europe, as well as the extremes, would disappear.

This was Smith's response to "the worlds blind ignorant censure" for the Virginia colonists' failure to find gold as the Spaniards had.[6] The Spaniards' good fortune had nothing to do with them, he insisted; they had stumbled on a populous land whose Indians were so highly developed that they had gold and silver as well as great abundance of food. In Virginia, "we chanced in a Land even as God made it" (p. 251). Everything that the southern Indians had accomplished still remained to be done in North America. God-given potential had to be converted into actual prosperity.

In his later works, Smith felt able to begin to judge the actual impact of English settlement on America. He was honest enough to see that it had not been entirely beneficial. Not only was the fertility of Bermuda thought to be in decline, but also the rats that had accidentally been introduced into those islands as well as to Virginia had become a plague. In the absence of natural enemies, the few that had escaped from the ships multiplied into thousands and drove the colonists to "our wits end" (p. 115). But on the whole Smith believed he could see, even within his own lifetime, the beneficial effects of European technology, calming and enriching the American environment.

So Smith held out the promise that with great industriousness all might eventually be as originally hoped. Tropical products could after

6. *The Proceedings of the English Colonie in Virginia* . . . , in Philip L. Barbour, ed., *The Complete Works of Captain John Smith (1580–1631)*, 3 vols. (Chapel Hill, N.C., 1986), I, 257.

all come from the southern parts of North America. This dream died hard. But in the meantime, Smith's message was twofold. Colonists must come prepared to work hard, and promoters must have reasonable expectations. The Virginia colony had been plagued by its failure to accomplish goals that had never been realistic. Smith ridiculed the "experts" who had declared North America barren because they had not found the riches they expected. "But if a man will goe at Christmas to gather Cherries in Kent, though there be plenty in Summer, he may be deceived; so here these plenties have each their seasons, as I have expressed" (p. 238). If you knew what you were doing and your expectations were reasonable, you could produce riches.

Smith was rare among writers of this early period in arguing that humble commodities would provide the returns investors sought. Smith pointed out that England was forced to buy many products from northern Europe; the American colonies could free the country of this economic burden. One class of such commodities, timber and wood products such as tars, potash, and turpentine, was especially important to an England almost denuded of woods.

Smith complained that the Virginia Company had criticized him for freighting their ship with cedar; his answer was that Jamestown's early problems stemmed in part from the colonists' neglect of the important job of building the settlement while they searched frantically for gold. He asked the company if they preferred the ships loaded with "gilded durt," "ore" that proved worthless when it was assayed at home.

Gold was the big issue. While Smith held out the hope that gold might one day be discovered, especially as rich mines were found in other countries in Virginia's latitude, he believed the search should be postponed. In the first place, no one in the early colonies had the skills to find and test ore. Smith himself thought he had seen tokens of gold in some of the mountains they passed. Quartz, for example, is often found in conjunction with gold, and the colonists knew that. But as Smith said, he was "no Alcumist"; unlike others, he would not "promise more then I know" (p. 232). He warned that most of the "mineral men" were more ignorant than he, but would "find" gold or other precious ores to encourage investors (p. 218).

There was a more fundamental reason why Smith wanted to see the search for gold dropped or postponed. The hope of immediate returns was not just foolish and self-defeating; it was also unworthy. If a new British nation was to be built in America, its foundations must be more secure. The great empires of the past were not built by "silvered idle golden Pharises, but industrious iron-steeled Publicans."[7]

IN MANY WAYS, Smith was a conventional Englishman of his time, loyal, pious, and xenophobic. In his early works, he carefully shielded the Virginia Company from charges of mismanagement, alleging that it had been deceived by its colonists, and he was loyal to his friends. Despite his wide experience, he shared the English distrust of foreigners, pouring much blame for Jamestown's troubles on the "damned Dutchmen" (actually German specialists) who he thought had betrayed the colony.

And he was scornful of any who challenged the standing order of England. He was angry that the extreme puritans who founded Plymouth in 1620 had been able to profit by his writings. Because the Pilgrims were convinced that the Church of England was beyond redemption, they were separatists; they had formed congregations outside the Anglican church. Smith called them Brownists, after a prominent early separatist leader. He found the puritans who settled Massachusetts Bay a decade later more acceptable; they professed themselves loyal to the Church of England, preferring to reform it from within.

Smith's religious feelings were conventional, but apparently deeply felt. He instituted daily religious services among his men even under the rough conditions of his exploring voyages, and his piety asserted itself constantly in his writings. He clearly saw the hand of God at work in his life, believing that it had intervened again and again to save him or the colonies. He concluded that God, who had thwarted Spanish attempts to settle in North America, had reserved that region for the Protestant English. This line of reasoning reinforced his belief that ample riches could be developed: God would provide the wherewithal for the establishment of colonies because he wanted the reformed religion in America. The Britons, who had been more savage than the Americans before the Romans had brought civilization and Christianity to their island, would now perform the same service for the Indians. England was working out God's plan, one the deity had clearly endorsed in his providential intercessions on the colonists' behalf.

7. *A Description of New England, ibid.*, 360.

Despite his conventionality, Smith offered a radical vision of the English future based on his experience and his model of colonization. His major writings were produced in a pivotal decade of English life, one which ended with the trickle of colonists turning into a mighty stream. The 1620s were a period of hardship for England; growing population and rising inflation met poor harvests occasioned by Little Ice Age conditions to produce famine and the lowest real wages for a century. At the end of the decade, Charles I, tired of the opposition of Parliament, decided to rule on his will alone; many thought his ultimate goal was to return the country to Roman Catholicism, or at least an English version of it. The 1630s saw massive migration to the English colonies in America by people who felt their options had run out at home.

The conception of colonization was also changing in the 1620s and 1630s, and Smith played a key role in this development. The earliest model had been an aristocratic one, developed by men like Sir Walter Ralegh; it had been anti-Spanish to the core but, ironically, had also drawn on Spanish examples. Gold figured heavily in this model. Ralegh's Roanoke colony had been originally intended as a base from which English privateers could prey on the Spanish treasure fleet, crippling the enemy and enriching backers at the same time. The Virginia Company's model was different (privateering had been outlawed by James I), but the expectation of easy wealth and the great-power confrontation between Protestant England and Roman Catholic Spain were still central. The company expected to set up military outposts run by gentlemen and aristocrats who would be given ample scope for swashbuckling exploits suitable to their station.

Smith was the first writer to say clearly that this model was both impossible and undesirable in North America. Instant wealth and derring-do did not build a country. This was the unwelcome message of Capt. John Smith, and it was addressed not to the aristocrats but to the merchants, the men of the future. If England was to become a great nation on the basis of an American empire, its model could not be the outdated one of Spain, bankrupt while Indian gold flowed through it to the banking houses of Europe, but rather that of Holland, whose great commercial empire was built on that "contemptible Trade of Fish" (p. 227).

Other easy options also must be avoided; there were too many snares to entice the unworthy. Looking back at the end of his life, Smith was sorry to see that the great promise of Virginia had been diverted entirely to growing tobacco. All opportunities to develop the commodities that English industry truly needed had been neglected while the colonists were "rooting in the ground about Tobacco like Swine" (p. 195). They had been seduced by the great commercial possibilities of tobacco, but an empire could not be built on smoke.

By calling fish "contemptible," Smith satirized the sensitivities of the gentlemen, who were attracted to colonization by the hope of profit but did not want to get their hands dirty. Woven throughout Smith's later works is the theme that "the sea is better then the richest Mine knowne" (p. 265), and its returns certain and self-renewing. Fish would be England's path to wealth as it had been Holland's.

In this program lies Smith's true radicalism; it goes much deeper than his scorn for the weak, effeminate gentlemen who pined for their luxuries in Jamestown, or his ridicule of the stay-at-home policy makers in London. He rejected the Elizabethan colonial tradition that focused on immense wealth won through exploits of great daring: raids on the Spanish treasure fleet or marches through hostile territory to discover gold mines. These were adventures suitable for gentlemen.

In pointing to fish and timber as England's way to wealth, Smith placed the merchants and their moneygrubbing in the forefront. The aristocratic tradition saw privateering as a way of striking at the national enemy, Spain, by seizing ships from the massive treasure fleets that traveled from the Caribbean every year. The reality was very different by the 1620s. Most privateers actually attacked small ships laden with commodities such as wine, hides, or tallow, and they were notoriously indiscriminate in their targets, sometimes even catching British ships in these sweeps. Smith argued that privateering most often robbed hardworking small merchants of the fruits of their labor by seizing their cargoes and ships. Though he did not say so explicitly, it seems clear that Smith rejected such a privately run foreign policy on behalf of all the small merchants of Europe. It was a system out of control.

Smith's sympathies were all with the merchants because he saw them as more valuable. Colonial ventures were better run when merchants were in control, and their activities would help build the nation's economy while they made their own fortunes. Wealth would come to the country in hundreds of small increments won by humble men in dirty jobs; patience and diligence would replace swashbuckling.

The aristocratic vision of colonization had involved the re-creation of a hierarchical society based on reciprocity, in which the landlord provided land, work, hospitality, and justice for members of society who could not care for themselves. Those who worked on the land were, in this model, tied to the landlord by a web of loyalty and reciprocal duties. Smith's view of the same relationship was one of preying, gouging landlords, victimizing their tenants by jacking up rents to an intolerable degree. The few tenants who tried to break free from the system and set up for themselves were confronted by the lawyers, who ensnared the unwary in a tangle of ruinous lawsuits.

Capt. John Smith's genius was that he saw, before anyone else, that America offered the chance of a new kind of middling order. Like the founders of Massachusetts Bay, he envisaged a society of landholders, excluding the extremes of rich and poor, in which each family worked for itself, producing the humble commodities that would constitute American gold. Through working for their own enrichment, these families would build a true commonwealth. The English poor could be set to work in America and could achieve the dignity of ownership and conversion to the middling ranks. Smith was an early apostle of the doctrine of hard work and self-reliance.

Smith saw his program as middling in another sense: it occupied a middle path between the self-indulgent exploitation of the aristocratic model and the rejection of order inherent in the separatism of Plymouth. He never meant to challenge the standing order, only to restore it and prune it of undesirable accretions. The disorder of the "multitude" would be destructive of the stability that was the underlying condition of success. Smith's middling families, owners of their own farms, ships, or shops, required freedom from threats that the fruits of their labor might be snatched from them. Free trade would enrich the worthy and cut out those who live by preying on others.

John Smith had maintained from the beginning that he alone spoke with authority because only he had experience sufficient to know the truth. It was experience that ultimately brought colonists and promoters to see that he was correct, that only the promise of independent ownership would lure the people capable of building a new English society in America. Each of the North American colonies ultimately offered such inducements to prospective English emigrants. They also took a step largely unforeseen by Smith when they converted unwilling colonists into property by enslaving Africans and importing them to labor on southern plantations. Smith, praising unrestricted free enterprise, had not encompassed the notion that his middling society, too, could become exploitive.

The seeds of such exploitation were, of course, in Smith's own writings, and form part of the confusion and self-contradictory elements in his work. He saw nothing wrong in harnessing the labor of Indians, but in his mind the gift of Christianity and civility would more than compensate them for this loss of independence. What their fate would have been after conversion in Smith's ideal colony was never spelled out. He also saw nothing wrong in harnessing the labor of English men and women to ensure survival of the commonwealth, just as he left English boys in Indian villages to develop skills that would be useful in the future. He implied that these rank-and-file colonists would be offered the chance to move into middling stations, but that, too, remained to be seen. The common multitudes had to be controlled, even forced to survive.

Ultimately Smith addressed his message to the small middling group in English society. His final book, *Advertisements for the Unexperienced Planters of New England, or Any Where. Or, the Path-way to Experience to Erect a Plantation* (1631), counseled the newly undertaken Massachusetts Bay colony. This puritan colony, sponsored by merchants and populated by lesser gentry and middling families, was independently organized on just the lines that Smith had recommended. As puritans, these emigrants had internalized the control that Smith saw as so essential to the enterprise, and their capacity for hard work, each family on its own land, was proven. Smith wrote approvingly of the colony. It is doubtful whether the admiration was reciprocal; Smith, with his image of the blustering war-horse, would not have been welcome in Boston. He died grieving that, despite all his contributions, the colonization movement had passed him by.

THE PUBLISHED WORKS OF

CAPT. JOHN SMITH

A True Relation of Such Occurrences and Accidents of Noate as Hath Hapned in Virginia (London, 1608).

This book, originally a long letter, was published without Smith's consent or knowledge. It was rushed into print full of errors, which were compounded by the fact that it was edited to eliminate parts of Smith's account of the early months in Jamestown that the sponsors felt should not be told.

A Map of Virginia. With a Description of the Countrey, the Commodities, People, Government and Religion (Oxford, 1612) and *The Proceedings of the English Colonie in Virginia since Their First Beginning from England in the Yeare of Our Lord 1606* (Oxford, 1612).

Smith's engraved map was published in the first of these two books, which describes the land and its people and products and is a basic source on the culture of the Chesapeake Algonquians. The second book, the *Proceedings*, often referred to as the *Map of Virginia*, Part II, retells the story of Jamestown's early months more coherently than the *True Relation* and carries the story up to the middle of 1610. Because the *Proceedings* extended past Smith's time in the colony, he was forced to rely on the relations of others for his material. At various places in the text, these men are listed as coauthors, but it is probable that the book was basically written by Smith. He was defying the Virginia Company in publishing it, which accounts for Oxford as the place of publication of both books, and the inclusion of multiple authors may have been intended to deflect official wrath.

A Description of New England (London, 1616).

This book describes New England and Smith's activities during his brief time there; the pronounced note of argument for colonies in this book is new.

New Englands Trials (London, 1620 and 1622).

The two editions of this book add an elaborate statistical analysis of the possibilities of the fishing industry in New England to a summary of the *Description*. The second edition tells of the founding of Plymouth colony by the Pilgrims and discusses the great Indian attack on the Virginia plantations of 1622. *Trials* refers to investigations to determine the truth, and the results produced by those investigations.

The Generall Historie of Virginia, New-England, and the Summer Isles: with the Names of the Adventurers, Planters, and Governours from Their First Beginning An: 1584. to This Present 1624. (London, 1624).

This is Smith's great work, which draws on the writings of many other authors and is punctuated by verses from classical sources. It was published just as the Virginia Company was losing its charter and Virginia was becoming a royal colony. Book I uses the collections of Richard Hakluyt to deal with colonization and exploration before Jamestown. Books II and III are reprints of the two parts of the *Map of Virginia* with changes and additions, particularly in Book III. Book IV is very confused, dealing as it does with Virginia after Smith had ceased to be active in its affairs. Book V relates the history of Bermuda (the Summer Islands) from the manuscripts of others, and Book VI draws on Smith's *Description of New England* and *New Englands Trials*. Though the book has many shortcomings, it was the first attempt to give a comprehensive narrative account of English colonization in America. Very little, even of Smith's own work, was reprinted exactly as it came to his hand. Smith reworked, analyzed, and commented on almost every passage in the *Generall Historie*.

An Accidence or the Path-way to Experience. Necessary for All Young Seamen, or Those That Are Desirous to Goe to Sea (London, 1626).

This is little more than a list of nautical terms.

A Sea Grammar, with the Plaine Exposition of Smiths Accidence for Young Sea-men, Enlarged (London, 1627).

This book undertakes to define the terms included; most of the definitions were taken from a manuscript by Sir Henry Mainwaring. This book and the *Accidence* show a side to Smith's experience and competence that has been largely overlooked.

The True Travels, Adventures, and Observations of Captaine John Smith,
in Europe, Asia, Affrica, and America, from Anno Domini 1593. to 1629.
(London, 1630).

It is in this book that John Smith tells the story of his life before
Jamestown for the first time, including adventures that many have
considered incredible. The autobiography form was almost unknown,
so the *True Travels* represents a departure not only for Smith but also
for the history of publishing. The last third brings the history of the
colonies up-to-date from the end of the *Generall Historie*, and the
whole book ends with an impassioned denunciation of pirates.

Advertisements for the Unexperienced Planters of New England, or Any
Where. Or, the Path-way to Experience to Erect a Plantation
(London, 1631).

This is Smith's most accomplished book. Though addressed to the
newly founded puritan settlement in Massachusetts Bay, it presents in
a considered and persuasive way all Smith's thoughts on colonization
and on his role in it. Captain Smith exhibits a sense of pride and
satisfaction in England's American accomplishments despite his own
disappointments.

John Smith was at work on another book, a history of the sea, when he
died on June 21, 1631.

In 1986 the University of North Carolina Press published for the Institute of Early American History and Culture Philip L. Barbour's definitive three-volume edition of *The Complete Works of Captain John Smith*.
This collection, the culmination of Philip Barbour's thirty years of
work on John Smith, includes much that was excluded from earlier
collections and provides the full scholarly context for Smith's work. It
is the first to bring together all of Smith's writing. Excerpts for this
select edition are taken from the three-volume collection; volume and
page numbers following selections refer to it.

SUGGESTIONS FOR
FURTHER READING

THE DEFINITIVE EDITION of the writings of Capt. John Smith is Philip L. Barbour, ed., *The Complete Works of Captain John Smith (1580–1631)*, 3 vols. (Chapel Hill, N.C., 1986). This contains everything he wrote with a wealth of detail about Smith and the milieu in which he worked, facsimiles of his maps, and an exhaustive bibliography. Philip L. Barbour edited all the documents connected with Jamestown's founding years in his *The Jamestown Voyages under the First Charter, 1606–1609*, 2 vols. (Cambridge, 1969). Smith has attracted many biographers. Among the best and most recent works are Philip L. Barbour, *The Three Worlds of Captain John Smith* (Boston, 1964) and Alden T. Vaughan, *American Genesis: Captain John Smith and the Founding of Virginia* (Boston, 1975). Everett H. Emerson's *Captain John Smith* (New York, 1971) discusses Smith's work as literature.

The set of concerns from which colonization emerged is fully presented in Kenneth R. Andrews, *Trade, Plunder, and Settlement: Maritime Enterprise and the Genesis of the British Empire, 1480–1630* (Cambridge, 1984). Projects for English domestic economic development provided a model for what colonies could accomplish. See Joan Thirsk, *Economic Policy and Projects: The Development of a Consumer Society in Early Modern England* (Oxford, 1978). Colonial promoters also drew on models that grew out of the colonization of Ireland. See Nicholas P. Canny, "The Ideology of English Colonization: From Ireland to America," *William and Mary Quarterly*, 3d Ser., XXX (1973), 575–598. See also the set of articles in Kenneth R. Andrews, N. P. Canny, and P. E. H. Hair, eds., *The Westward Enterprise: English Activities in Ireland, the Atlantic, and America, 1480–1650* (Detroit, Mich., 1979).

Much scholarly attention has centered on Jamestown's first years, particularly the high death rate and Smith's claims that he knew better than anyone else how to force the colonists to survive. Hypotheses about the causes of mortality are argued in Carville V. Earle, "Environment, Disease, and Mortality in Early Virginia," in Thad W. Tate and

David L. Ammerman, eds., *The Chesapeake in the Seventeenth Century: Essays on Anglo-American Society* (Chapel Hill, N.C., 1979), 96–125, and Karen Ordahl Kupperman, "Apathy and Death in Early Jamestown," *Journal of American History*, LXVI (1979), 24–40.

Edmund S. Morgan's *American Slavery, American Freedom: The Ordeal of Colonial Virginia* (New York, 1975) analyzes the developing relationships among colonists, between the settlement and London, and with the Indians. Wesley Frank Craven's *Dissolution of the Virginia Company: The Failure of a Colonial Experiment* (New York, 1932) remains the definitive work on the events and rivalries that led to Virginia's becoming a royal colony.

Discussion of Smith's role as publicist and mapmaker of New England is found in Douglas R. McManis, *European Impressions of the New England Coast, 1497–1620* (Chicago, 1972). The work of Smith's predecessors as mapmakers, ethnographers, and natural historians, Thomas Harriot and John White, is available in several forms. A definitive edition of White's paintings is Paul Hulton and David Beers Quinn, *The American Drawings of John White, 1577–1590*, 2 vols. (London and Chapel Hill, N.C., 1964); Paul Hulton has also produced an inexpensive edition of the Roanoke paintings, *America 1585: The Complete Drawings of John White* (Chapel Hill, N.C., and London, 1984). Dover Publications has issued a facsimile edition of Harriot's *A Briefe and True Report of the New Found Land of Virginia* (New York, 1972) with the woodcuts done from White's paintings by Theodor de Bry for the 1590 edition. The full scholarly edition of Harriot's book, his notes for White's paintings, and many other documents connected with the Roanoke colony is David Beers Quinn, ed., *The Roanoke Voyages, 1584–1590*, 2 vols. (London, 1955).

Recent work in ethnohistory has greatly increased the sophistication of our understanding of the Indians on whom the Jamestown settlers intruded. For overviews of the Indian cultures involved, see Charles Hudson, *The Southeastern Indians* (Knoxville, Tenn., 1976) and the Smithsonian Institution's *Handbook of North American Indians*, XV, *Northeast*, ed. Bruce G. Trigger (Washington, D.C., 1978). Despite its title, this volume of the *Handbook* includes the Indians of Virginia and North Carolina.

Nancy Oestreich Lurie's "Indian Cultural Adjustment to European Civilization," in James Morton Smith, ed., *Seventeenth-Century America: Essays in Colonial History* (Chapel Hill, N.C., 1959), 33–60, is a pioneering effort to overcome the ethnocentrism in the sources and understand the confrontation of Indians and English from the Powhatans' point of view. J. Frederick Fausz's dissertation, "The Powhatan Uprising of 1622: A Historical Study of Ethnocentrism and Cultural Conflict" (College of William and Mary, 1977) offers a complete picture from both sides of the developing confrontation. Fausz's work may be more accessible in his "Patterns of Anglo-Indian Aggression and Accommodation along the Mid-Atlantic Coast, 1584–1634," in William W. Fitzhugh, ed., *Cultures in Contact: The Impact of European Contacts on Native American Cultural Institutions, A.D. 1000–1800* (Washington, D.C., 1985), 225–268.

Karen Ordahl Kupperman, *Settling with the Indians: The Meeting of English and Indian Cultures in America, 1580–1640* (Totowa, N.J., 1980) discusses English attempts to understand and interpret the Indian cultures they encountered throughout the colonies. *Manitou and Providence: Indians, Europeans, and the Making of New England, 1500–1643* by Neal Salisbury (New York, 1982), treats Indian cultures of New England and the effects of European intrusion. Early chapters deal with Smith as an ethnographer.

PART ONE

JOHN SMITH

LIFE AND LEGEND

Capt. John Smith consciously gave his life a legendary quality. After his active service in America was over, he accepted the role of publicist and theorist. In presenting the cause of colonization, he simultaneously promoted himself; many of his Virginia stories were told and retold in successive books, becoming more dramatic and detailed with each rendition. In his own lifetime and ever since, many readers have reacted against the flamboyance of his narrative, in which Smith always played the leading role. Smith's justification for such self-glorification was that the "better sort" who dominated colonization would have left his part out altogether.

I

Toward the end of his life, John Smith wrote about his early years; his was one of the first autobiographies. Though many of his ideas were used in the colonies, Smith had been disappointed that his leadership was rejected. The True Travels *contains reflections on his life and presents his claims, based on broad experience, to superior knowledge. He began (using the third-person pronoun) with his early adventures in the European wars.*

H E WAS BORNE in Willoughby in Lincolne-shire, and a Scholler in the two Free-schooles of Alford and Louth. His father anciently descended from the ancient Smiths of Crudley in Lancashire; his mother from the Rickards at great Heck in York-shire.

His parents dying when he was about thirteene yeeres of age, left him a competent meanes, which hee not being capable to manage, little regarded; his minde being even then set upon brave adventures, sould his Satchell, bookes, and all he had, intending secretly to get to Sea, but that his fathers death stayed him. But now the Guardians of his estate more regarding it than him, he had libertie enough, though no meanes, to get beyond the Sea. About the age of fifteene yeeres hee was bound an Apprentice to Master Thomas Sendall of Linne, the greatest Merchant of all those parts; but because hee would not presently send him to Sea, he never saw his master in eight yeeres after.

At last he found meanes to attend Master Perigrine Barty into France, second sonne to the Right Honourable Perigrine, that generous Lord Willoughby, and famous Souldier; where comming to his brother Robert, then at Orleans, now Earle of Linsey, and Lord great Chamberlaine of England; being then but little youths under Tutorage: his service being needlesse, within a moneth or six weekes they sent him backe againe to his friends; who when he came from London they liberally gave him (but out of his owne estate) ten shillings to be rid of him; such oft is the share of fatherlesse children: but those two Honourable Brethren gave him sufficient to returne for England. But it was the least thought of his determination, for now being freely at libertie in Paris, growing acquainted with one Master David Hume,

Volume and page numbers following the selections refer to Philip L. Barbour's edition of *The Complete Works of Captain John Smith (1580–1631)*, 3 vols. (Chapel Hill, N.C., 1986).

who making some use of his purse, gave him Letters to his friends in
Scotland to preferre him to King James. Arriving at Roane, he better
bethinkes himselfe, seeing his money neere spent, downe the River he
went to Haver de grace, where he first began to learne the life of a
souldier: Peace being concluded in France, he went with Captaine
Joseph Duxbury into the Low-countries, under whose Colours having
served three or foure yeeres, he tooke his journey for Scotland, to
deliver his Letters.

At Ancusan he imbarked himselfe for Lethe, but as much danger, as
shipwracke and sicknesse could endure, hee had at the holy Ile in
Northumberland neere Barwicke: (being recovered) into Scotland he
went to deliver his Letters.

After much kinde usage amongst those honest Scots at Ripweth and
Broxmoth, but neither money nor meanes to make him a Courtier, he
returned to Willoughby in Lincolne-shire; where within a short time
being glutted with too much company, wherein he took small delight,
he retired himselfe into a little wooddie pasture, a good way from any
towne, invironed with many hundred Acres of other woods: Here by a
faire brook he built a Pavillion of boughes, where only in his cloaths
he lay. His studie was Machiavills Art of warre, and Marcus Aurelius;
his exercise a good horse, with his lance and Ring; his food was
thought to be more of venison than any thing else; what he wanted his
man brought him. The countrey wondering at such an Hermite; His
friends perswaded one Seignior Theadora Polaloga, Rider to Henry
Earle of Lincolne, an excellent Horse-man, and a noble Italian Gentleman, to insinuate into his wooddish acquaintances, whose Languages
and good discourse, and exercise of riding drew him to stay with him
at Tattersall. Long these pleasures could not content him, but hee
returned againe to the Low-Countreyes.[1]

T HUS WHEN France and Netherlands had taught him to ride a
Horse and use his Armes, with such rudiments of warre, as his
tender yeeres in those martiall Schooles could attaine unto; he was
desirous to see more of the world, and trie his fortune against the
Turkes, both lamenting and repenting to have seene so many Christians slaughter one another. Opportunitie casting him into the com-

---

1. Smith, back in England after his first taste of war and after his rejection as a
courtier in Scotland, portrays himself as a Renaissance man preparing for a future
role as a leader, a gentleman soldier.

pany of foure French Gallants well attended, faining to him the one to be a great Lord, the rest his Gentlemen, and that they were all devoted that way; over-perswaded him to goe with them into France, to the Dutchesse of Mercury, from whom they should not only have meanes, but also Letters of favour to her noble Duke, then Generall for the Emperour Rodolphus in Hungary; which he did, with such ill weather as winter affordeth, in the darke night they arrived in the broad shallow In-let of Saint Valleries sur Some in Picardie; his French Lord knowing he had good apparell, and better furnished with money than themselves, so plotted with the Master of the ship to set his and their owne trunckes a shore leaving Smith aboard till the boat could returne, which was the next day after towards evening; the reason hee alleaged was the sea went so high hee could come no sooner, and that his Lord was gone to Amiens where they would stay his comming; which treacherous villany, when divers other souldiers, and passengers understood, they had like to have slaine the Master, and had they knowne how, would have runne away with the ship.

Comming on shore hee had but one Carralue, was forced to sell his cloake to pay for his passage. One of the souldiers, called Curzianvere, compassionating his injury, assured him this great Lord Depreau was only the sonne of a Lawyer of Mortaigne in base Britany, and his Attendants Cursell, La Nelie, and Monferrat, three young citizens, as arrant cheats as himselfe; but if he would accompany him, he would bring him to their friends, but in the interim supplied his wants: thus travelling by Deepe, Codebeck, Humphla, Pount-demer in Normandie, they came to Cane in base Normandie; where both this noble Curzianvere, and the great Prior of the great Abbey of Saint Steven (where is the ruinous Tombe of William the Conquerour,) and many other of his friends kindly welcomed him, and brought him to Mortaigne, where hee found Depreau and the rest, but to small purpose; for Master Curzianvere was a banished man, and durst not be seene, but to his friends: yet the bruit of their cosenage occasioned the Lady Collumber, the Baron Larshan, the Lord Shasghe, and divers other honourable persons, to supply his wants, and with them to recreate himselfe so long as hee would: but such pleasant pleasures suited little with his poore estate, and his restlesse spirit, that could never finde content, to receive such noble favours, as he could neither deserve nor requite: but wandring from Port to Port to finde some man of war, spent that he had, and in a Forest, neere dead with griefe and cold, a rich Farmer found him by a faire Fountaine under a tree: This kinde

Pesant releeved him againe to his content, to follow his intent. Not long after, as he passed thorow a great grove of trees, betweene Pounterson and Dina in Britaine, it was his chance to meet Cursell, more miserable than himselfe: His piercing injuries had so small patience, as without any word they both drew, and in a short time Cursell fell to the ground, where from an old ruinated Tower the inhabitants seeing them, were satisfied, when they heard Cursell confesse what had formerly passed; and that how in the dividing that they had stolne from him, they fell by the ears amongst themselves, that were actors in it; but for his part, he excused himselfe to be innocent as well of the one, as of the other. In regard of his hurt, Smith was glad to be so rid of him, directing his course to an honourable Lord, the Earle of Ployer, who during the warre in France, with his two brethren, Viscount Poomory, and Baron d'Mercy, who had beene brought up in England; by him he was better refurnished than ever. When they had shewed him Saint Malo, Mount Saint Michael, Lambal, Simbreack, Lanion, and their owne faire Castle of Tuncadeck, Gingan, and divers other places in Britanny, (and their Brittish Cornwaile) taking his leave, he tooke his way to Raynes, the Britaines chiefe Citie, and so to Nantes, Poyters, Rochell, and Burdeaux. The rumour of the strength of Bayon in Biskay, caused him to see it; and from thence tooke his way from Leskar in Biearne, and Paw in the kingdom of Navar to Tolouza in Gascoigne, Bezers and Carcassone, Narbone, Montpellier, Nimes in Languedock, and thorow the Country of Avignion, by Arles to Marcellos in Province, there imbarking himselfe for Italy, the ship was enforced to Tolonne, and putting againe to sea, ill weather so grew upon them, they anchored close aboard the shore, under the little Isle of S. Mary, against Neice in Savoy. Here the inhumane Provincialls, with a rabble of Pilgrimes of divers Nations going to Rome, hourely cursing him, not only for a Hugonoit, but his Nation they swore were all Pyrats, and so vildly railed on his dread Soveraigne Queene Elizabeth, and that they never should have faire weather so long as hee was aboard them;[2] their disputations grew to that passion, that they threw him over-board, yet God brought him to that little Isle, where was no inhabitants, but a few kine and goats. The next morning he espied two

2. Huguenots are French Protestants. The Roman Catholic passengers on this ship believed that the storm was a sign of God's anger that a Protestant had been allowed aboard. Elizabeth I had placed England in the role of leader of the Protestant nations.

ships more riding by them, put in by the storme, that fetched him aboard, well refreshed him, and so kindly used him, that he was well contented to trie the rest of his fortune with them. After he had related unto them his former discourse, what for pitie, and the love of the Honourable Earle of Ployer, this noble Britaine his neighbour, Captaine la Roche of Saint Malo, regarded and entertained him for his well respected friend. With the next faire wind they sailed along by the Coast of Corsica and Sardinia, and crossing the gulfe of Tunis, passed by Cape Bona to the Isle of Lampadosa, leaving the coast of Barbary till they came at Cape Rosata, and so along the African shore, for Alexandria in Ægypt. There delivering their fraught, they went to Scandaroone; rather to view what ships was in the Roade, than any thing else: keeping their course by Cypres and the coast of Asia, sayling by Rhodes, the Archipellagans, Candia, and the coast of Grecia, and the Isle of Zaffalonia. They lay to and againe a few dayes betwixt the Isle of Corfue and the Cape of Otranto in the Kingdome of Naples, in the Entrance of the Adriatike sea.

B ETWIXT THE two Capes they meet with an Argosie of Venice, it seemed the Captaine desired to speake with them, whose untoward answer was such, as slew them a man; whereupon the Britaine presently gave them the broad-side, then his Sterne, and his other broad-side also, and continued the chase, with his chase peeces, till he gave them so many broad-sides one after another, that the Argosies sayles and tackling was so torne, she stood to her defence, and made shot for shot; twice in one houre and a halfe the Britaine boarded her, yet they cleared themselves, but clapping her aboard againe, the Argosie fired him, which with much danger to them both was presently quenched.[3] This rather augmented the Britaines rage, than abated his courage; for having reaccommodated himselfe againe, shot her so oft betweene wind and water, shee was readie to sinke, then they yeelded; the Britaine lost fifteene men, she twentie, besides divers were hurt, the rest went to worke on all hands; some to stop the leakes, others to guard the prisoners that were chained, the rest to rifle her. The Silkes, Velvets, Cloth of gold, and Tissue, Pyasters, Chicqueenes and Sultanies, which is gold and silver, they unloaded in foure and twentie houres, was wonderfull, whereof having sufficient, and tired with toile, they cast her off with her company, with as much good merchan-

3. An argosy is a carrack, a large merchant ship.

dize as would have fraughted such another Britaine, that was but two hundred Tunnes, she foure or five hundred.

To repaire his defects, hee stood for the coast of Calabria, but hearing there was six or seven Galleyes at Mesina hee departed thence for Malta, but the wind comming faire, he kept his course along the coast of the Kingdome of Sicilia by Sardinia and Corsica, till he came to the Road of Antibo in Peamon, where he set Smith on shore with five hundred chicqueenes, and a little box God sent him worth neere as much more. Here he left this noble Britaine, and embarked himselfe for Lygorne, being glad to have such opportunitie and meanes to better his experience by the view of Italy; and having passed Tuskany, and the Countrey of Sieana, where hee found his deare friends, the two Honourable Brethren, the Lord Willoughby and his Brother cruelly wounded, in a desperate fray, yet to their exceeding great honour. Then to Viterbo and many other Cities he came to Rome, where it was his chance to see Pope Clement the eight, with many Cardinalls, creepe up the holy Stayres, which they say are those our Saviour Christ went up to Pontius Pilate, where bloud falling from his head, being pricked with his crowne of thornes, the drops are marked with nailes of steele, upon them none dare goe but in that manner, saying so many *Ave-Maries* and *Pater-nosters*, as is their devotion, and to kisse the nailes of steele: But on each side is a paire of such like staires, up which you may goe, stand, or kneele, but divided from the holy Staires by two walls: right against them is a Chappell, where hangs a great silver Lampe, which burneth continually, yet they say the oyle neither increaseth nor diminisheth. A little distant is the ancient Church of Saint John de Laterane, where he saw him say Masse, which commonly he doth upon some Friday once a moneth. Having saluted Father Parsons, that famous English Jesuite, and satisfied himselfe with the rarities of Rome, he went downe the River of Tiber to Civita Vechia, where he embarked himselfe to satisfie his eye with the faire Citie of Naples, and her Kingdomes nobilitie; returning by Capua, Rome and Seana, he passed by that admired Citie of Florence, the Cities and Countries of Bolonia, Ferrara, Mantua, Padua and Venice, whose Gulfe he passed from Malamoco and the Adriatike Sea for Ragouza, spending some time to see that barren broken coast of Albania and Dalmatia, to Capo de Istria, travelling the maine of poore Slavonia by Lubbiano, till he came to Grates in Steria, the Seat of Ferdinando Arch-duke of Austria, now Emperour of Almania: where he met an English man, and an Irish Jesuite, who acquainted him with many brave Gentlemen of good qualitie, especially with the Lord Ebersbaught, with whom trying such conclusions, as he projected to undertake, preferred him to Baron Kisell, Generall of the Artillery, and he to a worthy Collonell, the Earle of Meldritch, with whom going to Vienne in Austria, under whose Regiment, in what service, and how he spent his time, this ensuing Discourse will declare. [*True Travels:* III, 153–162]

Smith here joined in the long war between the Holy Roman Empire of the Hapsburgs, centered in Austria, and the Turkish Ottoman Empire. The dynamic Turkish Moslems had, in the sixteenth century, swept into eastern Europe up to the very gates of Vienna. At the time Smith volunteered for service, much of Hungary and Transylvania, where he fought, was under a degree of Turkish control. Many of the people and places he mentioned can be identified; for example, his earl of Meldritch was the count of Modrusch, Duke Mercury was the duke of Mercoeur, and his General Zachel Moyses was Mózes Székely.

AFTER THE losse of Caniza, the Turkes with twentie thousand besieged the strong Towne of Olumpagh so straightly, as they were cut off from all intelligence and hope of succour; till John Smith, this English Gentleman, acquainted Baron Kisell, Generall of the Arch-dukes Artillery, he had taught the Governour, his worthy friend, such a Rule, that he would undertake to make him know any thing he intended, and have his answer, would they bring him but to some place where he might make the flame of a Torch seene to the Towne; Kisell inflamed with this strange invention; Smith made it so plaine, that forthwith hee gave him guides, who in the darke night brought him to a mountaine, where he shewed three Torches equidistant from other, which plainly appearing to the Towne, the Governour presently apprehended, and answered againe with three other fires in like manner; each knowing the others being and intent; Smith, though distant seven miles, signified to him these words: On Thursday at night I will charge on the East, at the Alarum, salley you; Ebersbaught answered he would, and thus it was done: First he writ his message as briefe, you see, as could be, then divided the Alphabet in two parts thus;

A. b. c. d. e. f. g. h. i. k. l.
I. I. I. I. I. I. I. I. I. I. I.

m. n. o. p. q. r. s. t. v. w. x. y. z.
2. 2. 2. 2. 2. 2. 2. 2. 2. 2. 2. 2. 2.

The first part from A. to L. is signified by shewing and hiding one linke, so oft as there is letters from A. to that letter you meane; the other part from M. to Z. is mentioned by two lights in like manner. The end of a word is signified by shewing of three lights, ever staying your light at that letter you meane, till the other may write it in a paper, and answer by his signall, which is one light, it is done, beginning to count the letters by the lights, every time from A. to M. by this meanes also the other returned his answer, whereby each did understand other. The Guides all this time having well viewed the Campe, returned to Kisell, who, doubting of his power being but ten thousand, was animated by the Guides, how the Turkes were so divided by the River in two parts, they could not easily second each other. To which Smith added this conclusion; that two or three thousand pieces of match fastened to divers small lines of an hundred fathome in length being armed with powder, might all be fired and stretched at an instant before the Alarum, upon the Plaine of Hysnaburg, supported by two staves, at each lines end, in that manner would seeme like so many Musketteers; which was put in practice; and being discovered by the Turkes, they prepared to encounter these false fires, thinking there had beene some great Armie: whilest Kisell with his ten thousand being entred the Turks quarter, who ranne up and downe as men amazed. It was not long ere Ebersbaught was pell-mell with them in their Trenches; in which distracted confusion, a third part of the Turkes, that besieged that side towards Knousbruck, were slaine; many of the rest drowned, but all fled. The other part of the Armie was so busied to resist the false fires, that Kisell before the morning put two thousand good souldiers in the Towne, and with small losse was retired; the Garrison was well releeved with that they found in the Turkes quarter, which caused the Turkes to raise their siege and returne to Caniza: and Kisell with much honour was received at Kerment, and occasioned the Author a good reward and preferment, to be Captaine of two hundred and fiftie Horse-men, under the Conduct of Colonell Voldo, Earle of Meldritch.

AGENERALL RUMOUR of a generall peace, now spred it selfe over all the face of those tormented Countries: but the Turke intended no such matter, but levied souldiers from all parts he could. The Emperour also, by the assistance of the Christian Princes, provided three Armies, the one led by the Arch-duke Mathias, the Emperours brother, and his Lieutenant Duke Mercury to defend Low Hungary, the second, by Ferdinando the Arch-duke of Steria, and the Duke of Mantua his Lieutenant to regaine Caniza; the third by Gonzago, Governour of High Hungary, to joyne with Georgio Busca, to make an absolute conquest of Transilvania.

Duke Mercury with an Armie of thirtie thousand, whereof neere ten thousand were French, besieged Stowlle-wesenburg, otherwise called Alba Regalis, a place so strong by Art and Nature, that it was thought impregnable. At his first comming, the Turkes sallied upon the Germane quarter, slew neere five hundred, and returned before they were thought on. The next night in like manner they did neere as much to the Bemers, and Hungarians; of which fortune still presuming, thinking to have found the French quarter as carelesse, eight or nine hundred of them were cut in pieces and taken prisoners. In this encounter Monsieur Grandvile, a brave French Colonell, received seven or eight cruell wounds, yet followed the Enemie to the Ports; he came off alive, but within three or foure dayes died.

Earle Meldritch, by the information of three or foure Christians, (escaped out of the Towne) upon every Alarum, where there was greatest assemblies and throng of people, caused Captaine Smith to put in practice his fiery Dragons, hee had demonstrated unto him, and the Earle Von Sulch at Comora, which hee thus performed: Having prepared fortie or fiftie round-bellied earthen pots, and filled them with hand Gunpowder, then covered them with Pitch, mingled with Brimstone and Turpentine; and quartering as many Musket-bullets, that hung together but only at the Center of the division, stucke them round in the mixture about the pots, and covered them againe with the same mixture, over that a strong Searcloth, then over all a good thicknesse of Towze-match well tempered with oyle of Lin-seed, Campheer, and powder of Brimstone, these he fitly placed in Slings, graduated so neere as they could to the places of these Assemblies. At midnight upon the Alarum, it was a fearfull sight to see the short flaming course of their flight in the aire, but presently after their fall, the lamentable noise of the miserable slaughtered Turkes was most wonderfull to heare: Besides, they had fired that Suburbe at the Port of Buda in two or three places, which so troubled the Turkes to quench, that had there beene any meanes to have assaulted them, they could hardly have resisted the fire, and their enemies. The Earle Rosworme, contrary to the opinion of all men, would needs undertake to finde meanes to surprize the Segeth and Suburbe of the Citie, strongly defended by a muddie Lake, which was thought unpassable.

The Duke having planted his Ordnance, battered the other side, whilest Rosworme, in the darke night, with every man a bundle of sedge and bavins still throwne before them, so laded up the Lake, as they surprized that unregarded Suburbe before they were discovered: upon which unexpected Alarum, the Turkes fled into the Citie, and the other Suburbe not knowing the matter, got into the Citie also, leaving their Suburbe for the Duke, who, with no great resistance, tooke it, with many peeces of Ordnance; the Citie, being of no such strength as the Suburbs, with their owne Ordnance was so battered, that it was taken perforce, with such a mercilesse execution, as was most pitifull to behold. The Bashaw notwithstanding drew together a partie of five hundred before his owne Pallace, where he intended to die; but seeing most of his men slaine before him, by the valiant Captaine Earle Meldritch, who tooke him prisoner with his owne hands; and with the hazard of himselfe saved him from the fury of other troopes, that did pull downe his Pallace, and would have rent him in peeces, had he not beene thus preserved. The Duke thought his victory much honoured with such a Prisoner; tooke order hee should bee used like a Prince, and with all expedition gave charge presently to repaire the breaches, and the ruines of this famous Citie, that had beene in the possession of the Turkes neere threescore yeares.

MAHOMET, the great Turke, during the siege, had raised an Armie of sixtie thousand men to have releeved it; but hearing it was lost, he sent Assan Bashaw, Generall of his Armie, the Bashaw of Buda, Bashaw Amaroz, to see if it were possible to regaine it; The Duke understanding there could be no great experience in such a new levied Armie as Assan had; having put a strong Garrison into it: and with the brave Colonell Rosworme, Culnits, Meldritch, the Rhine-Grave, Vahan and many others; with twenty thousand good souldiers, set forward to meet the Turke in the Plaines of Girke. Those two Armies encountred as they marched, where began a hot and bloudy Skirmish betwixt them, Regiment against Regiment, as they came in order, till the night parted them: Here Earle Meldritch was so invironed amongst those halfe circuler Regiments of Turkes, they supposed him their Prisoner, and his Regiment lost; but his two most couragious friends, Vahan and Culnits, made such a passage amongst them, that it was a terror to see how horse and man lay sprawling and tumbling, some one way, some another on the ground. The Earle there at that time made his valour shine more bright than his armour, which seemed then painted with Turkish bloud, he slew the brave Zanzack Bugola, and made his passage to his friends, but neere halfe his Regiment was slaine. Captain Smith had his horse slaine under him, and himselfe sore wounded; but he was not long unmounted, for there was choice enough of horses, that wanted masters. The Turke thinking the victory sure against the Duke, whose Armie, by the Siege and the Garrison, he had left behind him, was much weakned, would not be content with one, but he would have all; and lest the Duke should returne to Alba Regalis, he sent that night twenty thousand to besiege the Citie, assuring them he would keepe the Duke or any other from releeving them. Two or three dayes they lay each by other, entrenching themselves; the Turkes daring the Duke daily to a sett battell, who at length drew out his Army, led by the Rhine-Grave, Culnits and Meldritch, who upon their first encounter, charged with that resolute and valiant courage, as disordered not only the formost squadrons of the Turkes, but enforced all the whole Armie to retire to the Campe, with the losse of five or six thousand, with the Bashaw of Buda, and foure or five Zanzacks, with divers other great Commanders, two hundred Prisoners, and nine peeces of Ordnance. At that instant appeared, as it were, another Armie comming out of a valley over a plaine hill, that caused the Duke at that time to be contented, and to retire to his Trenches; which gave time to Assan to reorder his disordered squadrons: Here they lay nine or ten dayes, and more supplies repaired to them, expecting to try the event in a sett battell; but the souldiers on both parties, by reason of their great wants and approach of winter, grew so discontented, that they were ready of themselves to breake up the Leager; the Bashaw retiring himselfe to Buda, had some of the Reare Troopes cut off. Amaroz Bashaw hearing of this, found such bad welcome at Alba Regalis, and the Towne so strongly repaired, with so brave a Garrison, raised his siege, and retired to Zigetum.

The Duke understanding that the Arch-duke Ferdinando had so resolutely besieged Caniza, as what by the losse of Alba Regalis, and the Turks retreat to Buda, being void of hope of any reliefe, doubted not but it would become againe the Christians. To the furtherance whereof, the Duke divided his Armie into three parts. The Earle of Rosworme went with seven thousand to Caniza; the Earle of Meldritch with six thousand he sent to assist Georgio Busca against the Transilvanians, the rest went with himselfe to the Garrisons of Strigonium and Komara; having thus worthily behaved himselfe, he arrived at Vienne; where the Arch-dukes and the Nobilitie with as much honour received him, as if he had conquered all Hungaria; his very Picture they esteemed would make them fortunate, which thousands kept as curiously as a precious relique. To requite this honour, preparing himselfe to returne into France, to raise new Forces against the next yeare, with the two Arch-dukes, Mathias and Maximilian, and divers others of the Nobilitie, was with great magnificence conducted to Nurenburg, there by them royally feasted; (how it chanced is not knowne;) but the next morning he was found dead, and his brother in law died two dayes after; whose hearts, after this great triumph, with much sorrow were carried into France.

T HE WO RTH Y Lord Rosworme had not a worse journey to the miserable Seige of Caniza, (where by the extremitie of an extraordinary continuing tempest of haile, wind, frost and snow, in so much that the Christians were forced to leave their Tents and Artillery, and what they had; it being so cold that three or foure hundred of them were frozen to death in a night, and two or three thousand lost in that miserable flight in the snowie tempest, though they did know no enemie at all to follow them:) than the noble Earle of Meldritch had to Transilvania, where hearing of the death of Michael and the brave Duke Mercury, and knowing the policie of Busca, and the Prince his Roialtie, being now beyond all beleefe of men, in possession of the best part of Transilvania, perswaded his troopes, in so honest a cause, to assist the Prince against the Turke, rather than Busca against the Prince.

The souldiers being worne out with those hard payes and travells, upon hope to have free libertie to make bootie upon what they could get possession of from the Turkes, was easily perswaded to follow him whithersoever. Now this noble Earle was a Transilvanian borne, and his fathers Countrey yet inhabited by the Turkes; for Transilvania was yet in three divisions, though the Prince had the hearts both of Country and people; yet the Frontiers had a Garrison amongst the unpassable mountaines, some for the Emperour, some for the Prince, and some for the Turke: to regaine which small estate, hee desired leave of the Prince to trie his fortunes, and to make use of that experience, the time of twentie yeares had taught him in the Emperours service, promising to spend the rest of his dayes for his countries defence in his Excellencies service. The Prince glad of so brave a Commander, and so many expert and ancient souldiers, made him Campe-master of his Armie, gave him all necessary releefe for his troopes and what freedome they desired to plunder the Turkes.

The Earle having made many incursions into the Land of Zarkam among those rockie mountaines, where were some Turks, some Tartars, but most Bandittoes, Rennegadoes, and such like, which sometimes hee forced into the Plaines of Regall, where is a Citie not only of men and fortifications, strong of it selfe, but so environed with mountaines, that made the passages so difficult, that in all these warres no attempt had beene made upon it to any purpose: Having satisfied himselfe with the Situation, and the most convenient passages to bring his Armie unto it: The earth no sooner put on her greene habit, than the Earle overspread her with his armed troopes. To possesse himselfe first of the most convenient passage, which was a narrow valley betwixt two high mountaines; he sent Colonell Veltus with his Regiment, dispersed in companies to lye in Ambuscado, as he had directed them, and in the morning to drive all the cattell they could finde before a Fort in that passage, whom he supposed would sally, seeing but some small partie, to recover their prey; which tooke such good successe, that the Garrison was cut off by the Ambuscado, and Veltus seized on the Skonces, which was abandoned. Meldritch glad of so fortunate a beginning, it was six dayes ere he could with six thousand Pioners make passage for his Ordnance: The Turkes having such warning, strengthned the Towne so with men and provision, that they made a scorne of so small a number as Meldritch brought with him before the Citie, which was but eight thousand. Before they had pitched their Tents, the Turkes sallied in such abundance, as for an houre they had rather a bloudy battell than a skirmish, but with the losse of neere fifteene hundred on both sides. The Turkes were chased till the Cities Ordnance caused the Earle to retire. The next day Zachel Moyses, Generall of the Armie, pitched also his tents with nine thousand foot and horse, and six and twenty peeces of Ordnance; but in regard of the situation of this strong Fortresse, they did neither feare them nor hurt them, being upon the point of a faire promontory, environed on the one side within halfe a mile with an un-usefull mountaine, and on the other side with a faire Plaine, where the Christians encamped, but so commanded by their Ordnance, they spent neere a month in entrenching themselves, and raising their mounts to plant their batteries; which slow proceedings the Turkes oft derided, that their Ordnance were at pawne, and how they grew fat for want of exercise, and fearing lest they should depart ere they could assault their Citie, sent this Challenge to any Captaine in the Armie.

That to delight the Ladies, who did long to see some court-like pastime, the Lord Turbashaw did defie any Captaine, that had the command of a Company, who durst combate with him for his head: The matter being discussed, it was accepted, but so many questions grew for the undertaking, it was decided by lots, which fell upon Captaine Smith, before spoken of.

Truce being made for that time, the Rampiers all beset with faire Dames, and men in Armes, the Christians in Battalio; Turbashaw with a noise of Howboyes entred the field well mounted and armed; on his shoulders were fixed a paire of great wings, compacted of Eagles feathers within a ridge of silver, richly garnished with gold and precious stones, a Janizary before him, bearing his Lance, on each side another leading his horse; where long hee stayed not, ere Smith with a noise of Trumpets, only a Page bearing his Lance, passing by him with a courteous salute, tooke his ground with such good successe, that at the sound of the charge, he passed the Turke thorow the sight of his Beaver, face, head and all, that he fell dead to the ground, where alighting and unbracing his Helmet, cut off his head, and the Turkes tooke his body;[4] and so returned without any hurt at all. The head hee presented to the Lord Moses, the Generall, who kindly accepted it, and with joy to the whole armie he was generally welcomed.

The death of this Captaine so swelled in the heart of one Grualgo, his vowed friend, as rather inraged with madnesse than choller, he directed a particular challenge to the Conquerour, to regaine his friends head, or lose his owne, with his horse and Armour for advantage, which according to his desire, was the next day undertaken: as before upon the sound of the Trumpets, their Lances flew in peeces upon a cleare passage, but the Turke was neere unhorsed. Their Pistolls was the next, which marked Smith upon the placard; but the next shot the Turke was so wounded in the left arme, that being not able to rule his horse, and defend himselfe, he was throwne to the ground, and so bruised with the fall, that he lost his head, as his friend before

---

4. A beaver is the part of a helmet that protects the face.

him; with his horse and Armour; but his body and his rich apparell was sent backe to the Towne.

Every day the Turkes made some sallies, but few skirmishes would they endure to any purpose. Our workes and approaches being not yet advanced to that height and effect which was of necessitie to be performed; to delude time, Smith with so many incontradictable perswading reasons, obtained leave that the Ladies might know he was not so much enamoured of their servants heads, but if any Turke of their ranke would come to the place of combate to redeeme them, should have his also upon the like conditions, if he could winne it.

The challenge presently was accepted by Bonny Mulgro. The next day both the Champions entring the field as before, each discharging their Pistoll, having no Lances, but such martiall weapons as the defendant appointed, no hurt was done; their Battle-axes was the next, whose piercing bils made sometime the one, sometime the other to have scarce sense to keepe their saddles, specially the Christian received such a blow that he lost his Battle-axe, and failed not much to have fallen after it, wherat the supposing conquering Turk, had a great shout from the Rampiers. The Turk prosecuted his advantage to the uttermost of his power; yet the other, what by the readinesse of his horse, and his judgement and dexterity in such a businesse, beyond all mens expectation, by Gods assistance, not onely avoided the Turkes violence, but having drawne his Faulchion, pierced the Turke so under the Culets thorow backe and body, that although he alighted from his horse, he stood not long ere hee lost his head, as the rest had done.[5]

THIS GOOD successe gave such great encouragement to the whole Armie, that with a guard of six thousand, three spare horses, before each a Turkes head upon a Lance, he was conducted to the Generalls Pavillion with his Presents. Moyses received both him and them with as much respect as the occasion deserved, embracing him in his armes; gave him a faire Horse richly furnished, a Semitere and belt worth three hundred ducats; and Meldritch made him Sergeant major of his Regiment. But now to the siege, having mounted six and twenty peeces of Ordnance fifty or sixty foot above the Plaine, made them so plainly tell his meaning, that within fifteene dayes two breaches were made, which the Turkes as valiantly defended as men

5. Culets are overlapping plates of armor that protect the back of the body below the waist.

could; that day was made a darksome night, but by the light that proceeded from the murdering Muskets, and peace-making Canon, whilest their slothfull Governour lay in a Castle on the top of a high mountaine, and like a valiant Prince asketh what's the matter, when horrour and death stood amazed each at other, to see who should prevaile to make him victorious: Moyses commanding a generall assault upon the sloping front of the high Promontory, where the Barons of Budendorfe and Oberwin lost neere halfe their Regiments, by logs, bags of powder, and such like, tumbling downe the hill, they were to mount ere they could come to the breach; notwithstanding with an incredible courage they advanced to the push of the Pike with the defendants, that with the like courage repulsed, till the Earle Meldritch, Becklefield and Zarvana, with their fresh Regiments seconded them with that fury, that the Turks retired and fled into the Castle, from whence by a flag of truce they desired composition. The Earle remembring his fathers death, battered it with all the Ordnance in the Towne, and the next day tooke it; all he found could beare Armes he put to the sword, and set their heads upon stakes round about the walles, in the same manner they had used the Christians, when they tooke it. Moyses having repaired the Rampiers, and throwne downe the worke in his Campe, he put in it a strong Garrison, though the pillage he had gotten in the Towne was much, having beene for a long time an impregnable den of theeves; yet the losse of the Armie so intermingled the sowre with the sweet, as forced Moyses to seek a further revenge, that he sacked Veratio, Solmos, and Kupronka, and with two thousand prisoners, most women and children, came to Esenberg, not farre from the Princes Palace, where he there Encamped.[6]

Sigismundus comming to view his Armie, was presented with the Prisoners, and six and thirtie Ensignes; where celebrating thankes to Almightie God in triumph of those victories, hee was made acquainted with the service Smith had done at Olumpagh, Stowle-Wesenburg and Regall, for which with great honour hee gave him three Turkes heads

6. Because the European wars involved such scenes of revenge and destruction, the Virginia Company, while valuing Smith's experience and expertise, had good reason to try to force him and the colonists in general into a policy of good treatment and friendship toward the American Indians. The company did not want the brutal traditions of Europe to be carried thoughtlessly into the new relationship; their policy, which Smith scorned as weak and foolish, was founded on foresight and reflection.

in a Shield for his Armes, by Patent, under his hand and Seale, with an Oath ever to weare them in his Colours, his Picture in Gould, and three hundred Ducats, yearely for a Pension. [*True Travels:* III, 163–175]

I N   T H E valley of Veristhorne, betwixt the river of Altus, and the mountaine of Rottenton, was this bloudy encounter, where the most of the dearest friends of the noble Prince Sigismundus perished. Meldritch having ordered his eleven thousand in the best manner he could, at the foot of the mountaine upon his flancks, and before his front, he had pitched sharpe stakes, their heads hardned in the fire, and bent against the enemie, as three battalion of Pikes, amongst the which also there was digged many small holes. Amongst those stakes was ranged his footmen, that upon the charge was to retire, as there was occasion. The Tartar having ordered his 40000. for his best advantage, appointed Mustapha Bashaw to beginne the battell, with a generall shout, all their Ensignes displaying, Drummes beating, Trumpets and Howboyes sounding. Nederspolt and Mavazo with their Regiments of horse most valiantly encountred, and forced them to retire; the Tartar Begolgi with his Squadrons, darkening the skies with their flights of numberles arrowes, who was as bravely encountred by Veltus and Oberwin, which bloudie slaughter continued more than an houre, till the matchlesse multitude of the Tartars so increased, that they retired within their Squadrons of stakes, as was directed. The bloudy Tartar, as scorning he should stay so long for the victorie, with his massie troopes prosecuted the charge: but it was a wonder to see how horse and man came to the ground among the stakes, whose disordered troopes were there so mangled, that the Christians with a loud shout cryed Victoria; and with five or six field peeces, planted upon the rising of the mountaine, did much hurt to the enemy that still continued the battell with that furie, that Meldritch seeing there was no possibilitie long to prevaile, joyned his small troopes in one body, resolved directly to make his passage or die in the conclusion; and thus in grosse gave a generall charge, and for more than halfe an houre made his way plaine before him, till the maine battel of the Crym-Tartar with two Regiments of Turkes and Janizaries so overmatched them, that they were overthrowen. The night approaching, the Earle with some thirteene or fourteene hundred horse, swamme the River, some were drowned, all the rest slaine or taken prisoners: And thus in this bloudy field, neere 30000. lay, some headlesse, armelesse and leglesse, all cut and mangled; where breathing their last, they gave this knowledge to the world, that for the lives of so few, the Crym-Tartar never paid dearer. But now the Countreyes of Transilvania and Wallachia, (subjected to the Emperour) and Sigismundus that brave Prince his Subject and Pensioner, the most of his Nobilitie, brave Captaines and Souldiers, became a prey to the cruell devouring Turke: where had the Emperor been as ready to have assisted him, and those three Armies led by three such worthy Captaines, as Michael, Busca, and Himselfe, and had those three Armies joyned together against the Turke, let all men judge, how happie it might have beene for all Christendome: and have either regained Bulgaria, or at least have beat him out of Hungaria, where hee hath taken much more from the Emperour, than hath the Emperour from Transilvania.

In this dismal battell, where Nederspolt, Veltus, Zarvana, Mavazo, Bavell, and many other Earles, Barons, Colonels, Captaines, brave Gentlemen, and Souldiers were slaine. Give mee leave to remember the names of our owne Country-men with him in those exploits, that as resolutely as the best in the defence of Christ and his Gospell, ended their dayes, as Baskerfield, Hardwicke, Thomas Milemer, Robert Mullineux, Thomas Bishop, Francis Compton, George Davison, Nicholas Williams, and one John a Scot, did what men could doe, and when they could doe no more, left there their bodies in testimonie of their mindes; only Ensigne Carleton and Sergeant Robinson escaped: but Smith among the slaughtered dead bodies, and many a gasping soule, with toile and wounds lay groaning among the rest, till being found by the Pillagers hee was able to live, and perceiving by his armor and habit, his ransome might be better to them, than his death, they led him prisoner with many others; well they used him till his wounds were cured, and at Axopolis they were all sold for slaves, like beasts in a market-place, where everie Merchant, viewing their limbs and wounds, caused other slaves to struggle with them, to trie their strength, hee fell to the share of Bashaw Bogall, who sent him forthwith to Adrinopolis, so for Constantinople to his faire Mistresse for a slave. By twentie and twentie chained by the neckes, they marched in file to this great Citie, where they were delivered to their severall Masters, and he to the young Charatza Tragabigzanda.[7]

7. *Charatza Tragabigzanda* means "girl from Trebizond." She was the first in a long line of noblewomen who supported and cherished Smith in his story.

THIS NOBLE Gentlewoman tooke sometime occasion to shew him to some friends, or rather to speake with him, because shee could speake Italian, would feigne her selfe sick when she should goe to the Banians, or weepe over the graves, to know how Bogall tooke him prisoner; and if he were as the Bashaw writ to her, a Bohemian Lord conquered by his hand, as hee had many others, which ere long hee would present her, whose ransomes should adorne her with the glorie of his conquests.

But when she heard him protest he knew no such matter, nor ever saw Bogall till he bought him at Axopolis, and that hee was an English-man, onely by his adventures made a Captaine in those Countreyes. To trie the truth, shee found meanes to finde out many could speake English, French, Dutch, and Italian, to whom relating most part of these former passages he thought necessarie, which they so honestly reported to her, she tooke (as it seemed) much compassion on him; but having no use for him, lest her mother should sell him, she sent him to her brother, the Tymor Bashaw of Nalbrits, in the Countrey of Cambia, a Province in Tartaria.

Here now let us remember his passing in this speculative course from Constantinople by Sander, Screwe, Panassa, Musa, Lastilla, to Varna, an ancient Citie upon the Blacke Sea. In all which journey, having little more libertie, than his eyes judgement since his captivitie, he might see the Townes with their short Towers, and a most plaine, fertile, and delicate Countrey, especially that most admired place of Greece, now called Romania, but from Varna, nothing but the Blacke Sea water, till he came to the two Capes of Taur and Pergilos, where hee passed the Straight of Niger, which (as he conjectured) is some ten leagues long, and three broad, betwixt two low lands, the Channell is deepe, but at the entrance of the Sea Dissabacca, their are many great Osie-shoulds, and many great blacke rockes, which the Turkes said were trees, weeds, and mud, throwen from the in-land Countryes, by the inundations and violence of the Current, and cast there by the Eddy. They sayled by many low Iles, and saw many more of those muddy rockes, and nothing else, but salt water, till they came betwixt Susax and Curuske, only two white townes at the entrance of the river Bruapo appeared: In six or seven dayes saile, he saw foure or five seeming strong castles of stone, with flat tops and battlements about them, but arriving at Cambia, he was (according to their custome) well used. The river was there more than halfe a mile broad. The Castle was of a large circumference, fourteene or fifteene foot thicke, in the foundation some six foot from the wall, is a Pallizado, and then a Ditch of about fortie foot broad full of water. On the west side of it, is a Towne all of low flat houses, which as he conceived could bee of no great strength, yet it keepes all them barbarous Countreyes about it in admiration and subjection. After he had stayed there three dayes; it was two dayes more before his guides brought him to Nalbrits, where the *Tymor* then was resident, in a great vast stonie Castle with many great Courts about it, invironed with high stone wals, where was quartered their Armes, when they first subjected those Countreyes, which only live to labour for those tyrannicall Turkes.

To her unkinde brother, this kinde Ladie writ so much for his good usage, that hee halfe suspected, as much as she intended; for shee told him, he should there but sojourne to learne the language, and what it was to be a Turke, till time made her Master of her selfe. But the *Tymor* her brother, diverted all this to the worst of crueltie, for within an houre after his arrivall, he caused his *Drub-man* to strip him naked, and shave his head and beard so bare as his hand, a great ring of iron, with a long stalke bowed like a sickle, rivetted about his necke, and a coat made of Ulgries haire, guarded about with a peece of an undrest skinne. There were many more Christian slaves, and neere an hundred *Forsades* of Turkes and Moores, and he being the last, was slave of slaves to them all.[8] Among these slavish fortunes there was no great choice; for the best was so bad, a dog could hardly have lived to endure, and yet for all their paines and labours no more regarded than a beast. [*True Travels:* III, 184–189]

ALL THE hope he had ever to be delivered from this thraldome, was only the love of Tragabigzanda, who surely was ignorant of his bad usage; for although he had often debated the matter with some Christians, that had beene there a long time slaves, they could not finde how to make an escape, by any reason or possibility; but God beyond mans expectation or imagination helpeth his servants, when they least thinke of helpe, as it hapned to him. So long he lived in this miserable estate, as he became a thresher at a grange in a great field, more than a league from the *Tymors* house; the Bashaw as he oft used

8. *Drub-man* is Smith's rendition of the Turkish word *dragoman*, an interpreter. An argali (ulgrie) is a big-horned sheep. Forsades are galley slaves. Smith, relying on his slight knowledge of Italian, must have been dimly aware of what was happening and reconstructed the story of his travels with maps after his return to England.

to visit his granges, visited him, and tooke occasion so to beat, spurne, and revile him, that forgetting all reason, he beat out the *Tymors* braines with his threshing bat, for they have no flailes; and seeing his estate could be no worse than it was, clothed himselfe in his clothes, hid his body under the straw, filled his knapsacke with corne, shut the doores, mounted his horse, and ranne into the desart at all adventure; two or three dayes thus fearfully wandring he knew not whither, and well it was he met not any to aske the way; being even as taking leave of this miserable world, God did direct him to the great way or Castragan, as they call it, which doth crosse these large territories, and generally knowne among them by these markes.

In every crossing of this great way is planted a post, and in it so many bobs with broad ends, as there be wayes, and every bob the figure painted on it, that demonstrateth to what part that way leadeth; as that which pointeth towards the Cryms Country, is marked with a halfe Moone, if towards the Georgians and Persia, a blacke man, full of white spots, if towards China, the picture of the Sunne, if towards Muscovia, the signe of a Crosse, if towards the habitation of any other Prince, the figure whereby his standard is knowne. To his dying spirits thus God added some comfort in this melancholy journey, wherein if he had met any of that vilde generation, they had made him their slave, or knowing the figure engraven in the iron about his necke, (as all slaves have) he had beene sent backe againe to his master; sixteene dayes he travelled in this feare and torment, after the Crosse, till he arrived at Æcopolis, upon the river Don, a garrison of the Muscovites. The governour after due examination of those his hard events, tooke off his irons, and so kindly used him, he thought himselfe new risen from death, and the good Lady Callamata, largely supplied all his wants.

This is as much as he could learne of those wilde Countries, that the Country of Cambia is two dayes journy from the head of the great river Bruapo, which springeth from many places of the mountaines of Innagachi, that joyne themselves together in the Poole Kerkas; which they account for the head, and falleth into the Sea Dissabacca, called by some the lake Meotis, which receiveth also the river Tanais, and all the rivers that fall from the great Countries of the Circassi, the Cartaches, and many from the Tauricaes, Precopes, Cummani, Cossunka, and the Cryme; through which Sea he sailed, and up the river Bruapo to Nalbrits, and thence through the desarts of Circassi to Æcopolis, as is related; where he stayed with the Governour, till the Convoy went to Coragnaw; then with his certificate how hee found him, and had examined with his friendly letters sent him by Zumalacke to Caragnaw, whose Governour in like manner so kindly use him, that by this meanes he went with a safe conduct to Letch, and Donka, in Cologoske, and thence to Berniske, and Newgrod in Seberia, by Rezechica, upon the river Niper, in the confines of Littuania; from whence with as much kindnesse he was convoyed in like manner by Coroski, Duberesko, Duzihell, Drohobus, and Ostroge in Volonia; Saslaw and Lasco in Podolia; Halico and Collonia in Polonia; and so to Hermonstat in Transilvania. In all his life he seldome met with more respect, mirth, content, and entertainment; and not any Governour where he came, but gave him somewhat as a present, besides his charges; seeing themselves as subject to the like calamity. Through those poore continually forraged Countries there is no passage, but with the Carravans or Convoyes; for they are Countries rather to be pitied, than envied; and it is a wonder any should make warres for them. The Villages are onely here and there a few houses of straight Firre trees, laid heads and points above one another, made fast by notches at the ends more than a mans height, and with broad split boards, pinned together with woodden pinnes, as thatched for coverture.[9] In ten Villages you shall scarce finde ten iron nailes, except it be in some extraordinary mans house. For their Townes, Æcopolis, Letch, and Donko, have rampiers made of that woodden walled fashion, double, and betwixt them earth and stones, but so latched with crosse timber, they are very strong against any thing but fire; and about them a deepe ditch, and a Palizado of young Firre trees: but most of the rest have only a great ditch cast about them, and the ditches earth is all their rampier; but round well environed with Palizadoes. Some have some few small peeces of small Ordnance, and slings, calievers, and muskets, but their generallest weapons are the Russe bowes and arrowes; you shall find pavements over bogges, onely of young Firre trees laid crosse one over another, for two or three houres journey, or as the passage requires, and yet in two dayes travell you shall scarce see six habitations. Notwithstanding to see how their Lords, Governours, and Captaines are civilized, well attired and acoutred with Jewells, Sables, and Horses, and after their manner with curious furniture, it is wonderfull; but

9. Smith is describing log cabins, built by fitting together the notched ends of the logs instead of using nails. This construction was unknown in England.

they are all Lords or slaves, which makes them so subject to every invasion.

In Transilvania he found so many good friends, that but to see, and rejoyce himselfe (after all those encounters) in his native Country, he would ever hardly have left them, though the mirrour of vertue their Prince was absent. Being thus glutted with content, and neere drowned with joy, he passed high Hungaria by Fileck, Tocka, Cassovia, and Underoroway, by Ulmicht in Moravia, to Prague in Bohemia; at last he found the most gracious Prince Sigismundus, with his Colonell at Lipswick in Misenland, who gave him his Passe, intimating the service he had done, and the honours he had received, with fifteene hundred ducats of gold to repaire his losses: with this he spent some time to visit the faire Cities and Countries of Drasdon in Saxonie, Magdaburgh and Brunswicke; Cassell in Hessen; Wittenberg, Ullum, and Minikin in Bavaria; Aughsbrough, and her Universities; Hama, Franckford, Mentz, the Palatinate; Wormes, Speyre, and Strausborough; passing Nancie in Loraine, and France by Paris to Orleans, hee went downe the river of Loyer, to Angiers, and imbarked himselfe at Nantz in Britanny, for Bilbao in Biskay, to see Burgos, Valiadolid, the admired monasterie of the Escuriall, Madrill, Toledo, Cordua, Cuedyriall, Civill, Cheryes, Cales, and Saint Lucas in Spaine. [*True Travels:* III, 200–203]

Now Smith, "being thus satisfied with Europe and Asia," decided to travel in North Africa. After various adventures, including service on a French privateer, he returned to England, where he found preparations in hand for the new Virginia enterprise.

II

The most famous episode in the Smith legend was his captivity in Virginia under the "Great Emperor" Powhatan and his rescue by Powhatan's little daughter, Pocahontas. This story, told very briefly in his first book, the True Relation, *became very elaborate in its retellings, and the length of the captivity increased each time. The most complete version, reprinted here, was in his* Generall Historie, *published in 1624. Pocahontas, now grown up and married to John Rolfe, had come to England in 1616, where her presence created a sensation; it was natural that Smith would want to trade on his early association with her. Smith was captured during one of several exploring voyages on the rivers that emanate from Chesapeake Bay. The lines of poetry that punctuate the text are from various classical authors.*

B UT OUR Comædies never endured long without a Tragedie; some idle exceptions being muttered against Captaine Smith, for not discovering the head of Chickahamania river, and taxed by the Councell, to be too slow in so worthy an attempt. The next voyage hee proceeded so farre that with much labour by cutting of trees in sunder he made his passage, but when his Barge could passe no farther, he left her in a broad bay out of danger of shot, commanding none should goe a shore till his returne: himselfe with two English and two Salvages went up higher in a Canowe, but hee was not long absent, but his men went a shore, whose want of government, gave both occasion and opportunity to the Salvages to surprise one George Cassen, whom they slew, and much failed not to have cut of the boat and all the rest. Smith little dreaming of that accident, being got to the marshes at the rivers head, twentie myles in the desert, had his two men slaine (as is supposed) sleeping by the Canowe, whilst himselfe by fowling sought them victuall, who finding he was beset with 200. Salvages, two of them hee slew, still defending himselfe with the ayd of a Salvage his guid, whom he bound to his arme with his garters, and used him as a buckler, yet he was shot in his thigh a little, and had many arrowes that stucke in his cloathes but no great hurt, till at last they tooke him prisoner.[10] When this newes came to James towne, much was their sorrow for his losse, fewe expecting what ensued. Six or seven weekes those Barbarians kept him prisoner, many strange triumphes and conjurations they made of him, yet hee so demeaned himselfe amongst them, as he not onely diverted them from surprising the Fort, but procured his owne libertie, and got himselfe and his company such

10. When attacked, Smith seized one of the Indians who had been serving as his guides, tied the guide to his arm with his sash or belt, called a garter, and made him serve as a shield, a buckler. The word *savage*, which may have meant little more than the modern term *native*, was often spelled *salvage*. The word *desert* refers to any uninhabited wild region.

John Smith's capture in 1607.

Robert Vaughan engraved these scenes illustrating Smith's story for the Generall
Historie of Virginia, New-England, and the Summer Isles. *In many cases Vaughan
borrowed images from the Roanoke colonist John White's drawings
of the Carolina Algonquians. Here White's rendition of a harvest festival is
changed into an Indian dance of triumph at the capture of John Smith.
Courtesy of the Princeton University Library.*

estimation amongst them, that those Salvages admired him more then their owne *Quiyouckosucks*.[11] The manner how they used and delivered him, is as followeth.

The Salvages having drawne from George Cassen whether Captaine Smith was gone, prosecuting that oportunity they followed him with 300. bowmen, conducted by the King of Pamaunkee, who in divisions searching the turnings of the river, found Robinson and Emry by the fire side, those they shot full of arrowes and slew. Then finding the Captaine, as is said, that used the Salvage that was his guide as his sheld (three of them being slaine and divers other so gauld) all the rest would not come neere him. Thinking thus to have returned to his boat, regarding them, as he marched, more then his way, slipped up to the middle in an oasie creeke and his Salvage with him, yet durst they not come to him till being neere dead with cold, he threw away his armes. Then according to their composition they drew him forth and led him to the fire, where his men were slaine. Diligently they chafed his benummed limbs. He demanding for their Captaine, they shewed him Opechankanough, King of Pamaunkee, to whom he gave a round Ivory double compass Dyall. Much they marvailed at the playing of the Fly and Needle, which they could see so plainely, and yet not touch it, because of the glasse that covered them. But when he demonstrated by that Globe-like Jewell, the roundnesse of the earth, and skies, the spheare of the Sunne, Moone, and Starres, and how the Sunne did chase the night round about the world continually; the greatnesse of the Land and Sea, the diversitie of Nations, varietie of complexions, and how we were to them Antipodes, and many other such like matters, they all stood as amazed with admiration.[12] Notwithstanding, within an houre after they tyed him to a tree, and as many as could

---

11. Smith was actually away from Jamestown a little more than three weeks. *Quiyouckosucks* refers to Indian "pettie" gods; in his earlier rendition of the same story, Smith said that the Indians "admired him as a demi-God."

12. Smith, having killed three Indians, galled, or broke the spirit of the others with his gun, so that he was able to retreat toward his boat still behind his human shield. Because his eye was on the Indian attackers, he stepped into a muddy bog, in which he was imprisoned and finally forced to surrender. The Indians, led by Opechancanough, half-brother and eventual successor to Powhatan, made a "composition," an agreement, which they honored, and took him to Orapaks, a temporary hunting village. The cosmography lesson, since each side's understanding of the other's language was rudimentary at best, must have been an interesting exercise in nonverbal communication.

stand about him prepared to shoot him, but the King holding up the Compass in his hand, they all laid downe their Bowes and Arrowes, and in a triumphant manner led him to Orapaks, where he was after their manner kindly feasted, and well used.

Their order in conducting him was thus; Drawing themselves all in fyle, the King in the middest had all their Peeces and Swords borne before him.[13] Captaine Smith was led after him by three great Salvages, holding him fast by each arme: and on each side six went in fyle with their Arrowes nocked. But arriving at the Towne (which was but onely thirtie or fortie hunting houses made of Mats, which they remove as they please, as we our tents) all the women and children staring to behold him, the souldiers first all in fyle performed the forme of a Bissone so well as could be; and on each flanke, officers as Serjeants to see them keepe their order.[14] A good time they continued this exercise, and then cast themselves in a ring, dauncing in such severall Postures, and singing and yelling out such hellish notes and screeches; being strangely painted, every one his quiver of Arrowes, and at his backe a club; on his arme a Fox or an Otters skinne, or some such matter for his vambrace; their heads and shoulders painted red, with Oyle and *Pocones* mingled together, which Scarlet-like colour made an exceeding handsome shew;[15] his Bow in his hand, and the skinne of a Bird with her wings abroad dryed, tyed on his head, a peece of copper, a white shell, a long feather, with a small rattle growing at the tayles of their snakes tyed to it, or some such like toy. All this while Smith and the King stood in the middest guarded, as before is said, and after three dances they all departed. Smith they conducted to a long house, where thirtie or fortie tall fellowes did guard him, and ere long more bread and venison was brought him then would have served twentie men, I thinke his stomacke at that time was not very good; what he left they put in baskets and tyed over his head. About midnight they set the meate againe before him, all this time not one of them would eate a bit

13. A peece is a gun. These weapons must have been taken from Smith's slain men.
14. *Bissone*, or *besom*, could refer to a bundle of switches used either as a broom or to punish; it could also refer to the act of sweeping clean. Smith may have been recording the kind of welcoming ritual that often greeted captives, one designed ceremonially to "beat the whiteness" out of the newcomer and prepare the captive for adoption into Indian life. See James Axtell, "The White Indians of Colonial America," *William and Mary Quarterly*, 3d Ser., XXXII, 55–88.
15. *Vambrace* refers to protective armor for the forearm. *Pocones* is a red vegetable dye.

with him, till the next morning they brought him as much more, and then did they eate all the old, and reserved the new as they had done the other, which made him thinke they would fat him to eat him. Yet in this desperate estate to defend him from the cold, one Maocassater brought him his gowne, in requitall of some beads and toyes Smith had given him at his first arrivall in Virginia.

Two dayes after a man would have slaine him (but that the guard prevented it) for the death of his sonne, to whom they conducted him to recover the poore man then breathing his last. Smith told them that at James towne he had a water would doe it, if they would let him fetch it, but they would not permit that; but made all the preparations they could to assault James towne, craving his advice, and for recompence he should have life, libertie, land, and women. In part of a Table booke he writ his minde to them at the Fort, what was intended, how they should follow that direction to affright the messengers, and without fayle send him such things as he writ for.[16] And an Inventory with them. The difficultie and danger, he told the Salvages, of the Mines, great gunnes, and other Engins exceedingly affrighted them, yet according to his request they went to James towne, in as bitter weather as could be of frost and snow, and within three dayes returned with an answer.

But when they came to James towne, seeing men sally out as he had told them they would, they fled; yet in the night they came againe to the same place where he had told them they should receive an answer, and such things as he had promised them, which they found accordingly, and with which they returned with no small expedition, to the wonder of them all that heard it, that he could either divine, or the paper could speake: then they led him to the Youghtanunds, the Mattapanients, the Payankatanks, the Nantaughtacunds, and Onawmanients upon the rivers of Rapahanock, and Patawomek, over all those rivers, and backe againe by divers other severall Nations, to the Kings habitation at Pamaunkee, where they entertained him with most strange and fearefull Conjurations;

16. Smith was taken to see a man he had mortally wounded when he was captured; it was thought that the Englishman might have the capacity to cure the wound. Smith, though he could do nothing, encouraged the idea that back at the fort the soldiers had medicines capable of such cures. He was able to warn the fort of an impending attack by persuading his captors to deliver a message he wrote in his notebook (table book).

As if neare led to hell,
Amongst the Devils to dwell.

Not long after, early in a morning a great fire was made in a long house, and a mat spread on the one side, as on the other, on the one they caused him to sit, and all the guard went out of the house, and presently came skipping in a great grim fellow, all painted over with coale, mingled with oyle; and many Snakes and Wesels skins stuffed with mosse, and all their tayles tyed together, so as they met on the crowne of his head in a tassell; and round about the tassell was as a Coronet of feathers, the skins hanging round about his head, backe, and shoulders, and in a manner covered his face; with a hellish voyce and a rattle in his hand. With most strange gestures and passions he began his invocation, and environed the fire with a circle of meale; which done, three more such like devils came rushing in with the like antique tricks, painted halfe blacke, halfe red: but all their eyes were painted white, and some red stroakes like Mutchato's, along their cheekes:[17] round about him those fiends daunced a pretty while, and then came in three more as ugly as the rest; with red eyes, and white stroakes over their blacke faces, at last they all sat downe right against him; three of them on the one hand of the chiefe Priest, and three on the other. Then all with their rattles began a song, which ended, the chiefe Priest layd downe five wheat cornes: then strayning his armes and hands with such violence that he sweat, and his veynes swelled, he began a short Oration: at the conclusion they all gave a short groane; and then layd down three graines more. After that, began their song againe, and then another Oration, ever laying downe so many cornes as before, till they had twice incirculed the fire; that done, they tooke a bunch of little stickes prepared for that purpose, continuing still their devotion, and at the end of every song and Oration, they layd downe a sticke betwixt the divisions of Corne. Till night, neither he nor they did either eate or drinke, and then they feasted merrily, with the best provisions they could make. Three dayes they used this Ceremony; the meaning whereof they told him, was to know if he intended them well or no. The circle of meale signified their Country, the circles of corne the bounds of the Sea, and the stickes his Country. They imagined the

---

17. By *antique* Smith means "grotesque." *Mutchato* means "moustache"; on birds, stripes down the side of the face such as Smith describes are called moustaches.

world to be flat and round, like a trencher, and they in the middest.[18] After this they brought him a bagge of gunpowder, which they carefully preserved till the next spring, to plant as they did their corne; because they would be acquainted with the nature of that seede. Opitchapam the Kings brother invited him to his house, where, with as many platters of bread, foule, and wild beasts, as did environ him, he bid him wellcome; but not any of them would eate a bit with him, but put up all the remainder in Baskets. At his returne to Opechancanoughs, all the Kings women, and their children, flocked about him for their parts, as a due by Custome, to be merry with such fragments.

But his waking mind in hydeous dreames did oft see wondrous shapes,
Of bodies strange, and huge in growth, and of stupendious makes.

At last they brought him to Meronocomoco, where was Powhatan their Emperor. Here more then two hundred of those grim Courtiers stood wondering at him, as he had beene a monster; till Powhatan and his trayne had put themselves in their greatest braveries. Before a fire upon a seat like a bedsted, he sat covered with a great robe, made of Rarowcun skinnes, and all the tayles hanging by.[19] On either hand did sit a young wench of 16 or 18 yeares, and along on each side the house, two rowes of men, and behind them as many women, with all their heads and shoulders painted red; many of their heads bedecked with the white downe of Birds; but every one with something: and a great chayne of white beads about their necks. At his entrance before the King, all the people gave a great shout. The Queene of Appamatuck was appointed to bring him water to wash his hands, and another brought him a bunch of feathers, in stead of a Towell to dry them: having feasted him after their best barbarous manner they could, a long consultation was held, but the conclusion was, two great stones were brought before Powhatan: then as many as could layd hands on him, dragged him to them, and thereon laid his head, and being ready with their clubs, to beate out his braines, Pocahontas the Kings dearest daughter, when no intreaty could prevaile, got his head in her armes, and laid her owne upon his to save him from death: whereat the Emperour was contented he should live to make him hatchets, and her

18. A trencher is a large flat wooden platter. Smith is describing a ceremony of divination.
19. *Greatest braveries* means "finest attire." Powhatan's seat was actually *Werowocomoco*. *Rarowcun* is an early spelling of *raccoon*.

bells, beads, and copper; for they thought him as well of all occupations as themselves.[20] For the King himselfe will make his owne robes,
shooes, bowes, arrowes, pots; plant, hunt, or doe any thing so well as
the rest.

> *They say he bore a pleasant shew,*
> *But sure his heart was sad.*
> *For who can pleasant be, and rest,*
> *That lives in feare and dread:*
> *And having life suspected, doth*
> *It still suspected lead.*

Two dayes after, Powhatan having disguised himselfe in the most
fearefullest manner he could, caused Captaine Smith to be brought
forth to a great house in the woods, and there upon a mat by the fire
to be left alone. Not long after from behinde a mat that divided the
house, was made the most dolefullest noyse he ever heard; then Powhatan more like a devill then a man with some two hundred more as
blacke as himselfe, came unto him and told him now they were friends,
and presently he should goe to James towne, to send him two great
gunnes, and a gryndstone, for which he would give him the Country
of Capahowosick, and for ever esteeme him as his sonne Nantaquoud.
So to James towne with 12 guides Powhatan sent him. That night they
quarterd in the woods, he still expecting (as he had done all this long
time of his imprisonment) every houre to be put to one death or
other: for all their feasting. But almightie God (by his divine providence) had mollified the hearts of those sterne Barbarians with compassion. The next morning betimes they came to the Fort, where
Smith having used the Salvages with what kindnesse he could, he
shewed Rawhunt, Powhatans trusty servant two demi-Culverings and
a millstone to carry Powhatan: they found them somewhat too heavie;
but when they did see him discharge them, being loaded with stones,

20. Whether Pocahontas, who was about 11 years old at this time, actually saved
Smith's life has been hotly debated ever since. It seems likely that it was a symbolic
rather than a real death, that Smith was undergoing a ceremony signifying the
death of the old self and his "rebirth" as an Indian and a werowance, or subchief
under Powhatan. Adolescent Indian boys, and sometimes girls, went through a
ritual called the *huskenaw* in which the child symbolically died and the full tribal
member emerged. Powhatan, who now called Smith "friend" and "son" and made
him werowance of Capahowosick, obviously thought the captain could be useful
to him.

among the boughs of a great tree loaded with Isickles, the yce and branches came so tumbling downe, that the poore Salvages ran away halfe dead with feare. But at last we regained some conference with them, and gave them such toyes, and sent to Powhatan, his women, and children such presents, as gave them in generall full content. Now in James Towne they were all in combustion, the strongest preparing once more to run away with the Pinnace; which with the hazzard of his life, with Sakre falcon and musket shot, Smith forced now the third time to stay or sinke.[21] Some no better then they should be, had plotted with the President, the next day to have put him to death by the Leviticall law, for the lives of Robinson and Emry, pretending the fault was his that had led them to their ends: but he quickly tooke such order with such Lawyers, that he layd them by the heeles till he sent some of them prisoners for England.[22] Now ever once in foure or five dayes, Pocahontas with her attendants, brought him so much provision, that saved many of their lives, that els for all this had starved with hunger.

> *Thus from numbe death our good God sent reliefe,*
> *The sweete asswager of all other griefe.*

His relation of the plenty he had seene, especially at Werawocomoco, and of the state and bountie of Powhatan, (which till that time was unknowne) so revived their dead spirits (especially the love of Pocahontas) as all mens feare was abandoned. Thus you may see what difficulties still crossed any good indevour: and the good successe of the businesse being thus oft brought to the very period of destruction; yet you see by what strange means God hath still delivered it. As for the insufficiency of them admitted in Commission, that error could not be prevented by the Electors; there being no other choise, and all strangers to each others education, qualities, or disposition. And if any deeme it a shame to our Nation to have any mention made of those inormities, let them peruse the Histories of the Spanyards Discoveries and Plantations, where they may see how many mutinies, disorders,

21. Demi-culverins, sacres, and falcons are all small cannon.
22. "Leviticall law": Smith's rivals in Jamestown wanted to punish him for the deaths of his men under the biblical formula of Leviticus 24, which called for punishment equivalent to the offense, such as an eye for an eye. He was saved by the arrival that same evening of the supply ships from London under Capt. Christopher Newport.

and dissentions have accompanied them, and crossed their attempts: which being knowne to be particular mens offences; doth take away the generall scorne and contempt, which malice, presumption, covetousnesse, or ignorance might produce; to the scandall and reproach of those, whose actions and valiant resolutions deserve a more worthy respect. [*Generall Historie:* II, 146–153]

When Pocahontas came to London with her husband John Rolfe and their infant son, Smith wrote to Queen Anne, wife of James I, with the intention of demonstrating that he, of all the English colonists, had the earliest association with Powhatan's daughter. The account of his captivity and rescue reprinted above would not be published for another eight years. Smith's letter to Queen Anne and his account of Pocahontas in London were published at the same time.

DURING THIS TIME, the Lady Rebecca, alias Pocahontas, daughter to Powhatan, by the diligent care of Master John Rolfe her husband and his friends, was taught to speake such English as might well bee understood, well instructed in Christianitie, and was become very formall and civill after our English manner;[23] shee had also by him a childe which she loved most dearely, and the Treasurer and Company tooke order both for the maintenance of her and it, besides there were divers persons of great ranke and qualitie had beene very kinde to her; and before she arrived at London, Captaine Smith to deserve her former courtesies, made her qualities knowne to the Queenes most excellent Majestie and her Court, and writ a little booke to this effect to the Queene: An abstract whereof followeth.

To the most high and vertuous Princesse Queene Anne
of Great Brittanie.

Most admired Queene,

The love I beare my God, my King and Countrie, hath so oft emboldened mee in the worst of extreme dangers, that now honestie doth constraine mee presume thus farre beyond my selfe, to present your

23. Pocahontas was given the English name Rebecca when she was baptized.

Pocahontas, age twenty. When she visited London in 1616 with her husband,
John Rolfe, and her infant son, Pocahontas created a sensation; she was buried
at Gravesend in 1617. Her portrait was engraved by Simon van de Passe.
Courtesy of the Trustees of the British Museum.

Majestie this short discourse: if ingratitude be a deadly poyson to all honest vertues, I must bee guiltie of that crime if I should omit any meanes to bee thankfull. So it is,

That some ten yeeres agoe being in Virginia, and taken prisoner by the power of Powhatan their chiefe King, I received from this great Salvage exceeding great courtesie, especially from his sonne Nanta-quaus, the most manliest, comeliest, boldest spirit, I ever saw in a Salvage, and his sister Pocahontas, the Kings most deare and wel-beloved daughter, being but a childe of twelve or thirteene yeeres of age, whose compassionate pitifull heart, of my desperate estate, gave me much cause to respect her: I being the first Christian this proud King and his grim attendants ever saw: and thus inthralled in their barbarous power, I cannot say I felt the least occasion of want that was in the power of those my mortall foes to prevent, notwithstanding al their threats. After some six weeks fatting amongst those Salvage Courtiers, at the minute of my execution, she hazarded the beating out of her owne braines to save mine, and not onely that, but so prevailed with her father, that I was safely conducted to James towne, where I found about eight and thirtie miserable poore and sicke creatures, to keepe possession of all those large territories of Virginia, such was the weaknesse of this poore Common-wealth, as had the Salvages not fed us, we directly had starved.

And this reliefe, most gracious Queene, was commonly brought us by this Lady Pocahontas, notwithstanding all these passages when inconstant Fortune turned our peace to warre, this tender Virgin would still not spare to dare to visit us, and by her our jarres have beene oft appeased, and our wants still supplyed; were it the policie of her father thus to imploy her, or the ordinance of God thus to make her his instrument, or her extraordinarie affection to our Nation, I know not: but of this I am sure; when her father with the utmost of his policie and power, sought to surprize mee, having but eighteene with mee, the darke night could not affright her from comming through the irkesome woods, and with watered eies gave me intelli-gence, with her best advice to escape his furie; which had hee knowne, hee had surely slaine her. James towne with her wild traine she as freely frequented, as her fathers habitation; and during the time of two or three yeeres, she next under God, was still the instrument to pre-serve this Colonie from death, famine and utter confusion, which if in those times had once beene dissolved, Virginia might have line as it

Pocahontas intervenes to save John Smith's life. Engraved by Robert Vaughan.
Courtesy of the Princeton University Library.

was at our first arrivall to this day.[24] Since then, this businesse having beene turned and varied by many accidents from that I left it at: it is most certaine, after a long and troublesome warre after my departure, betwixt her father and our Colonie, all which time shee was not heard of, about two yeeres after shee her selfe was taken prisoner, being so detained neere two yeeres longer, the Colonie by that meanes was relieved, peace concluded, and at last rejecting her barbarous condition, was maried to an English Gentleman, with whom at this present she is in England;[25] the first Christian ever of that Nation, the first Virginian ever spake English, or had a childe in mariage by an Englishman, a matter surely, if my meaning bee truly considered and well understood, worthy a Princes understanding.

Thus most gracious Lady, I have related to your Majestie, what at your best leasure our approved Histories will account you at large, and done in the time of your Majesties life, and however this might bee presented you from a more worthy pen, it cannot from a more honest heart, as yet I never begged any thing of the state, or any, and it is my want of abilitie and her exceeding desert, your birth, meanes and authoritie, hir birth, vertue, want and simplicitie, doth make mee thus bold, humbly to beseech your Majestie to take this knowledge of her, though it be from one so unworthy to be the reporter, as my selfe, her husbands estate not being able to make her fit to attend your Majestie: the most and least I can doe, is to tell you this, because none so oft hath tried it as my selfe, and the rather being of so great a spirit, how ever her stature: if she should not be well received, seeing this Kingdome may rightly have a Kingdome by her meanes; her present love to us and Christianitie, might turne to such scorne and furie, as to divert all this good to the worst of evill, where finding so great a Queene should doe her some honour more than she can imagine, for being so kinde to your servants and subjects, would so ravish her with content, as endeare her dearest bloud to effect that, your Majestie and all the Kings honest subjects most earnestly desire: And so I humbly kisse your gracious hands.[26]

Being about this time preparing to set saile for New-England, I could not stay to doe her that service I desired, and she well deserved;

---

24. *Line* is a variant spelling of *lain*.

25. Powhatan removed his daughter from contact with the English when she moved from childhood into puberty; she was found and kidnapped by an English trading ship in 1613.

26. The letter to Queen Anne ends here.

but hearing shee was at Branford with divers of my friends, I went to see her: After a modest salutation, without any word, she turned about, obscured her face, as not seeming well contented; and in that humour her husband, with divers others, we all left her two or three houres, repenting my selfe to have writ she could speake English. But not long after, she began to talke, and remembred mee well what courtesies shee had done: saying, You did promise Powhatan what was yours should bee his, and he the like to you; you called him father being in his land a stranger, and by the same reason so must I doe you: which though I would have excused, I durst not allow of that title, because she was a Kings daughter; with a well set countenance she said, Were you not afraid to come into my fathers Countrie, and caused feare in him and all his people (but mee) and feare you here I should call you father; I tell you then I will, and you shall call mee childe, and so I will bee for ever and ever your Countrieman. They did tell us alwaies you were dead, and I knew no other till I came to Plimoth; yet Powhatan did command Uttamatomakkin to seeke you, and know the truth, because your Countriemen will lie much.

This Salvage, one of Powhatans Councell, being amongst them held an understanding fellow; the King purposely sent him, as they say, to number the people here, and informe him well what wee were and our state. Arriving at Plimoth, according to his directions, he got a long sticke, whereon by notches hee did thinke to have kept the number of all the men hee could see, but he was quickly wearie of that taske: Comming to London, where by chance I met him, having renewed our acquaintance, where many were desirous to heare and see his behaviour, hee told me Powhatan did bid him to finde me out, to shew him our God, the King, Queene, and Prince, I so much had told them of: Concerning God, I told him the best I could, the King I heard he had seene, and the rest hee should see when he would; he denied ever to have seene the King, till by circumstances he was satisfied he had: Then he replyed very sadly, You gave Powhatan a white Dog, which Powhatan fed as himselfe, but your King gave me nothing, and I am better than your white Dog.

The small time I staid in London, divers Courtiers and others, my acquaintances, hath gone with mee to see her, that generally concluded, they did thinke God had a great hand in her conversion, and they have seene many English Ladies worse favoured, proportioned and behavioured, and as since I have heard, it pleased both the King and Queenes Majestie honourably to esteeme her, accompanied with that honourable Lady the Lady De la Ware, and that honourable Lord her husband, and divers other persons of good qualities, both publikely at the maskes and otherwise,[27] to her great satisfaction and content, which doubtlesse she would have deserved, had she lived to arrive in Virginia.[28] [*Generall Historie:* II, 258–262]

III

Smith often made the point that simply having been to America did not make one an expert. Many of the colonists had never left the vicinity of the fort; yet, so it appeared to Smith, those weak and discontented men were the most vocal when they returned to England. It was they who had criticized Smith's administration while contributing nothing themselves, and they who had led many at home to believe that Virginia was a poor place for a colony.

AND THIS IS as much as my memory can call to minde worthy of note; which I have purposely collected, to satisfie my friends of the true worth and qualitie of Virginia. Yet some bad natures will not sticke to slander the Countrey, that will slovenly spit at all things, especially in company where they can finde none to contradict them. Who though they were scarce ever ten myles from James Towne, or at the most but at the falles; yet holding it a great disgrace that amongst so much action, their actions were nothing, exclaime of all things, though they never adventured to know any thing; nor ever did any thing but devoure the fruits of other mens labours. Being for most part of such tender educations, and small experience in Martiall accidents, because they found not English Cities, nor such faire houses, nor at their owne wishes any of their accustomed dainties, with feather beds and downe pillowes, Tavernes and Alehouses in every breathing place, neither such plentie of gold and silver and dissolute libertie, as they expected, had little or no care of any thing, but to pamper their bellies, to fly away with our Pinnaces, or procure their meanes to

27. Masques were great pageants held at court that combined music, poetry, and drama; courtiers and the ladies of the court performed the parts.
28. Pocahontas died in England as her ship was about to leave for America; she had been away less than a year. John Rolfe returned to Virginia leaving their son in England. By *deserved* Smith means "requited."

returne for England. For the Country was to them a misery, a ruine, a death, a hell, and their reports here, and their actions there according.

Some other there were that had yearely stipends to passe to and againe for transportation: who to keepe the mysterie of the businesse in themselves, though they had neither time nor meanes to know much of themselves; yet all mens actions or relations they so formally tuned to the temporizing times simplicitie, as they could make their ignorances seeme much more, then all the true actors could by their experience. And those with their great words deluded the world with such strange promises, as abused the businesse much worse then the rest. For the businesse being builded upon the foundation of their fained experience, the planters, the money and meanes have still miscarried: yet they ever returning, and the planters so farre absent, who could contradict their excuses? which, still to maintaine their vaine glory and estimation, from time to time have used such diligence as made them passe for truths, though nothing more false. And that the adventurers might be thus abused, let no man wonder; for the wisest living is soonest abused by him that hath a faire tongue and a dissembling heart.

There were many in Virginia meerely projecting, verball, and idle contemplators, and those so devoted to pure idlenesse, that though they had lived two or three yeares in Virginia, lordly, necessitie it selfe could not compell them to passe the Peninsula, or Pallisadoes of James Towne, and those witty spirits, what would they not affirme in the behalfe of our transporters, to get victuall from their ships, or obtaine their good words in England, to get their passes. Thus from the clamors, and the ignorance of false informers, are sprung those disasters that sprung in Virginia: and our ingenious verbalists were no lesse plague to us in Virginia, then the Locusts to the Egyptians. For the labour of twentie or thirtie of the best onely preserved in Christianitie by their industry, the idle livers of neare two hundred of the rest: who living neere ten moneths of such naturall meanes, as the Country naturally of it selfe afforded, notwithstanding all this, and the worst fury of the Salvages, the extremitie of sicknesse, mutinies, faction, ignorances, and want of victuall; in all that time I lost but seaven or eight men, yet subjected the salvages to our desired obedience, and received contribution from thirtie five of their Kings, to protect and assist them against any that should assault them, in which order they continued true and faithfull, and as subjects to his Majestie, so long after as I did governe there, untill I left the Countrey: since, how they have revolted, the Countrie lost, and againe replanted, and the businesses hath succeded from time to time, I referre you to the relations of them returned from Virginia, that have beene more diligent in such Observations.

John Smith writ this with his owne hand.

[*Generall Historie:* II, 128–129]

In his last book, Advertisements for the Unexperienced Planters of New England, or Any Where, *Smith, now in the final year of his life, reflected on what he had contributed and how little he had been valued by those in a position to sponsor colonies. This presents the Smith legend as he thought it should be and as it actually was in his lifetime. He is here writing what could have been his own epitaph: John Smith told the truth, and no one wanted to hear it.*

N OW I F you but truly consider how many strange accidents have befallen those plantations and my selfe, how oft up, how oft downe, sometimes neere despaire, and ere long flourishing; how many scandals and Spanolized English have sought to disgrace them, bring them to ruine, or at least hinder them all they could; how many have shaven and couzened both them and me, and their most honourable supporters and well-willers, cannot but conceive Gods infinite mercy both to them and me.[29] Having beene a slave to the Turks, prisoner amongst the most barbarous Salvages, after my deliverance commonly discovering and ranging those large rivers and unknowne Nations with such a handfull of ignorant companions, that the wiser sort often gave mee for lost, always in mutinies, wants and miseries, blowne up with gunpowder; A long time prisoner among the French Pyrats, from whom escaping in a little boat by my selfe, and adrift, all such a stormy winter night when their ships were split, more than an hundred thousand pound lost, wee had taken at sea, and most of them drownd upon the Ile of Ree, not farre from whence I was driven on shore in my little boat, etc.[30] And many a score of the worst of winter moneths lived in

29. Smith here asserts that he and the colonies were cheated and stripped of resources ("shaven and couzened") by "Spanolized English," that is, by Englishmen who had taken on characteristics, particularly inconstancy and craftiness, that his countrymen associated with the Spaniard.

30. The Ile de Ré is off La Rochelle in Brittany.

the fields, yet to have lived neere 37. yeares in the midst of wars, pestilence and famine; by which, many an hundred thousand have died about mee, and scarce five living of them went first with me to Virginia, and see the fruits of my labours thus well begin to prosper: Though I have but my labour for my paines, have I not much reason both privately and publikely to acknowledge it and give God thankes, whose omnipotent power onely delivered me to doe the utmost of my best to make his name knowne in those remote parts of the world, and his loving mercy to such a miserable sinner.

Had my designes beene to have perswaded men to a mine of gold, as I know many have done that knew no such matter; though few doe conceive either the charge or paines in refining it, nor the power nor care to defend it; or some new invention to passe to the South sea, or some strange plot to invade some strange Monastery; or some chargeable Fleet to take some rich Charaques, or letters of mart, to rob some poore Merchant or honest fisher men;[31] what multitudes of both people and money would contend to be first imployed. But in those noble indevours now how few, unlesse it bee to begge them as Monopolies, and those seldome seeke the common good, but the commons goods, as the 217. the 218. and the 219. pages in the generall history will shew. But only those noble Gentlemen and their associates, for whose better incouragements I have recollected those experienced memorandums, as an Apologie against all calumniating detracters, as well for my selfe as them.

Now since them called Brownists went, some few before them also having my bookes and maps, presumed they knew as much as they desired, many other directers they had as wise as themselves, but that was best that liked their owne conceits;[32] for indeed they would not be knowne to have any knowledge of any but themselves, pretending

---

31. A carrack is a great ship, and letters of mart, or marque, are a license to engage in privateering. Smith is lamenting that more investment money was forthcoming for projects to prey on shipping than to build honest colonies.

32. By Brownists, Smith means the Pilgrims who settled in Plymouth in 1620. Puritans who believed that the Church of England was beyond redemption and who therefore wanted to separate from it and form independent congregations were popularly known as Brownists. The name, that of an early separatist leader, was somewhat scornful. Smith castigated the Pilgrims in a marginal note ("Miserablenesse no good husbandry") because they refused to make use of superior knowledge such as his and made a virtue of their frugal life and poor yields. What they thought of as humility, he said was full of self-pride.

onely Religion their governour, and frugality their counsell, when indeed it was onely their pride, and singularity, and contempt of authority; because they could not be equals, they would have no superiours: in this fooles Paradise, they so long used that good husbandry, they have payed soundly in trying their owne follies, who undertaking in small handfuls to make many plantations, and to bee severall Lords and Kings of themselves, most vanished to nothing, to the great disparagement of the generall businesse, therefore let them take heed that doe follow their example. [*Advertisements:* III, 284–286]

PART TWO

JAMESTOWN

JOHN SMITH AS LEADER

I

The first months in Jamestown after the ships had returned to England were miserable; the colonists' misery was compounded by mismanagement and misappropriation of supplies by those on the governing council and by lack of purpose among the "lower sort." Smith later insisted, though, especially after the Pilgrims began to use America to challenge established religion, that religious worship, and the good order it ordained, had been instituted from the beginning in Virginia.

NOW BECAUSE I have spoke so much for the body, give me leave to say somewhat of the soule; and the rather because I have beene demanded by so many, how we beganne to preach the Gospell in Virginia, and by what authority, what Churches we had, our order of service, and maintenance for our Ministers, therefore I thinke it not amisse to satisfie their demands, it being the mother of all our Plantations, intreating pride to spare laughter, to understand her simple beginning and proceedings.

When I went first to Virginia, I well remember, wee did hang an awning (which is an old saile) to three or foure trees to shadow us from the Sunne, our walls were rales of wood, our seats unhewed trees, till we cut plankes, our Pulpit a bar of wood nailed to two neighbouring trees, in foule weather we shifted into an old rotten tent, for we had few better, and this came by the way of adventure for new; this was our Church, till wee built a homely thing like a barne, set upon Cratchets, covered with rafts, sedge, and earth, so was also the walls: the best of our houses of the like curiosity,[1] but the most part farre much worse workmanship, that could neither well defend wind nor raine, yet wee had daily Common Prayer morning and evening, every Sunday two Sermons, and every three moneths the holy Communion, till our Minister died, but our Prayers daily, with an Homily on Sundaies; we continued two or three yeares after till more Preachers came, and surely God did most mercifully heare us, till the continuall inundations of mistaking directions, factions, and numbers of unprovided Libertines neere consumed us all, as the Israelites in the wildernesse.

Notwithstanding, out of the relicks of our miseries, time and experi-

---

1. Smith describes buildings constructed with earth and mat walls over a scaffoldlike structure. *Curiosity* refers to precise, careful workmanship.

ence had brought that Country to a great happinesse, had they not so much doated on their Tabacco, on whose fumish foundation there is small stability: there being so many good commodities besides, yet by it they have builded many pretty Villages, faire houses, and Chapels.[2] [*Advertisements:* III, 295–296]

What happened till the first supply.

B EING THUS left to our fortunes, it fortuned that within ten dayes scarce ten amongst us could either goe, or well stand, such extreame weaknes and sicknes oppressed us. And thereat none need marvaile, if they consider the cause and reason, which was this; whilest the ships stayed, our allowance was somewhat bettered, by a daily proportion of Bisket, which the sailers would pilfer to sell, give, or exchange with us, for money, Saxefras, furres, or love.[3] But when they departed, there remained neither taverne, beere-house, nor place of reliefe, but the common Kettell. Had we beene as free from all sinnes as gluttony, and drunkennesse, we might have beene canonized for Saints; But our President would never have beene admitted, for in-grossing to his private, Oatmeale, Sacke, Oyle, Aquavitæ, Beefe, Egges, or what not, but the Kettell;[4] that indeed he allowed equally to be distributed, and that was halfe a pint of wheat, and as much barley boyled with water for a man a day, and this having fryed some 26. weekes in the ships hold, contained as many wormes as graines; so that we might truely call it rather so much bran then corne, our drinke was water, our lodgings Castles in the ayre: with this lodging and dyet, our extreame toile in bearing and planting Pallisadoes, so strained and bruised us, and our continuall labour in the extremitie of the heat had so weakened us, as were cause sufficient to have made us as miserable

2. In these last few lines, Smith describes what Virginia had become by the end of his life.

3. Sassafras (saxefras) was a valuable commodity because it was considered a cure for syphilis. Since syphilis had appeared in Europe in an extremely virulent form just about the time Columbus's ships returned from America, it was commonly thought that the disease had New World origins. Early modern science taught that the remedy for any disease would be found in the place where the disease had originated, so sassafras, as an American plant, was prized.

4. Sack is white wine from Spain or the Canary Islands, and aquavitae is any strong spirit, such as brandy.

in our native Countrey, or any other place in the world. From May, to September, those that escaped, lived upon Sturgeon, and Sea-crabs, fiftie in this time we buried, the rest seeing the Presidents projects to escape these miseries in our Pinnace by flight (who all this time had neither felt want nor sicknes) so moved our dead spirits, as we deposed him; and established Ratcliffe in his place, (Gosnoll being dead) Kendall deposed, Smith newly recovered, Martin and Ratcliffe was by his care preserved and relieved, and the most of the souldiers recovered, with the skilfull diligence of Master Thomas Wotton our Chirurgian generall.[5] But now was all our provision spent, the Sturgeon gone, all helps abandoned, each houre expecting the fury of the Salvages; when God the patron of all good indevours, in that desperate extremitie so changed the hearts of the Salvages, that they brought such plenty of their fruits, and provision, as no man wanted.

And now where some affirmed it was ill done of the Councell to send forth men so badly provided, this incontradictable reason will shew them plainely they are too ill advised to nourish such ill conceits; first, the fault of our going was our owne, what could be thought fitting or necessary we had, but what we should find, or want, or where we should be, we were all ignorant, and supposing to make our passage in two moneths, with victuall to live, and the advantage of the spring to worke; we were at Sea five moneths, where we both spent our victuall and lost the opportunitie of the time, and season to plant, by the unskilfull presumption of our ignorant transporters, that understood not at all, what they undertooke.

Such actions have ever since the worlds beginning beene subject to such accidents, and every thing of worth is found full of difficulties, but nothing so difficult as to establish a Common-wealth so farre remote from men and meanes, and where mens mindes are so untoward as neither doe well themselves, nor suffer others. But to proceed.

The new President and Martin, being little beloved, of weake judgement in dangers, and lesse industrie in peace, committed the managing of all things abroad to Captaine Smith: who by his owne example, good words, and faire promises, set some to mow, others to binde thatch, some to build houses, others to thatch them, himselfe alwayes bearing the greatest taske for his owne share, so that in short time, he provided most of them lodgings, neglecting any for himselfe. This done, seeing the Salvages superfluitie beginne to decrease (with some

---

5. *Chirurgian* (or *chirurgeon*) was the contemporary spelling of *surgeon*.

of his workemen) shipped himselfe in the Shallop to search the Country for trade. The want of the language, knowledge to mannage his boat without sailes, the want of a sufficient power, (knowing the multitude of the Salvages) apparell for his men, and other necessaries, were infinite impediments, yet no discouragement. Being but six or seaven in company he went downe the river to Kecoughtan, where at first they scorned him, as a famished man, and would in derision offer him a handfull of Corne, a peece of bread, for their swords and muskets, and such like proportions also for their apparell. But seeing by trade and courtesie there was nothing to be had, he made bold to try such conclusions as necessitie inforced, though contrary to his Commission:[6] Let fly his muskets, ran his boat on shore, whereat they all fled into the woods. So marching towards their houses, they might see great heapes of corne: much adoe he had to restraine his hungry souldiers from present taking of it, expecting as it hapned that the Salvages would assault them, as not long after they did with a most hydeous noyse. Sixtie or seaventie of them, some blacke, some red, some white, some party-coloured, came in a square order, singing and dauncing out of the woods, with their *Okee* (which was an Idoll made of skinnes, stuffed with mosse, all painted and hung with chaines and copper) borne before them: and in this manner being well armed, with Clubs, Targets, Bowes and Arrowes, they charged the English, that so kindly received them with their muskets loaden with Pistoll shot, that downe fell their God, and divers lay sprauling on the ground; the rest fled againe to the woods, and ere long sent one of their *Quiyoughkasoucks* to offer peace, and redeeme their *Okee*.[7] Smith told them, if onely six of them would come unarmed and loade his boat, he would not only be their friend, but restore them their *Okee*, and give them Beads, Copper, and Hatchets besides: which on both sides was to their contents performed: and then they brought him Venison, Turkies, wild foule, bread, and what they had, singing and dauncing in signe of friendship till they departed. In his returne he discovered the Towne and Country of Warraskoyack.

6. "though contrary to his Commission": The colonists had been ordered by the Virginia Company not to offend the Indians or take their goods by force. Smith here illustrates his contention that the Indians had nothing but scorn for a policy of weakness.

7. *Quiyoughkasoucks* were identified by Smith as "pettie gods" and their priests.

Thus God unboundlesse by his power,
Made them thus kind, would us devour.

Smith perceiving (notwithstanding their late miserie) not any regarded but from hand to mouth (the company being well recovered) caused the Pinnace to be provided with things fitting to get provision for the yeare following; but in the interim he made 3. or 4. journies and discovered the people of Chickahamania: yet what he carefully provided the rest carelesly spent. . . . And now the winter approaching, the rivers became so covered with swans, geese, duckes, and cranes, that we daily feasted with good bread, Virginia pease, pumpions, and putchamins, fish, fowle, and diverse sorts of wild beasts as fat as we could eate them:[8] so that none of our Tuftaffaty humorists desired to goe for England.[9] [*Generall Historie:* II, 142–146]

II

Before he became president in Jamestown, Captain Smith took on the role of chief explorer and negotiator with the Indians. Since the colonists were dependent on the Indians for food and basic information about the environment, such functions were of great immediate, as well as long-range, importance. His heroic exploits in these twin roles form an important part of the Smith legend.

In their two voyages of discovery, Smith and his men thoroughly explored Chesapeake Bay and many of the rivers and inlets leading off it. They first traveled across the mouth of Chesapeake Bay to Cape Charles, and then coasted up the peninsula, staying close to the eastern shore. From the point where the bay narrows, they moved to the western shore, which is easier to coast along. Though they had meetings with many Indians along the eastern shore, they saw no one beyond the narrowing of the bay. For almost two weeks, they traveled in isolation, without fresh food to replenish their own rotting stock. The Indians may have been practicing a strategy that was an effective alternative to attack: to leave the ill-prepared Englishmen to their

8. Pumpions and putchamins are pumpkins and persimmons.
9. By "Tuftaffaty humorists" Smith is satirizing the idle gentlemen who remained in the fort dressed luxuriously and who were given to fantastic, ever-changing humors or opinions.

own devices. Finally, the men prevailed on Smith to turn around at a point just above the Patapsco River, which he called the Bolus.

Returning south, they found the mouth of the Potomac River (Patawomeck), which had been one of the main objects of their search as it was reputed to be the location of precious minerals. The men explored the Potomac past the site of Washington, D.C. They next prepared to go up the Rappahannock River, but the attack of a stingray ended that plan, and the wounded captain and his men returned to Jamestown. On the way, they lied to the Indians at Kecoughtan at the mouth of the James, telling them that they had vanquished the mighty Massawomecks, when in reality they had obtained Indian goods through trade.

The situation was bad in Jamestown when they arrived; the settlers were sick and the president and his administration were corrupt. Since the president's term had only two months to run, Smith and his allies put Matthew Scrivener in his place and the captain left to complete the job that his first voyage had failed to do. He planned to return in time for the new election, which he expected would name him president; meanwhile, he wanted to be away from the wrangling in the fort.

The party went back to the head of Chesapeake Bay and explored its intricacies. Smith probably went as far as the present borders of Delaware and Pennsylvania with Maryland. Here the men actually met warriors of the Massawomecks, and "gyant-like" men from the great Susquehannock tribe of modern Pennsylvania came to see Smith. On their return voyage, the explorers traveled up the Patuxent River and then up the Rappahannock probably past the site of Fredericksburg and into the territory of the Mannahoacks. On the journey back down the Rappahannock, Smith apparently acted as peacemaker between the warring Rappahannocks and the Moraughtacunds; both sides were impressed that he had survived an encounter with the Mannahoacks.

Rather than return to Jamestown prematurely, Smith then decided to explore further south of the fort. His party journeyed along the south shore of the James and up the Nansemond, where he taught the Indians a graphic lesson about the vengefulness of the English when they had the upper hand. He returned to the settlement in time for his election as president.

THE PRODIGALITIE of the Presidents state went so deepe into our small store, that Smith and Scrivener tyed him and his Parasites to the rules of proportion. But now Smith being to depart, the Presidents authoritie so oversto swayed the discretion of Master Scrivener, that our store, our time, our strength and labours were idely consumed to fulfill his phantasies. The second of June 1608. Smith left the Fort to performe his Discovery with this Company.

Walter Russell, *Doctor of Physicke.*
Ralfe Murton.
Thomas Momford.
William Cantrill.
Richard Fetherston. } *Gentlemen.*
James Burne.
Michell Sicklemore.

Jonas Profit.
Anas Todkill.
Robert Small.
James Watkins. } *Souldiers.*
John Powell.
James Read.
Richard Keale.

These being in an open Barge neare three tuns burthen, leaving the *Phœnix* at Cape Henry, they crossed the Bay to the Easterne shore, and fell with the Isles called Smiths Isles, after our Captaines name. The first people we saw were two grim and stout Salvages upon Cape Charles, with long poles like Javelings, headed with bone, they boldly demanded what we were, and what we would; but after many circumstances they seemed very kinde, and directed us to Accomack, the habitation of their Werowance, where we were kindly intreated. This King was the comliest, proper, civill Salvage we incountred. His Country is a pleasant fertile clay soyle, some small creekes; good Harbours for small Barks, but not for Ships. He told us of a strange accident lately happened him, and it was, two children being dead; some extreame passions, or dreaming visions, phantasies, or affection moved their parents againe to revisit their dead carkases, whose benummed bodies reflected to the eyes of the beholders such delightfull countenances, as though they had regained their vitall spirits. This as a miracle drew many to behold them, all which being a great part of his people, not long after dyed, and but few escaped. They spake the language of Powhatan, wherein they made such descriptions of the Bay, Isles, and rivers, that often did us exceeding pleasure. Passing

John Smith's map of Virginia showing the distribution of the Indians and the intricacies of the landscape. Crosses mark the farthest extent of Smith's own exploring voyages. Engraved by William Hole from Smith's sketches and notes. William Hole, like Robert Vaughan, borrowed images from John White's drawings of the Carolina Algonquians for the insets of Indian life. Powhatan addressing his people is adapted from White's picture of a carved wooden figure that watched over the remains of dead village leaders. Vaughan also used this image (see p. 150).
Courtesy of the Newberry Library, Chicago.

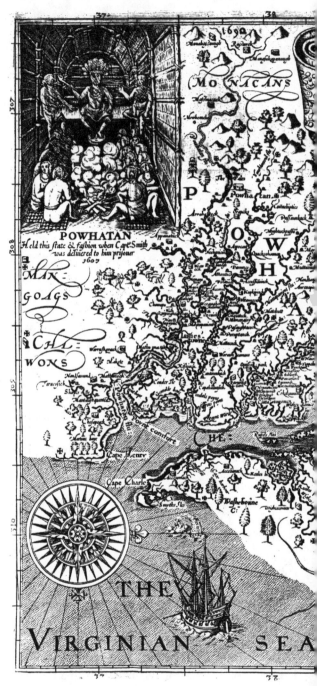

along the coast, searching every inlet, and Bay, fit for harbours and habitations. Seeing many Isles in the midst of the Bay we bore up for them, but ere we could obtaine them, such an extreame gust of wind, rayne, thunder, and lightening happened, that with great danger we escaped the unmercifull raging of that Ocean-like water. The highest land on the mayne, yet it was but low, we called Keales hill, and these uninhabited Isles, Russels Isles. The next day searching them for fresh water, we could find none, the defect whereof forced us to follow the next Easterne Channell, which brought us to the river of Wighco-comoco. The people at first with great fury seemed to assault us, yet at last with songs and daunces and much mirth became very tractable, but searching their habitations for water, we could fill but three barri-coes, and that such puddle, that never till then we ever knew the want of good water.[10] We digged and searched in many places, but before two daies were expired, we would have refused two barricoes of gold for one of that puddle water of Wighcocomoco. Being past these Isles which are many in number, but all naught for habitation, falling with a high land upon the mayne, we found a great Pond of fresh water, but so exceeding hot wee supposed it some bath; that place we called poynt Ployer, in honor of that most honourable House of Mousay in Britaine, that in an extreame extremitie once relieved our Captaine. From Wighcocomoco to this place, all the coast is low broken Isles of Morap, growne a myle or two in breadth, and ten or twelve in length, good to cut for hay in Summer, and to catch fish and foule in Winter: but the Land beyond them is all covered over with wood, as is the rest of the Country.

Being thus refreshed in crossing over from the maine to other Isles, we discovered the winde and waters so much increased with thunder, lightning, and raine, that our mast and sayle blew overbord and such mighty waves overracked us in that small barge that with great labour we kept her from sinking by freeing out the water. Two dayes we were inforced to inhabite these uninhabited Isles which for the extremitie of gusts, thunder, raine, stormes, and ill wether we called Limbo. Repair-ing our saile with our shirts, we set sayle for the maine and fell with a pretty convenient river on the East called Cuskarawaok, the people ran as amazed in troups from place to place, and divers got into the tops of trees, they were not sparing of their arrowes, nor the greatest passion

---

10. *Mayne*, or *maine*, simply means "mainland." *Barricoe* means "cask" or "keg."

they could expresse of their anger. Long they shot, we still ryding at an Anchor without there reatch making all the signes of friendship we could. The next day they came unarmed, with every one a basket, dancing in a ring, to draw us on shore: but seeing there was nothing in them but villany, we discharged a volly of muskets charged with pistoll shot, whereat they all lay tumbling on the grownd, creeping some one way, some another into a great cluster of reedes hard by; where there companies lay in Ambuscado.[11] Towards the evening we wayed, and approaching the shoare, discharging five or six shot among the reedes, we landed where there lay a many of baskets and much bloud, but saw not a Salvage. A smoake appearing on the other side the river, we rowed thither, where we found two or three little houses, in each a fire, there we left some peeces of copper, beads, bells, and looking glasses, and then went into the bay, but when it was darke we came backe againe. Early in the morning foure Salvages came to us in their Canow, whom we used with such courtesie, not knowing what we were, nor had done, having beene in the bay a fishing, bade us stay and ere long they would returne, which they did and some twentie more with them; with whom after a little conference, two or three thousand men women and children came clustring about us, every one presenting us with something, which a little bead would so well requite, that we became such friends they would contend who should fetch us water, stay with us for hostage, conduct our men any whither, and give us the best content. Here doth inhabite the people of Sarapinagh, Nause, Arseek, and Nantaquak the best Marchants of all other Salvages. They much extolled a great nation called Massawomekes, in search of whom we returned by Limbo: this river but onely at the entrance is very narrow, and the people of small stature as them of Wighcocomoco, the Land but low, yet it may prove very commodious, because it is but a ridge of land betwixt the Bay and the maine Ocean. Finding this Easterne shore, shallow broken Isles, and for most part without fresh water, we passed by the straites of Limbo for the Westerne shore: so broad is the bay here, we could scarce perceive the great high clifts on the other side: by them we Anchored that night and called them Riccards Cliftes. 30. leagues we sayled more Northwards not finding any inhabitants, leaving all the Easterne shore, lowe Islandes, but overgrowne with wood, as all the Coast beyond them so farre as wee could

11. *Ambuscado* means "ambush"; like *barricoe*, it had a Spanish flavor.

see: the Westerne shore by which we sayled we found all along well
watered, but very mountanous and barren, the vallies very fertill, but
extreame thicke of small wood so well as trees, and much frequented
with Wolves, Beares, Deere and other wild beasts. We passed many
shallow creekes, but the first we found Navigable for a ship, we called
Bolus, for that the clay in many places under the clifts by the high
water marke, did grow up in red and white knots as gum out of trees;
and in some places so participated together as though they were all of
one nature, excepting the coulour, the rest of the earth on both sides
being hard sandy gravell, which made us thinke it Bole-Armoniack
and Terra sigillata.[12] When we first set sayle some of our Gallants
doubted nothing but that our Captaine would make too much hast
home, but having lien in this small barge not above 12. or 14. dayes, oft
tyred at the Oares, our bread spoyled with wet so much that it was
rotten (yet so good were their stomacks that they could disgest it) they
did with continuall complaints so importune him now to returne, as
caused him bespeake them in this manner.

> Gentlemen if you would remember the memorable history of Sir
> Ralph Layne,[13] how his company importuned him to proceed in
> the discovery of Moratico, alleadging they had yet a dog, that
> being boyled with Saxafras leaves, would richly feede them in
> their returnes; then what a shame would it be for you (that have
> bin so suspitious of my tendernesse) to force me returne, with so
> much provision as we have, and scarce able to say where we have
> beene, nor yet heard of that we were sent to seeke? You cannot say
> but I have shared with you in the worst which is past; and for
> what is to come, of lodging, dyet, or whatsoever, I am contented
> you allot the worst part to my selfe. As for your feares that I will
> lose my selfe in these unknowne large waters, or be swallowed up
> in some stormie gust; abandon these childish feares, for worse
> then is past is not likely to happen: and there is as much danger to
> returne as to proceede. Regaine therefore your old spirits for re-

---

12. Bole Armoniack and Terra sigillata are both clays with astringent properties
that were used for medicinal purposes and imported into England; the discovery
of a deposit of either might help the colonists repay the investors in London.
13. Ralph Lane was the governor of Sir Walter Ralegh's Roanoke colony of 1585–
1586. Smith is trying to shame his men by telling the story of the fortitude of Lane's
colonists in a similar exploring voyage.

turne I will not (if God please) till I have seene the Massawomeks, found Patawomek, or the head of this water you conceit to be endlesse.

Two or 3. dayes we expected winde and wether, whose adverse extremities added such discouragement, that three or foure fell sicke, whose pittifull complaints caused us to returne, leaving the bay some nine miles broad, at nine and ten fadome water.

The 16. of June we fell with the river Patowomek: feare being gone, and our men recovered, we were all content to take some paines, to know the name of that seven mile broad river: for thirtie myles sayle, we could see no inhabitants: then we were conducted by two Savages up a little bayed creeke, towards Onawmanient, where all the woods were layd with ambuscado's to the number of three or foure thousand Salvages, so strangely paynted, grimed and disguised, shouting, yelling and crying as so many spirits from hell could not have shewed more terrible. Many bravado's they made, but to appease their fury, our Captaine prepared with as seeming a willingnesse (as they) to incounter them. But the grazing of our bullets upon the water (many being shot on purpose they might see them) with the Ecco of the woods so amazed them, as downe went their bowes and arrowes; (and exchanging hostage) James Watkins was sent six myles up the woods to their Kings habitation. We were kindly used of those Salvages, of whom we understood, they were commanded to betray us, by the direction of Powhatan, and he so directed from the discontents at James towne, because our Captaine did cause them stay in their country against their wills.[14]

The like incounters we found at Patowomek, Cecocawonee and divers other places: but at Moyaones, Nacotchtant and Toags the people did their best to content us. Having gone so high as we could with the bote, we met divers Salvages in Canowes, well loaden with the flesh of Beares, Deere, and other beasts, whereof we had part, here we found mighty Rocks, growing in some places above the grownd as high as the shrubby trees, and divers other solid quarries of divers tinctures: and divers places where the waters had falne from the high

14. Smith indicates that he believed the malcontents in Jamestown conspired with Powhatan to eliminate him so that they could return to England. James Watkins is here being exchanged for an Indian to ensure good behavior on both sides.

mountaines they had left a tinctured spangled skurfe, that made many
bare places seeme as guilded. Digging the growne above in the highest
clifts of rocks, we saw it was a claie sand so mingled with yeallow
spangles as if it had beene halfe pin-dust.[15] In our returne inquiring
still for this Matchqueon, the king of Patawomeke gave us guides to
conduct us up a little river called Quiyough, up which we rowed so
high as we could. Leaving the bote, with six shot, and divers Salvages,
he marched seven or eight myle before they came to the mine: leading
his hostages in a small chaine they were to have for their paines, being
proud so richly to be adorned. The mine is a great Rocky mountaine
like Antimony; wherein they digged a great hole with shells and hatchets: and hard by it, runneth a fayre brooke of Christal-like water,
where they wash a way the drosse and keepe the remainder, which they
put in little baggs and sell it all over the country to paint there bodyes,
faces, or Idols; which makes them looke like Blackmores dusted over
with silver. With so much as we could carry we returned to our bote,
kindly requiting this kinde king and all his kinde people. The cause of
this discovery was to search this mine, of which Newport did assure us
that those small baggs (we had given him) in England he had tryed to
hold halfe silver; but all we got proved of no value: also to search what
furrs, the best whereof is at Cuscarawaoke, where is made so much
Rawranoke or white beads that occasion as much dissention among the
Salvages, as gold and silver amongst Christians;[16] and what other
mineralls, rivers, rocks, nations, woods, fishings, fruites, victuall, and
what other commodities the land afforded: and whether the bay were
endlesse or how farre it extended: of mines we were all ignorant, but a
few Bevers, Otters, Beares, Martins and minkes we found, and in
divers places that aboundance of fish, lying so thicke with their heads
above the water, as for want of nets (our barge driving amongst them)
we attempted to catch them with a frying pan: but we found it a bad
instrument to catch fish with:[17] neither better fish, more plenty, nor

---

15. *Skurfe* means "a crusted deposit, a thin layer." Pindust is the dust left from the
grinding of brass pins. Smith is indicating that there is some evidence of precious
metals in Virginia, though he, unlike others, would not make extravagant claims.
16. *Rawranoke:* roanoke, beads made of shell, elsewhere called *wampum*.
17. It is revealing that, despite Smith's bravado, his party had not brought along
any equipment to catch fish; this meant that they would be dependent on the
Indians they met for fresh food.

more variety for smal fish, had any of us ever seene in any place so swimming in the water, but they are not to be caught with frying pans: some small codd also we did see swim close by the shore by Smiths Iles, and some as high as Riccards Clifts. And some we have found dead upon the shore.

To express all our quarrels, trecheries and incounters amongst those Salvages I should be too tedious: but in breefe, at all times we so incountred them, and curbed their insolencies, that they concluded with presents to purchase peace; yet we lost not a man: at our first meeting our Captaine ever observed this order to demand their bowes and arrowes, swordes, mantells and furrs, with some childe or two for hostage, whereby we could quickly perceive, when they intended any villany. Having finished this discovery (though our victuall was neere spent) he intended to see his imprisonment-acquaintances upon the river of Rapahanock, by many called Toppahanock, but our bote by reason of the ebbe, chansing to grownd upon a many shoules lying in the entrances, we spyed many fishes lurking in the reedes: our Captaine sporting himselfe by nayling them to the grownd with his sword, set us all a fishing in that manner: thus we tooke more in owne houre then we could eate in a day.[18] But it chansed our Captaine taking a fish from his sword (not knowing her condition) being much of the fashion of a Thornback, but a long tayle like a ryding rodde, whereon the middest is a most poysoned sting, of two or three inches long, bearded like a saw on each side, which she strucke into the wrest of his arme neere an inch and a halfe: no bloud nor wound was seene, but a little blew spot, but the torment was instantly so extreame, that in foure houres had so swolen his hand, arme and shoulder, we all with much sorrow concluded his funerall, and prepared his grave in an Island by, as himselfe directed: yet it pleased God by a precious oyle Doctor Russell at the first applyed to it when he sounded it with probe (ere night) his tormenting paine was so well asswaged that he eate of the fish to his supper, which gave no lesse joy and content to us then ease to himselfe, for which we called the Island Stingray Isle after the name of the fish.

Having neither Chirurgian, nor Chirurgery, but that preservative oyle we presently set sayles for James towne, passing the mouthes of the rivers of Payankatank, and Pamaunkee, the next day we safely

18. *Owne* for *one*.

arrived at Kecougtan.[19] The simple Salvages seeing our Captaine hurt, and an other bloudy by breaking his shinne, our numbers of bowes, arrowes, swords, mantles, and furrs, would needes imagine we had beene at warres (the truth of these accidents would not satisfie them) but impatiently importuned us to know with whom. Finding their aptnesse to beleeve we fayled not (as a great secret) to tell them any thing that might affright them, what spoyle we had got and made of the Massawomeks. This rumor went faster up the river then our Barge, that arrived at Waraskoyack the 20 of July; where trimming her with painted streamers, and such devises as we could, we made them at James towne jealous of a Spanish Frigot, where we all God be thanked safely arrived the 21 of July. There we found the last Supply were all sicke, the rest some lame, some bruised, all unable to doe any thing but complaine of the pride and unreasonable needlesse crueltie of the silly President, that had riotously consumed the store: and to fulfill his follies about building him an unnecessary building for his pleasure in the woods, had brought them all to that misery; that had we not arrived, they had as strangely tormented him with revenge: but the good newes of our Discovery, and the good hope we had by the Salvages relation, that our Bay had stretched into the South Sea, or somewhat neare it, appeased their fury; but conditionally that Ratliffe should be deposed, and that Captaine Smith would take upon him the government, as by course it did belong.[20] Their request being effected, he substituted Master Scrivener his deare friend in the Presidency, equally distributing those private provisions the other had ingrossed, appointing more honest officers to assist master Scrivener (who then lay exceeding sicke of a Callenture) and in regard of the weaknesse of

19. Surgeons dealt with wounds and open sores, whereas physicians were trained to maintain health by keeping the humors balanced through the use of purgatives; therefore, a surgeon was more useful on an exploring expedition.

20. Smith and his exploring party arrived to find the last supply, that is, those men who had arrived most recently, sick and unable to work. Captain Smith contrasts his leadership and self-sacrifice with the corrupt regime in Jamestown that consumed the colonists' food "riotously" and diverted labor to building a special house for the president, who was "silly," meaning weak, foolish, and lacking in judgment. Smith appointed Matthew Scrivener president despite the latter's being sick with a calenture, a fever associated with hot climates.

Captain Smith probably wrote most or all of the passages, but added other names to make it clear that his opinions were not unique. The illusion of multiple authorship may have made publication possible after Smith had offended the powerful Virginia Company with his criticisms.

the company, and heate of the yeare, they being unable to worke, he left them to live at ease, to recover their healths, but imbarked himselfe to finish his Discovery.

Written by Walter Russell, Anas Todkill, and Thomas Momford.

T HE 24 of July, Captaine Smith set forward to finish the discovery with twelve men: their names were

Nathaniell Powell.	
Thomas Momford.	
Richard Fetherston.	
Michell Sicklemore.	*Gentlemen.*
James Bourne.	
Anthony Bagnall, *Chirurgian.*	
Jonas Profit.	
Anas Todkill.	
Edward Pising.	*Souldiers.*
Richard Keale.	
James Watkins.	
William Ward.	

The wind being contrary caused our stay two or three dayes at Kecoughtan: the King feasted us with much mirth, his people were perswaded we went purposely to be revenged of the Massawomeks. In the evening we fired a few rackets, which flying in the ayre so terrified the poore Salvages, they supposed nothing unpossible we attempted; and desired to assist us. The first night we anchored at Stingray Isle. The next day crossed Patawomeks river, and hasted to the river Bolus. We went not much further before we might see the Bay to divide in two heads, and arriving there we found it divided in foure, all which we searched so farre as we could sayle them. Two of them we found inhabited, but in crossing the Bay, we incountred 7 or 8 Canowes full of Massawomeks. We seeing them prepare to assault us, left our Oares and made way with our sayle to incounter them, yet were we but five with our Captaine that could stand, for within 2 dayes after we left Kecoughtan, the rest (being all of the last supply) were sicke almost to death, untill they were seasoned to the Country. Having shut them under our Tarpawling, we put their hats upon stickes by the Barges side, and betwixt two hats a man with two peeces, to make us seeme many, and so we thinke the Indians supposed those hats to be men, for they fled with all possible speed to the shore, and there stayed, staring at the sayling of our barge till we anchored right against them. Long it was ere we could draw them to come unto us. At last they sent two of their company unarmed in a Canow, the rest all followed to second them if neede required. These two being but each presented with a bell, brought aboord all their fellowes, presenting our Captaine with venison, beares flesh, fish, bowes, arrowes, clubs, targets, and beareskinnes. We understood them nothing at all, but by signes, whereby they signified unto us they had beene at warres with the Tockwoghes, the which they confirmed by shewing us their greene wounds,[21] but the night parting us, we imagined they appointed the next morning to meete, but after that we never saw them.

Entring the river of Tockwogh, the Salvages all armed, in a fleete of boats, after their barbarous manner, round invironed us; so it chanced one of them could speake the language of Powhatan, who perswaded the rest to a friendly parley. But when they saw us furnished with the Massawomeks weapons, and we faining the invention of Kecoughtan, to have taken them perforce;[22] they conducted us to their pallizadoed towne, mantelled with the barkes of trees, with scaffolds like mounts, brested about with brests very formally. Their men, women, and children with daunces, songs, fruits, furres, and what they had, kindly welcommed us, spreading mats for us to sit on, stretching their best abilities to expresse their loves.

Many hatchets, knives, peeces of iron, and brasse, we saw amongst them, which they reported to have from the Sasquesahanocks, a mightie people and mortall enemies with the Massawomeks.[23] The

---

21. Green wounds are fresh wounds.
22. Smith and his men kept up the fiction that they had defeated the Massawomecks in battle, and the Tockwoghs took them to see their fortified town, which featured a palisade covered with tree bark and earthworks to repel attacks.
23. The iron and brass tools supposed to have come from the Susquehannocks were significant, because they might indicate that these inland Indians were in contact with other Europeans. The hope of all the colonists and their backers was that the explorers would find a way through the continent to the Pacific and the rich Eastern trades. Smith had already reported, on his earlier return to Jamestown, that Chesapeake Bay might extend to the South Sea, the Pacific.

Latitude could be calculated with great accuracy, but it would be another century before longitude could be known; therefore, even though Europeans had sailed to both sides of the American continents, it was difficult to know how far west a ship had actually gone in traveling up the west coast. In the case of the Susquehannocks, Smith was soon satisfied that their European goods came from the French in Canada.

Sasquesahanocks inhabit upon the chiefe Spring of these foure branches of the Bayes head, two dayes journey higher then our barge could passe for rocks, yet we prevailed with the Interpreter to take with him another Interpreter, to perswade the Sasquesahanocks to come visit us, for their language are different. Three or foure dayes we expected their returne, then sixtie of those gyant-like people came downe, with presents of Venison, Tobacco-pipes three foot in length, Baskets, Targets, Bowes and Arrowes. Five of their chiefe Werowances came boldly aboord us to crosse the Bay for Tockwhogh, leaving their men and Canowes; the wind being so high they durst not passe.

Our order was daily to have Prayer, with a Psalme, at which solemnitie the poore Salvages much wondred, our Prayers being done, a while they were busied with a consultation till they had contrived their businesse. Then they began in a most passionate manner to hold up their hands to the Sunne, with a most fearefull song, then imbracing our Captaine, they began to adore him in like manner: though he rebuked them, yet they proceeded till their song was finished: which done with a most strange furious action, and a hellish voyce, began an Oration of their loves; that ended, with a great painted Beares skin they covered him: then one ready with a great chayne of white Beads, weighing at least six or seaven pound, hung it about his necke, the others had 18 mantels, made of divers sorts of skinnes sowed together; all these with many other toyes they layd at his feete, stroking their ceremonious hands about his necke for his Creation to be their Governour and Protector, promising their aydes, victualls, or what they had to be his, if he would stay with them, to defend and revenge them of the Massawomeks. But we left them at Tockwhogh, sorrowing for our departure, yet we promised the next yeare againe to visit them. Many descriptions and discourses they made us, of Atquanachuck, Massawomek, and other people, signifying they inhabit upon a great water beyond the mountaines, which we understood to be some great lake, or the river of Canada: and from the French to have their hatchets and Commodities by trade. These know no more of the territories of Powhatan, then his name, and he as little of them, but the Atquanachuks are on the Ocean Sea.

The highest mountaine we saw Northward wee called Perigrines mount, and a rocky river, where the Massawomeks went up, Willowbyes river, in honor of the towne our Captaine was borne in, and that honorable house the Lord Willowby, his most honored good friend. The Sasquesahanocks river we called Smiths falles; the next poynt to

Tockwhogh, Pisings poynt; the next it poynt Bourne. Powells Isles and
Smals poynt is by the river Bolus; and the little Bay at the head Profits
poole; Watkins, Reads, and Momfords poynts are on each side Limbo;
Ward, Cantrell, and Sicklemore, betwixt Patawomek and Pamaunkee,
after the names of the discoverers. In all those places and the furthest
we came up the rivers, we cut in trees so many crosses as we would,
and in many places made holes in trees, wherein we writ notes, and in
some places crosses of brasse, to signifie to any, Englishmen had beene
there.

Thus having sought all the inlets and rivers worth noting, we returned to discover the river of Pawtuxunt; these people we found very
tractable, and more civill then any. We promised them, as also the
Patawomeks to revenge them of the Massawomeks, but our purposes
were crossed.

In the discovery of this river some call Rapahanock, we were kindly
entertained by the people of Moraughtacund; here we incountered our
old friend Mosco, a lusty Salvage of Wighcocomoco upon the river of
Patawomek. We supposed him some French mans sonne, because he
had a thicke blacke bush beard, and the Salvages seldome have any at
all, of which he was not a little proud, to see so many of his Countrymen.[24] Wood and water he would fetch us, guide us any whether, nay,
cause divers of his Countrymen helpe us towe against winde or tyde
from place to place till we came to Patawomek: there he rested till we
returned from the head of the river, and occasioned our conduct to the
mine we supposed Antimony. And in the place he fayled not to doe us
all the good he could, perswading us in any case not to goe to the
Rapahanocks, for they would kill us for being friends with the Moraughtacunds that but lately had stolne three of the Kings women.
This we did thinke was but that his friends might onely have our trade:
so we crossed the river to the Rapahanocks. There some 12 or 16
standing on the shore, directed us a little Creeke where was good
landing, and Commodities for us in three or foure Canowes we saw lie
there: but according to our custome, we demanded to exchange a man
in signe of love, which after they had a little consulted, foure or five

24. Mosco, whose beard indicated possible European parentage on one side, is an
interesting case. He apparently was not fully at home in either Indian or English
society; he sought recognition and friendship from Smith and his party. Part of
this description is a "flashback" to the first voyage and the expedition to the mine
of antimony.

came up to the middles, to fetch our man, and leave us one of them, shewing we need not feare them, for they had neither clubs, bowes, nor arrowes. Notwithstanding, Anas Todkill, being sent on shore to see if he could discover any Ambuscadoes, or what they had, desired to goe over the playne to fetch some wood, but they were unwilling, except we would come into the Creeke, where the boat might come close ashore. Todkill by degrees having got some two stones throwes up the playne, perceived two or three hundred men (as he thought) behind the trees, so that offering to returne to the Boat, the Salvages assayed to carry him away perforce, that he called to us we were betrayed, and by that he had spoke the word, our hostage was overboord, but Watkins his keeper slew him in the water. Immediately we let fly amongst them, so that they fled, and Todkill escaped, yet they shot so fast that he fell flat on the ground ere he could recover the boat. Here the Massawomek Targets stood us in good stead, for upon Mosco's words, we had set them about the forepart of our Boat like a forecastle, from whence we securely beat the Salvages from off the plaine without any hurt: yet they shot more then a thousand Arrowes, and then fled into the woods. Arming our selves with these light Targets (which are made of little small sticks woven betwixt strings of their hempe and silke grasse, as is our Cloth, but so firmely that no arrow can possibly pierce them:) we rescued Todkill, who was all bloudy by some of them who were shot by us that held him, but as God pleased he had no hurt; and following them up to the woods, we found some slaine, and in divers places much bloud. It seems all their arrowes were spent, for we heard no more of them. Their Canows we tooke; the arrowes we found we broke, save them we kept for Mosco, to whom we gave the Canowes for his kindnesse, that entertained us in the best triumphing manner, and warlike order in armes of conquest he could procure of the Moraughtacunds.

The rest of the day we spent in accomodating our Boat, in stead of thoules wee made stickes like Bedstaves, to which we fastened so many of our Massawomek Targets, that invironed her as wast clothes.[25] The next morning we went up the river, and our friend Mosco followed us along the shore, and at last desired to goe with us in our Boat. But as we passed by Pisacack, Matchopeak, and Mecuppom, three Townes

---

25. Targets are shields. Thoules, or tholes, are pegs driven into the side of the ship that function as oarlocks, and wast clothes are hangings that both decorate a boat and screen its occupants from view.

situated upon high white clay clifts; the other side all a low playne marish, and the river there but narrow. Thirtie or fortie of the Rapahanocks, had so accommodated themselves with branches, as we tooke them for little bushes growing among the sedge, still seeing their arrowes strike the Targets, and dropped in the river: whereat Mosco fell flat in the Boat on his face, crying the Rapahanocks, which presently we espied to be the bushes, which at our first volley fell downe in the sedge: when wee were neare halfe a myle from them, they shewed themselves dauncing and singing very merrily.

The Kings of Pissassack, Nandtaughtacund, and Cuttatawomen, used us kindly, and all their people neglected not any thing to Mosco to bring us to them. Betwixt Secobeck and Massawteck is a small Isle or two, which causeth the river to be broader then ordinary; there it pleased God to take one of our Company called Master Fetherstone, that all the time he had beene in this Country, had behaved himselfe, honestly, valiantly, and industriously, where in a little Bay we called Fetherstones Bay wee buryed him with a volley of shot: the rest notwithstanding their ill dyet, and bad lodging, crowded in so small a Barge, in so many dangers never resting, but always tossed to and againe, had all well recovered their healths. The next day wee sayled so high as our Boat would float, there setting up crosses, and graving our names in the trees.[26] Our Sentinell saw an arrow fall by him, though we had ranged up and downe more then an houre in digging in the earth, looking of stones, herbs, and springs, not seeing where a Salvage could well hide himselfe.

Upon the alarum by that we had recovered our armes, there was about an hundred nimble Indians skipping from tree to tree, letting fly their arrows so fast as they could: the trees here served us for Baricadoes as well as they. But Mosco did us more service then we expected, for having shot away his quiver of Arrowes, he ran to the Boat for more. The Arrowes of Mosco at the first made them pause upon the matter, thinking by his bruit and skipping, there were many Salvages. About halfe an houre this continued, then they all vanished as suddainly as they approached. Mosco followed them so farre as he could see us, till they were out of sight. As we returned there lay a Salvage as dead, shot in the knee, but taking him up we found he had life, which Mosco seeing, never was Dog more furious against a Beare, then Mosco was to have beat out his braines, so we had him to our Boat,

26. The English boats could not go above the fall line.

where our Chirurgian who went with us to cure our Captaines hurt of the Stingray, so dressed this Salvage that within an houre after he looked somewhat chearefully, and did eate and speake. In the meane time we contented Mosco in helping him to gather up their arrowes, which were an armefull, whereof he gloried not a little. Then we desired Mosco to know what he was, and what Countries were beyond the mountaines; the poore Salvage mildly answered, he and all with him were of Hasinninga, where there are three Kings more, like unto them, namely the King of Stegora, the King of Tauxuntania, and the King of Shakahonea, that were come to Mohaskahod, which is onely a hunting Towne, and the bounds betwixt the Kingdome of the Manna-hocks, and the Nandtaughtacunds, but hard by where we were. We demanded why they came in that manner to betray us, that came to them in peace, and to seeke their loves; he answered, they heard we were a people come from under the world, to take their world from them. We asked him how many worlds he did know, he replyed, he knew no more but that which was under the skie that covered him, which were the Powhatans, with the Monacans, and the Massawo-meks, that were higher up in the mountaines. Then we asked him what was beyond the mountaines, he answered the Sunne: but of any thing els he knew nothing; because the woods were not burnt.[27] These and many such questions wee demanded, concerning the Massawomeks, the Monacans, their owne Country, and where were the Kings of Stegora, Tauxsintania, and the rest. The Monacans he sayd were their neighbours and friends, and did dwell as they in the hilly Countries ۱٫y small rivers, living upon rootes and fruits, but chiefly by hunting. The Massawomeks did dwell upon a great water, and had many boats, and so many men that they made warre with all the world. For their Kings, they were gone every one a severall way with their men on hunting: But those with him came thither a fishing till they saw us, notwith-standing they would be altogether at night at Mahaskahod. For his relation we gave him many toyes, with perswasions to goe with us, and he as earnestly desired us to stay the comming of those Kings that for his good usage should be friends with us, for he was brother to Hasin-ninga. But Mosco advised us presently to be gone, for they were all naught, yet we told him we would not till it was night. All things we made ready to entertain what came, and Mosco was as diligent in

27. Indians along the coast of North America burned the underbrush in the woods periodically in order to facilitate travel and hunting.

trimming his arrowes. The night being come we all imbarked, for the river was so narrow, had it beene light the land on the one side was so high, they might have done us exceeding much mischiefe. All this while the King of Hasinninga was seeking the rest, and had consultation a good time what to doe. But by their espies seeing we were gone, it was not long before we heard their arrowes dropping on every side the Boat; we caused our Salvages to call unto them, but such a yelling and hallowing they made that they heard nothing, but now and then a peece, ayming so neare as we could where we heard the most voyces. More then 12 myles they followed us in this manner; then the day appearing, we found our selves in a broad Bay, out of danger of their shot, where wee came to an anchor, and fell to breakfast. Not so much as speaking to them till the Sunne was risen; being well refreshed, we untyed our Targets that covered us as a Deck, and all shewed our selves with those shields on our armes, and swords in our hands, and also our prisoner Amoroleck; a long discourse there was betwixt his Countrimen and him, how good wee were, how well wee used him, how wee had a Patawomek with us, loved us as his life, that would have slaine him had we not preserved him, and that he should have his libertie would they be but friends; and to doe us any hurt it was impossible. Upon this they all hung their Bowes and Quivers upon the trees, and one came swimming aboord us with a Bow tyed on his head, and another with a Quiver of Arrowes, which they delivered our Captaine as a present, the Captaine having used them so kindly as he could, told them the other three Kings should doe the like, and then the great King of our world should be their friend, whose men we were. It was no sooner demanded but performed, so upon a low Moorish poynt of Land we went to the shore, where those foure Kings came and received Amoroleck: nothing they had but Bowes, Arrowes, Tobacco-bags, and Pipes: what we desired, none refused to give us, wondering at every thing we had, and heard we had done: our Pistols they tooke for pipes, which they much desired, but we did content them with other Commodities, and so we left foure or five hundred of our merry Mannahocks, singing, dauncing, and making merry, and set sayle for Moraughtacund.

In our returnes we visited all our friends, that rejoyced much at our Victory against the Mannahocks, who many times had Warres also with them, but now they were friends, and desired we would be friends with the Rapahanocks, as we were with the Mannahocks. Our Captaine told them, they had twise assaulted him that came onely in love to doe them good, and therefore he would now burne all their houses, destroy their corne, and for ever hold them his enemies, till they made him satisfaction; they desired to know what that should be: he told them they should present him the Kings Bow and Arrowes, and not offer to come armed where he was; that they should be friends with the Moraughtacunds his friends, and give him their Kings sonne in pledge to performe it, and then all King James his men should be their friends. Upon this they presently sent to the Rapahanocks to meete him at the place where they first fought, where would be the Kings of Nantautacund and Pissassac: which according to their promise were there so soone as we; where Rapahanock presented his Bow and Arrowes, and confirmed all we desired, except his sonne, having no more but him he could not live without him, but in stead of his sonne he would give him the three women Moraughtacund had stolne. This was accepted: and so in three or foure Canowes, so many as could went with us to Moraughtacund, where Mosco made them such relations, and gave to his friends so many Bowes and Arrowes, that they no lesse loved him then admired us. The 3 women were brought our Captaine, to each he gave a chayne of Beads: and then causing Moraughtacund, Mosco, and Rapahanock stand before him, bid Rapahanock take her he loved best, and Moraughtacund chuse next, and to Mosco he gave the third. Upon this away went their Canowes over the water, to fetch their venison, and all the provision they could, and they that wanted Boats swam over the river: the darke commanded us then to rest. The next day there was of men, women, and children, as we conjectured, six or seaven hundred, dauncing, and singing, and not a Bow nor Arrow seene amongst them. Mosco changed his name Uttasantasough, which we interpret Stranger, for so they call us. All promising ever to be our friends, and to plant Corne purposely for us; and we to provide hatchets, beads, and copper for them, we departed, giving them a Volley of shot, and they us as loud shouts and cryes as their strengths could utter. That night we anchored in the river of Payankatank, and discovered it so high as it was navigable, but the people were most a hunting, save a few old men, women, and children, that were tending their corne, of which they promised us part when we would fetch it, as had done all the Nations where ever we had yet beene.

In a fayre calme, rowing towards poynt Comfort, we anchored in Gosnolls Bay, but such a suddaine gust surprised us in the night with thunder and rayne, that we never thought more to have seene James

Towne. Yet running before the wind, we sometimes saw the Land by
the flashes of fire from heaven, by which light onely we kept from the
splitting shore, untill it pleased God in that blacke darknesse to preserve us by that light to finde poynt Comfort: there refreshing our
selves, because we had onely but heard of the Chisapeacks and Nandsamunds, we thought it as fit to know all our neighbours neare home,
as so many Nations abroad.

So setting sayle for the Southerne shore, we sayled up a narrow river
up the country of Chisapeack; it hath a good channell, but many
shoules about the entrance. By that we had sayled six or seaven myles,
we saw two or three little garden plots with their houses, the shores
overgrowne with the greatest Pyne and Firre trees wee ever saw in the
Country. But not seeing nor hearing any people, and the river very
narrow, we returned to the great river, to see if we could finde any of
them. Coasting the shore towards Nandsamund, which is most Oys-
ter-bankes; at the mouth of that river, we espied six or seaven Salvages
making their wires, who presently fled:[28] ashore we went, and where
they wrought we threw divers toyes, and so departed. Farre we were
not gone ere they came againe, and began to sing, and daunce, and
recall us: and thus we began our first acquaintance. At last one of them
desired us to goe to his house up that river, into our Boat voluntarily
he came, the rest ran after us by the shore with all shew of love that
could be. Seaven or eight myles we sayled up this narrow river: at last
on the Westerne shore we saw large Cornefields, in the midst a little
Isle, and in it was abundance of Corne; the people he told us were all a
hunting, but in the Isle was his house, to which he invited us with
much kindnesse: to him, his wife, and children, we gave such things as
they seemed much contented them. The others being come, desired us
also to goe but a little higher to see their houses: here our host left us,
the rest rowed by us in a Canow, till we were so far past the Isle the
river became very narrow. Here we desired some of them to come
abord us, wherat pausing a little, they told us they would but fetch
their bows and arrowes and goe all with us, but being a-shore and thus
armed, they perswaded us to goe forward, but we could neither perswade them into their Canow, nor into our Boat. This gave us cause to
provide for the worst. Farre we went not ere seaven or eight Canowes
full of men armed appeared following us, staying to see the conclusion. Presently from each side the river came arrowes so fast as two or

28. *Wires* is probably for *weirs*, traps set in the river to catch fish.

three hundred could shoot them, whereat we returned to get the open. They in the Canowes let fly also as fast, but amongst them we bestowed so many shot, the most of them leaped overboord and swam ashore, but two or three escaped by rowing. Being against their playnes:[29] our Muskets they found shot further then their Bowes, for wee made not twentie shot ere they all retyred behind the next trees. Being thus got out of their trap, we seised on all their Canowes, and moored them in the midst of the open. More then an hundred arrowes stucke in our Targets, and about the boat, yet none hurt, onely Anthony Bagnall was shot in his Hat, and another in his sleeve. But seeing their multitudes, and suspecting as it was, that both the Nandsamunds, and the Chisapeacks were together, we thought it best to ryde by their Canowes a while, to bethinke if it were better to burne all in the Isle, or draw them to composition, till we were provided to take all they had, which was sufficient to feed all our Colony: but to burne the Isle at night it was concluded. In the interim we began to cut in peeces their Canowes, and they presently to lay downe their bowes, making signes of peace: peace we told them we would accept, would they bring us their Kings bowes and arrowes, with a chayne of pearle; and when we came againe give us foure hundred baskets full of Corne, otherwise we would breake all their boats, and burne their houses, and corne, and all they had. To performe all this they alledged onely the want of a Canow; so we put one a drift and bad them swim to fetch her: and till they performed their promise, wee would but onely breake their Canowes. They cryed to us to doe no more, all should be as we would: which presently they performed, away went their bowes and arrowes, and tagge and ragge came with their baskets: so much as we could carry we tooke, and so departing good friends, we returned to James Towne, where we safely arrived the 7. of September, 1608. There we found Master Scrivener, and divers others well recovered: many dead; some sicke: the late President prisoner for mutiny: by the honest diligence of Master Scrivener, the harvest gathered, but the provision in the store much spoyled with rayne. Thus was that summer (when little wanted) consumed and spent, and nothing done (such was the government of Captaine Ratliffe) but onely this discovery; wherein to expresse all the dangers, accidents, and incounters this

29. By "being against their playnes," Smith apparently means that the fleeing Indians were escaping into an open meadow or plain that formed a background against which their figures stood out clearly.

small number passed in that small Barge, by the scale of proportion, about three thousand myles,[30] with such watery dyet in those great waters and barbarous Countries (till then to any Christian utterly unknowne) I rather referre their merit to the censure of the courteous and experienced Reader, then I would be tedious or partiall being a partie. [*Generall Historie:* II, 162–180]

III

Smith began his presidency with characteristic energy.

THE 10. of September 1608. by the election of the Councel, and request of the company Captaine Smith received the letters patents, and tooke upon him the place of President, which till then by no meanes he would accept though hee were often importuned thereunto. Now the building of Ratcliffes pallas staide as a thing needlesse; The church was repaired, the storehouse recovered; buildings prepared for the supply we expected. The fort reduced to the forme of this figure, the order of watch renued, the squadrons (each setting of the watch) trained. The whole company every Satturday exercised in a fielde prepared for that purpose; the boates trimmed for trade. . . . [*Proceedings:* I, 233–234]

THE PRESIDENT dispersed many as were able, some for glasse, others for pitch, tarre and sope ashes, leaving them, (with the fort) to the Councels oversight.[31] But 30 of us he conducted 5. myles from the fort to learn to make clapbord, cut downe trees, and ly in woods; amongst the rest he had chosen Gabriell Beadell, and John Russell the only two gallants of this last supply, and both proper gentlemen: strange were these pleasures to their conditions, yet lodging eating, drinking, working, or playing they doing but as the President, all these things were carried so pleasantly, as within a weeke they

---

30. Three thousand miles is an extreme exaggeration of the two voyages.
31. Colonial investors had high hopes for the importation of clapboard and wood by-products such as pitch, tar, and potash. England suffered a severe wood shortage, which it was thought the colonies could help rectify. Most timber products proved too bulky to be carried economically.

became Masters, making it their delight to heare the trees thunder as they fell, but the axes so oft blistered there tender fingers, that commonly every third blow had a lowd oath to drowne the eccho; for remedy of which sin the President devised howe to have everie mans oathes numbred, and at night, for every oath to have a can of water powred downe his sleeve, with which every offender was so washed (himselfe and all) that a man should scarse heare an oath in a weeke.

By this, let no man think that the President, or these gentlemen spent their times as common wood-hackers at felling of trees, or such like other labours, or that they were pressed to any thing as hirelings or common slaves, for what they did (being but once a little inured) it seemed, and they conceited it only as a pleasure and a recreation. Yet 30 or 40 of such voluntary Gentlemen would doe more in a day then 100 of the rest that must bee prest to it by compulsion.[32] Master Scrivener, Captaine Waldo, and Captaine Winne at the fort, every one in like manner carefully regarded their charge. The President returning from amongst the woodes, seeing the time consumed, and no provision gotten, (and the ship lay Idle, and would do nothing) presently imbarked himselfe in the discovery barge, giving order to the Councell, to send Master Persey after him with the next barge that arrived at the fort; 2. barges, he had himselfe, and 20. men, but arriving at Chickahamina, that dogged nation was too wel acquainted with our wants, refusing to trade, with as much scorne and insolencie as they could expresse. The President perceiving it was Powhatans policy to starve us, told them he came not so much for their corne, as to revenge his imprisonment, and the death of his men murdered by them, and so landing his men, and ready to charge them, they immediatly fled; but then they sent their imbassadours, with corne, fish, fowl, or what they had to make their peace, (their corne being that year bad) they complained extreamly of their owne wants, yet fraughted our boats with 100 bushels of corne, and in like manner Master Persies, that not long after us arrived; they having done the best they could to content us, within 4. or 5. daies we returned to James Towne.

Though this much contented the company (that then feared nothing but starving) yet some so envied his good successe, that they rather desired to starve, then his paines should prove so much more effectuall

32. When this passage was reprinted in the *Generall Historie* 12 years later, Smith added "but twentie good workemen had beene better then them all" (Barbour edition, II, 186).

then theirs; some projects there was, not only to have deposed him but to have kept him out of the fort, for that being President, he would leave his place, and the fort without their consents; but their hornes were so much too short to effect it, as they themselves more narrowly escaped a greater mischiefe.

All this time our old taverne made as much of all them that had either mony or ware as could bee desired;[33] and by this time they were become so perfect on all sides (I meane Souldiers, Sailers, and Salvages,) as there was ten-times more care to maintaine their damnable and private trade, then to provide for the Colony things that were necessary. Neither was it a small pollicy in the mariners, to report in England wee had such plenty and bring us so many men without victuall, when they had so many private factors in the fort, that within 6. or 7. weekes after the ships returne, of 2. or 300. hatchets, chissels, mattocks, and pickaxes scarce 20 could be found, and for pike-heads, knives, shot, powder, or any thing (they could steale from their fellowes) was vendible; They knew as well (and as secretly) how to convay them to trade with the Salvages, for furres, baskets, mussaneekes,[34] young beastes or such like commodities, as exchange them with the sailers, for butter, cheese, biefe, porke, aquavitæ, beere, bisket, and oatmeale; and then faine, all was sent them from their friends. And though Virginia afford no furs for the store, yet one mariner in one voyage hath got so many, as hee hath confessed to have solde in England for 30[l].

Those are the Saint-seeming worthies of Virginia, that have notwithstanding all this, meate, drinke, and pay, but now they begin to grow weary, their trade being both perceived and prevented; none hath bin in Virginia (that hath observed any thing) which knowes not this to be true, and yet the scorne, and shame was the poore souldiers, gentlemen and carelesse governours, who were all thus bought and solde, the adventurers cousened, and the action overthrowne by their false excuses, informations, and directions, by this let all the world Judge, how this businesse coulde prosper, being thus abused by such pilfering occasions. [*Proceedings:* I, 238–240]

33. By "our old taverne" Smith means the supply ship that was anchored off Jamestown. The sailors carried on a private trade in provisions and alcohol with both colonists and Indians. Smith believed that the mariners traded in commodities sent by the Virginia Company for the good of the colony while the settlers kept for such commerce products that should have gone to reimburse the company.
34. *Mussaneekes* may be gray squirrels.

In 1624, when Captain Smith republished his account of his presidency, the Virginia Company was under investigation for mismanagement by a royal commission and Smith, who no longer looked to Virginia for his future, was more forthright about blaming the company for the misery endured in the settlement's early years. He printed a letter sent by him from Jamestown to London when he was president, in which he angrily and plainly answered the company's charges that the colonists were idly spending their time spinning factions instead of producing commodities that would repay investors and make the colony strong. Smith's reply argued that it was the confused and contradictory instructions from London that caused the most trouble.

The Copy of a Letter sent to the Treasurer
and Councell of Virginia from Captaine Smith,
then President in Virginia.

Right Honorable, etc.

I Received your Letter, wherein you write, that our minds are so set upon faction, and idle conceits in dividing the Country without your consents, and that we feed You but with ifs and ands, hopes, and some few proofes; as if we would keepe the mystery of the businesse to our selves: and that we must expresly follow your instructions sent by Captain Newport: the charge of whose voyage amounts to neare two thousand pounds, the which if we cannot defray by the Ships returne, we are like to remain as banished men. To these particulars I humbly intreat your Pardons if I offend you with my rude Answer.

For our factions, unlesse you would have me run away and leave the Country, I cannot prevent them: because I do make many stay that would els fly any whether. For the idle Letter sent to my Lord of Salisbury, by the President and his confederats, for dividing the Country etc.[35] What it was I know not, for you saw no hand of mine to it; nor ever dream't I of any such matter. That we feed you with hopes, etc. Though I be no scholer, I am past a schoole-boy; and I desire but to know, what either you, and these here doe know, but that I have learned to tell you by the continuall hazard of my life. I have not

35. The president referred to was John Ratcliffe, also known as John Sicklemore; Smith and he had been allies, but had fallen out.

concealed from you any thing I know; but I feare some cause you to beleeve much more then is true.

Expresly to follow your directions by Captaine Newport, though they be performed, I was directly against it; but according to our Commission, I was content to be overruled by the major part of the Councell, I feare to the hazard of us all; which now is generally confessed when it is too late. Onely Captaine Winne and Captaine Waldo I have sworne of the Councell, and Crowned Powhatan according to your instructions.

For the charge of this Voyage of two or three thousand pounds,[36] we have not received the value of an hundred pounds. And for the quartred Boat to be borne by the Souldiers over the Falles, Newport had 120 of the best men he could chuse. If he had burnt her to ashes, one might have carried her in a bag; but as she is, five hundred cannot, to a navigable place above the Falles. And for him at that time to find in the South Sea, a Mine of gold; or any of them sent by Sir Walter Raleigh:[37] at our Consultation I told them was as likely as the rest. But during this great discovery of thirtie myles, (which might as well have beene done by one man, and much more, for the value of a pound of Copper at a seasonable tyme) they had the Pinnace and all the Boats with them, but one that remained with me to serve the Fort.[38] In their absence I followed the new begun workes of Pitch and Tarre, Glasse, Sope-ashes, and Clapboord, whereof some small quantities we have sent you. But if you rightly consider, what an infinite toyle it is in

36. In this paragraph, Smith is pointing out how unrealistic the company's plans and directions were, and that they trusted the wrong people. Though the company claimed to have spent two or three thousand pounds on the supply voyage, Smith said the colonists received goods to the value only of a hundred. The "quartred Boat" was a boat sent in pieces that the Virginia Company hoped the men could carry around the falls, then put together and proceed along the James River in search of the Pacific Ocean.

37. Those sent by Sir Walter Ralegh were the Lost Colonists of Roanoke, who had been abandoned in 1587. They had intended to go overland to Chesapeake Bay and settle there, and the Jamestown colonists heard persistent rumors of Europeans in the region. Had the Virginia colonists been able to learn from the Roanoke colonists' 20 years of experience, the lessons would have been invaluable.

38. "This great discovery of thirtie myles . . .": Captain Newport, commander of the supply fleet, went exploring while he was in America on a special commission from the Virginia Company. Smith implicitly compares Newport's accomplishments with his own explorations.

Russia and Swethland,[39] where the woods are proper for naught els, and though there be the helpe both of man and beast in those ancient Common-wealths, which many an hundred yeares have used it, yet thousands of those poore people can scarce get necessaries to live, but from hand to mouth. And though your Factors there can buy as much in a week as will fraught you a ship, or as much as you please; you must not expect from us any such matter, which are but a many of ignorant miserable soules, that are scarce able to get wherewith to live, and defend our selves against the inconstant Salvages: finding but here and there a tree fit for the purpose, and want all things els the Russians have. For the Coronation of Powhatan, by whose advice you sent him such presents, I know not; but this give me leave to tell you, I feare they will be the confusion of us all ere we heare from you againe. At your Ships arrivall, the Salvages harvest was newly gathered, and we going to buy it, our owne not being halfe sufficient for so great a number. As for the two ships loading of Corne Newport promised to provide us from Powhatan, he brought us but foureteene Bushels; and from the Monacans nothing, but the most of the men sicke and neare famished. From your Ship we had not provision in victuals worth twenty pound, and we are more then two hundred to live upon this: the one halfe sicke, the other little better. For the Saylers (I confesse) they daily make good cheare, but our dyet is a little meale and water, and not sufficient of that. Though there be fish in the Sea, foules in the ayre, and Beasts in the woods, their bounds are so large, they so wilde, and we so weake and ignorant, we cannot much trouble them. Captaine Newport we much suspect to be the Authour of those inventions. Now that you should know, I have made you as great a discovery as he, for lesse charge then he spendeth you every meale; I have sent you this Mappe of the Bay and Rivers, with an annexed Relation of the Countries and Nations that inhabit them, as you may see at large. Also two barrels of stones, and such as I take to be good Iron ore at the least; so devided, as by their notes you may see in what places I found them. The Souldiers say many of your officers maintaine their families out of that you send us: and that Newport hath an hundred pounds a yeare for carrying newes. For every master you have yet sent can find the way as well as he, so that an hundred pounds might be spared, which is more then we have all, that helpe to pay him wages. Captaine

39. Sweden.

Ratliffe is now called Sicklemore, a poore counterfeited Imposture. I have sent you him home, least the company should cut his throat. What he is, now every one can tell you: if he and Archer returne againe, they are sufficient to keepe us alwayes in factions. When you send againe I intreat you rather send but thirty Carpenters, husband-men, gardiners, fisher men, blacksmiths, masons, and diggers up of trees, roots, well provided; then a thousand of such as we have: for except wee be able both to lodge them, and feed them, the most will consume with want of necessaries before they can be made good for any thing. Thus if you please to consider this account, and of the unnecessary wages to Captaine Newport, or his ships so long lingering and staying here (for notwithstanding his boasting to leave us victuals for 12 moneths, though we had 89 by this discovery lame and sicke, and but a pinte of Corne a day for a man, we were constrained to give him three hogsheads of that to victuall him homeward) or yet to send into Germany or Poleland for glasse-men and the rest, till we be able to sustaine our selves, and relieve them when they come. It were better to give five hundred pound a tun for those grosse Commodities in Denmarke, then send for them hither, till more necessary things be provided. For in over-toyling our weake and unskilfull bodies, to satisfie this desire of present profit, we can scarce ever recover our selves from one Supply to another. And I humbly intreat you hereafter, let us know what we should receive, and not stand to the Saylers courtesie to leave us what they please, els you may charge us with what you will, but we not you with any thing. These are the causes that have kept us in Virginia, from laying such a foundation, that ere this might have given much better content and satisfaction; but as yet you must not looke for any profitable returnes: so I humbly rest. [*Generall Historie:* II, 187–190]

Once the supply ships left and Smith was in command, he set out to make the colony thrive.

N O W W E so quietly followed our businesse, that in three moneths wee made three or foure Last of Tarre, Pitch, and Sope ashes;[40]

40. A last is twelve barrels.

produced a tryall of Glasse; made a Well in the Fort of excellent sweet water, which till then was wanting; built some twentie houses; recovered our Church; provided Nets and Wires for fishing; and to stop the disorders of our disorderly theeves, and the Salvages, built a Block-house in the neck of our Isle, kept by a Garrison to entertaine the Salvages trade, and none to passe nor repasse Salvage nor Christian without the presidents order. Thirtie or forty Acres of ground we digged and planted. Of three sowes in eighteene moneths, increased 60, and od Piggs. And neere 500. chickings brought up themselves without having any meat given them: but the Hogs were transported to Hog Isle: where also we built a block-house with a garison to give us notice of any shipping, and for their exercise they made Clapbord and waynscot, and cut downe trees. We built also a fort for a retreat neere a convenient River upon a high commanding hill, very hard to be assalted and easie to be defended, but ere it was finished this defect caused a stay.

In searching our casked corne, we found it halfe rotten, and the rest so consumed with so many thousands of Rats that increased so fast, but there originall was from the ships, as we knew not how to keepe that little we had.[41] This did drive us all to our wits end, for there was nothing in the country but what nature afforded. Untill this time Kemps and Tassore were fettered prisoners, and did double taske and taught us how to order and plant our fields:[42] whom now for want of victuall we set at liberty, but so well they liked our companies they did not desire to goe from us. And to expresse their loves for 16. dayes continuance, the Countrie people brought us (when least) 100. a day, of Squirrils, Turkyes, Deere and other wilde beasts: But this want of corne occasioned the end of all our works, it being worke sufficient to provide victuall. 60. or 80. with Ensigne Laxon was sent downe the river to live upon Oysters, and 20. with liutenant Percy to try for fishing at Poynt Comfort: but in six weekes they would not agree once to cast out the net, he being sicke and burnt sore with Gunpouder. Master West with as many went up to the falls, but nothing could be found but a few Acornes; of that in store every man had their equall

41. The rats had escaped from the ships and multiplied in the absence of natural enemies; they were not native to North America.
42. Kemps and Tassore were two Indians taken prisoner to put pressure on Powhatan.

proportion.[43] Till this present, by the hazard and indevours of some thirtie or fortie, this whole Colony had ever beene fed. We had more Sturgeon, then could be devoured by Dog and Man, of which the industrious by drying and pounding, mingled with Caviare, Sorell and other wholesome hearbes would make bread and good meate: others would gather as much *Tockwhogh* roots,[44] in a day as would make them bread a weeke, so that of those wilde fruites, and what we caught, we lived very well in regard of such a diet. But such was the strange condition of some 150, that had they not beene forced *nolens, volens*, perforce to gather and prepare their victuall they would all have starved or have eaten one another.[45] Of those wild fruits the Salvages often brought us, and for that, the President would not fullfill the unreasonable desire, of those distracted Gluttonous Loyterers, to sell not only our kettles, hows,[46] tooles, and Iron, nay swords, pieces, and the very Ordnance and howses, might they have prevayled to have beene but Idle: for those Salvage fruites, they would have had imparted all to the Salvages, especially for one basket of Corne they heard of to be at Powhatans, fifty myles from our Fort. Though he bought neere halfe of it to satisfie their humors, yet to have had the other halfe, they would have sould their soules, though not sufficient to have kept them a weeke. Thousands were their exclamations, suggestions and devises, to force him to those base inventions to have made it an occasion to abandon the Country. Want perforce constrained him to indure their exclaiming follies, till he found out the author, one Dyer a most crafty fellow and his ancient Maligner, whom he worthily punished, and with the rest he argued the case in this maner.

Fellow souldiers, I did little thinke any so false to report, or so many to be so simple to be perswaded, that I either intend to starve you, or that Powhatan at this present hath corne for him-

---

43. Smith dispersed his men to live off the land as best they could, hoping that they would, at the same time, learn more about the American environment.

44. *Tockwhogh* (tuckahoe) is green arrow arum.

45. Smith describes the colonists as falling into a state of apathy, a phenomenon known as "fatal withdrawal." For two analyses of the physical and psychological condition of the settlers, see Carville V. Earle, "Environment, Disease, and Mortality in Early Virginia," in Thad W. Tate and David L. Ammerman, eds., *The Chesapeake in the Seventeenth Century: Essays on Anglo-American Society* (Chapel Hill, N.C., 1979), 96–125, and Karen Ordahl Kupperman, "Apathy and Death in Early Jamestown," *Journal of American History*, LXVI (1979), 24–40.

46. *How* may be Smith's spelling of *hoe*.

selfe, much lesse for you; or that I would not have it, if I knew where it were to be had. Neither did I thinke any so malitious as now I see a great many; yet it shal not so passionate me, but I will doe my best for my worst maligner. But dreame no longer of this vaine hope from Powhatan, nor that I will longer forbeare to force you, from your Idlenesse, and punish you if you rayle. But if I finde any more runners for Newfoundland with the Pinnace, let him assuredly looke to arive at the Gallows. You cannot deny but that by the hazard of my life many a time I have saved yours, when (might your owne wills have prevailed) you would have starved; and will doe still whether I will or noe; But I protest by that God that made me, since necessitie hath not power to force you to gather for your selves those fruites the earth doth yeeld, you shall not onely gather for your selves, but those that are sicke. As yet I never had more from the store then the worst of you: and all my English extraordinary provision that I have, you shall see me divide it amongst the sick. And this Salvage trash you so scornfully repine at; being put in your mouthes your stomackes can disgest, if you would have better you should have brought it; and therefore I will take a course you shall provide what is to be had. The sick shall not starve, but equally share of all our labours; and he that gathereth not every day as much as I doe, the next day shall be set beyond the river, and be banished from the Fort as a drone, till he amend his conditions or starve.

But some would say with Seneca.

> *I know those things thou sayst are true good Nurse,*
> *But fury forceth me to follow worse.*
> *My minde is hurried headlong up and downe:*
> *Desiring better counsell, yet finds none.*

This order many murmured was very cruell, but it caused the most part so well bestirre themselves, that of 200. (except they were drowned) there died not past seven: as for Captaine Winne and Master Leigh they were dead ere this want hapned, and the rest dyed not for want of such as preserved the rest. Many were billetted amongst the Salvages, whereby we knew all their passages, fields and habitations, how to gather and use there fruits as well as themselves; for they did know wee had such a commanding power at James towne they durst not wrong us of a pin.

So well those poore Salvages used us that were thus billetted, that divers of the Souldiers ran away to search Kemps and Tassore our old prisoners. Glad were these Salvages to have such an oportunity to testifie their love unto us, for in stead of entertaining them, and such things as they had stollen, with all their great Offers, and promises they made them how to revenge their injuryes upon Captaine Smith; Kemps first made himselfe sport, in shewing his countrie men (by them) how he was used, feeding them with this law, who would not work must not eat, till they were neere starved indeede, continually threatning to beate them to death: neither could they get from him, till hee and his consorts brought them perforce to our Captaine, that so well contented him and punished them, as many others that intended also to follow them, were rather contented to labour at home, then adventure to live idlely amongst the Salvages; (of whom there was more hope to make better Christians and good subjects, then the one halfe of those that counterfeited themselves both.) For so affraide was al those kings and the better sort of the people to displease us, that some of the baser sort that we have extreamly hurt and punished for there villanies would hire us, we should not tell it to their kings, or countrymen, who would also repunish them, and yet returne them to James towne to content the President for a testimony of their loves.

Master Sicklemore well returned from Chawwonoke; but found little hope and lesse certaintie of them were left by Sir Walter Raleigh. The river, he saw was not great, the people few, the countrey most over growne with pynes, where there did grow here and there straglingly *Pemminaw*, we call silke grasse. But by the river the ground was good, and exceeding furtill;

Master Nathanael Powell and Anas Todkill were also by the Quiyoughquohanocks conducted to the Mangoags to search them there: but nothing could they learne but they were all dead. This honest proper good promise-keeping king, of all the rest did ever best affect us, and though to his false Gods he was very zealous, yet he would confesse our God as much exceeded his as our Gunns did his Bow and Arrowes, often sending our President many presents, to pray to his God for raine or his corne would perish, for his Gods were angry. Three dayes jorney they conducted them through the woods, into a high country towards the Southwest: where they saw here and there a little corne field, by some little spring or smal brooke, but no river they could see: the people in all respects like the rest, except there language: they live most upon rootes, fruites and wilde beasts; and trade with them towards the sea and the fatter countrys for dryed fish and corne, for skins.

All this time to recover the Dutch-men and one Bentley another fugitive, we imployed one William Volday, a Zwitzar by birth, with Pardons and promises to regaine them.[47] Little we then suspected this double villane, of any villany; who plainly taught us, in the most trust was the greatest treason; for this wicked hypocrite, by the seeming hate he bore to the lewd conditions of his cursed country men, (having this oportunity by his imployment to regaine them) convayed them every thing they desired to effect their projects, to distroy the Colony. With much devotion they expected the Spaniard, to whom they intended good service, or any other, that would but carry them from us. But to begin with the first oportunity; they seeing necessitie thus inforced us to disperse our selves, importuned Powhatan to lend them but his forces, and they would not onely distroy our Hoggs, fire our towne, and betray our Pinnace; but bring to his service and subjection the most of our company. With this plot they had acquainted many Discontents, and many were agreed to there Devilish practise. But one Thomas Douse, and Thomas Mallard (whose christian hearts relented at such an unchristian act) voluntarily revealed it to Captaine Smith, who caused them to conceale it, perswading Douse and Mallard to proceed in their confedracie: onely to bring the irreclamable Dutch men and the inconstant Salvages in such a maner amongst such Ambuscado's as he had prepared, that not many of them should returne from our Peninsula. But this brute[48] comming to the eares of the impatient multitude they so importuned the President to cut off those Dutch men, as amongst many that offered to cut their throats before

47. The English were extremely ethnocentric and distrusted foreigners; ironically, because they lacked skills, they were forced to import foreigners into the colony to test minerals and to set up ironworks, glassworks, and later, silk manufacture. The "Dutchmen," who were actually Germans, were sent as construction experts. In answer to a request from Powhatan and in order to cement relations with him, Smith had sent several of the Dutchmen to build an English-style house for him. Smith believed that these men had proved traitors and had informed Powhatan of the colony's weakness and managed to bleed tools and weapons out of the settlement for their Indian hosts. The "Zwitzar" may have actually been Dutch, or Swiss. This account contains a phrase that could have been Smith's motto: "in the most trust was the greatest treason." For further descriptions of the Dutchmen's activities, see Part Three, Section II.

48. *Brute* for *bruit*, report.

the face of Powhatan, the first was Lieutenant Percy, and Master John Cuderington, two Gentlemen of as bold resolute spirits as could possibly be found. But the President had occasion of other imploiment for them, and gave way to Master Wyffin and Sarjeant Jeffrey Abbot, to goe and stab them or shoot them. But the Dutch men made such excuses, accusing Volday whom they supposed had revealed their project, as Abbot would not, yet Wyffing would, perceiving it but deceit. The King understanding of this their imployment, sent presently his messengers to Captaine Smith to signifie it was not his fault to detaine them, nor hinder his men from executing his command: nor did he nor would he mantaine them, or any to occasion his displeasure.

But whilst this businesse was in hand, Arrived one Captaine Argall, and Master Thomas Sedan, sent by Master Cornelius to truck with the Collony,⁴⁹ and fish for Sturgeon, with a ship well furnished, with wine and much other good provision. Though it was not sent us, our necessities was such as inforced us to take it. He brought us newes of a great supply and preparation for the Lord La Warre, with letters that much taxed our President for his heard dealing with the Salvages, and not returning the shippes fraughted.⁵⁰ Notwithstanding we kept this ship tell the fleete arrived. True it is Argall lost his voyage, but we revictualled him, and sent him for England, with a true relation of the causes of our defailments, and how imposible it was to returne that wealth they expected, or observe there instructions to indure the Salvages insolencies, or doe any thing to any purpose, except they would send us men and meanes that could produce that they so much desired: otherwise all they did was lost, and could not but come to confusion. The villany of Volday we still dissembled. Adam upon his pardon came home but Samuell still stayed with Powhatan to heare further of there estates by this supply. Now all their plots Smith so well understood, they were his best advantages to secure us from any trechery, could be done by them or the Salvages: which with facility he could revenge when he would, because all those countryes more feared him then Powhatan, and hee had such parties with all his bordering neighbours: and many of the rest for love or feare would have done any thing he would have them, upon any commotion, though these fugitives had done all they could to perswade Powhatan, King James would kill Smith, for using him and his people so unkindly.

---

49. To truck is to trade.
50. Heard dealing is hard dealing.

By this you may see for all those crosses, trecheries, and dissentions, how hee wrestled and overcame (without bloudshed) all that happened: also what good was done; how few dyed; what food the Countrey naturally affoordeth; what small cause there is men should starve, or be murthered by the Salvages, that have discretion to mannage them with courage and industrie. The first two yeares, though by his adventures, he had oft brought the Salvages to a tractable trade, yet you see how the envious authoritie ever crossed him, and frustrated his best endevours. But it wrought in him that experience and estimation amongst the Salvages, as otherwise it had bin impossible, he had ever effected that he did. Notwithstanding the many miserable, yet generous and worthy adventures, he had oft and long endured in the wide world, yet in this case he was againe to learne his Lecture by experience. Which with thus much adoe having obtained, it was his ill chance to end, when he had but onely learned how to begin. And though he left those unknowne difficulties (made easie and familiar) to his unlawfull successors, (who onely by living in James Towne, presumed to know more then all the world could direct them:) Now though they had all his Souldiers, with a tripple power, and twice tripple better meanes; by what they have done in his absence, the world may see what they would have done in his presence, had he not prevented their indiscretions: it doth justly prove, what cause he had to send them for England; and that he was neither factious, mutinous, nor dishonest. But they have made it more plaine since his returne for England; having his absolute authoritie freely in their power, with all the advantages and opportunitie that his labours had effected. As I am sorry their actions have made it so manifest, so I am unwilling to say what reason doth compell me, but onely to make apparant the truth, least I should seeme partiall, reasonlesse, and malicious. [*Generall Historie:* II, 212–218]

IV

In 1609, the Virginia Company, distressed by the tales told by those who had returned from Jamestown, decided to redesign the colony. To this end they set up a new government, and because they thought part of the problem was that the body of colonists was too small, they sent five hundred new settlers in a huge fleet of nine ships. The part of this fleet that carried the new government, the admiral or flagship, was wrecked in a hurricane (Herycano) off

Bermuda and only arrived much later. The ships that got through to James-
town carried the news that Smith and his government had been replaced,
but they could offer no proof. Moreover these tidings were relayed by Smith's
old enemies, the very men he had warned the Virginia Company not to send
back to America (see p. 114, above). There ensued a power struggle between
Smith and these men, John Ratcliffe (or Sicklemore), Gabriel Archer, and
John Martin. Captain Smith tried to deal with the problems partly by
dividing the colonists and setting up new plantations along the river.

To REDRESSE those jarres and ill proceedings, the Councell in
England altered the governement and devolved the authoritie to
the Lord De-la-ware. Who for his deputie, sent Sir Thomas Gates, and
Sir George Somers, with 9 ships and 500 persons, they set saile from
England in May 1609. A smal catch perished at sea in a Herycano. The
Admirall, with 150 men, with the two knights, and their new commission, their bils of loading with al manner of directions, and the most
part of their provision arived not. With the other 7 (as Captaines)
arived Ratliffe, whose right name was Sickelmore, Martin, and Archer.
Who as they had been troublesome at sea, beganne againe to marre all
ashore. For though, as is said, they were formerly deposed and sent for
England: yet now returning againe, graced by the title of Captaines of
the passengers, seeing the admirall wanting, and great probabilitie of
her losse, strengthned themselves with those newe companies, so rail-
ing and exclaiming against Captaine Smith, that they mortally hated
him, ere ever they see him. Who understanding by his scouts the
arivall of such a fleet (little dreaming of any such supply) supposing
them Spaniards, hee so determined and ordered his affaires, as wee
little feared their arivall, nor the successe of our incounter, nor were
the Salvages any way negligent or unwilling, to aide and assist us with
their best power. Had it so beene, wee had beene happy. For we would
not have trusted them but as our foes, whereas receiving those as our
countriemen and friends, they did their best to murder our President,
to surprise the store, the fort, and our lodgings, to usurp the governement, and make us all their servants, and slaves to our owne merit.
To 1000 mischiefes those lewd Captaines led this lewd company,[51]

51. *Lewd* means "ignorant, ill-bred." The unruly gallants were presumably courtiers,
fashionable men sent out to the colony to avoid punishment for their infractions at
home.

wherein were many unruly gallants packed thether by their friends to escape il destinies, and those would dispose and determine of the governement, sometimes one, the next day another, to day the old commission, to morrow the new, the next day by neither. In fine, they would rule all or ruine all; yet in charitie we must endure them thus to destroy us, or by correcting their follies, have brought the worlds censure upon us to have beene guiltie of their bloods. Happy had we bin had they never arrived; and we for ever abandoned, and (as we were) left to our fortunes, for on earth was never more confusion, or miserie, then their factions occasioned.

The President seeing the desire those braves had to rule, seeing how his authoritie was so unexpectedly changed, would willingly have left all and have returned for England, but seeing there was smal hope this newe commission would arive, longer hee would not suffer those factious spirits to proceed. It would bee too tedious, too strange, and almost incredible, should I particularly relate the infinite dangers, plots, and practises, hee daily escaped amongst this factious crue, the chiefe whereof he quickly laid by the heeles, til his leasure better served to doe them justice; and to take away al occasions of further mischiefe, Master Persie had his request granted to returne for England, and Master West with 120 went to plant at the falles. Martin with neare as many to Nansamund, with their due proportions, of all provisions, according to their numbers.

Now the Presidents yeare being neere expired, he made Martin President, who knowing his own insufficiencie, and the companies scorne, and conceit of his unworthinesse, within 3 houres resigned it againe to Captaine Smith, and at Nansamund thus proceeded. The people being contributers used him kindly: yet such was his jealous feare, and cowardize, in the midst of his mirth, hee did surprize this poore naked king, with his monuments, houses, and the Ile he inhabited; and there fortified himselfe, but so apparantly distracted with fear, as imboldned the Salvages to assalt him, kill his men, redeeme their king, gather and carrie away more then 1000 bushels of corne, hee not once daring to intercept them. But sent to the President then at the Falles for 30 good shotte, which from James towne immediatly were sent him, but hee so well imploid them, as they did just nothing, but returned, complaining of his childishnesse, that with them fled from his company, and so left them to their fortunes.

Master West having seated his men at the Falles, presently returned to revisit James Towne, the President met him by the way as he followed him to the falles: where he found this company so inconsiderately seated, in a place not only subject to the rivers inundation, but round invironed with many intollerable inconveniences. For remedy whereof, he sent presently to Powhatan to sell him the place called Powhatan, promising to defend him against the Monacans, and these should be his conditions (with his people) to resigne him the fort and houses and all that countrie for a proportion of copper: that all stealing offenders should bee sent him, there to receive their punishment: that every house as a custome should pay him a bushell of corne for an inch square of copper, and a proportion of *Pocones*[52] as a yearely tribute to King James, for their protection as a dutie: what else they could spare to barter at their best discreation.

But both this excellent place and those good conditions did those furies refuse, contemning both him, his kind care and authoritie. The worst they could to shew their spite, they did. I doe more then wonder to thinke how only with 5 men, he either durst, or would adventure as he did, (knowing how greedy they were of his blood) to land amongst them and commit to imprisonment the greatest spirits amongst them, till by their multitudes being 120. they forced him to retire; yet in that retreate hee surprised one of the boates, wherewith hee returned to their shippe, wherein was their provisions, which also hee tooke. And well it chaunced hee found the marriners so tractable and constant, or there had beene small possibility he had ever escaped. Notwithstanding there were many of the best, I meane of the most worthy in Judgement, reason or experience, that from their first landing hearing the generall good report of his old souldiers, and seeing with their eies his actions so wel managed with discretion, as Captaine Wood, Captaine Web, Captaine Mone, Captaine Phitz-James, Master Partridge, Master White, Master Powell and divers others. When they perceived the malice and condition of Ratliffe, Martin, and Archer, left their factions; and ever rested his faithfull friends: But the worst was, the poore Salvages that dailie brought in their contribution to the President. That disorderlie company so tormented those poore naked soules, by stealing their corne, robbing their gardens, beating them, breaking their houses, and keeping some prisoners; that they dailie complained to Captaine Smith he had brought them for protectors worse enimies then the Monocans themselves; which though till then, (for his love) they had indured: they desired pardon, if hereafter they

52. *Pocones* is a root that produces a red dye.

defended themselves, since he would not correct them, as they had long expected he would: so much they importuned him to punish their misdemeanores, as they offered (if hee would conduct them) to fight for him against them. But having spent 9. daies in seeking to reclaime them, shewing them how much they did abuse themselves with their great guilded hopes of seas, mines, commodities, or victories they so madly conceived. Then (seeing nothing would prevaile with them) he set saile for James Towne: now no sooner was the ship under saile but the Salvages assaulted those 120 in their fort, finding some stragling abroad in the woods they slew manie, and so affrighted the rest, as their prisoners escaped, and they scarse retired, with the swords and cloaks of these they had slaine. But ere we had sailed a league our shippe grounding, gave us once more libertie to summon them to a parlie. Where we found them all so stranglie amazed with this poore simple assault, as they submitted themselves upon anie tearmes to the Presidents mercie. Who presentlie put by the heeles 6 or 7 of the chiefe offenders, the rest he seated gallantlie at Powhatan, in their Salvage fort they built and pretilie fortified with poles and barkes of trees sufficient to have defended them from all the Salvages in Virginia, drie houses for lodgings 300 acres of grounde readie to plant, and no place so strong, so pleasant and delightful in Virginia, for which we called it Nonsuch. The Salvages also he presentlie appeased; redelivering to every one their former losses. Thus al were friends, new officers appointed to command, and the President againe readie to depart. But at that Instant arrived Master West, whose good nature with the perswasions and compassion of those mutinous prisoners was so much abused, that to regaine their old hopes new turboiles arose.[53] For the rest being possessed of al their victuall munition and everie thing, they grew to that height in their former factions, as there the President left them to their fortunes, they returning againe to the open aire at West Fort, abandoning Nonsuch, and he to James Towne with his best expedition, but this hapned him in that Journie.

Sleeping in his boat, (for the ship was returned 2 daies before,) accidentallie, one fired his powder bag, which tore his flesh from his bodie and thighes, 9. or 10. inches square in a most pittifull manner; but to quench the tormenting fire, frying him in his cloaths he leaped over bord into the deepe river, where ere they could recover him he was neere drownd. In this estat, without either Chirurgion, or chirur-

53. *Turboils* may be Smith's combination of *turmoils* and *garboils* (brawls).

gery he was to go neare 100. miles. Ariving at James Towne causing all things to bee prepared for peace or warres to obtain provision, whilest those things were providing, Martin, Ratliffe, and Archer, being to have their trials, their guiltie consciences fearing a just reward for their deserts, seeing the President unable to stand, and neare bereft of his senses by reason of his torment, they had plotted to have murdered him in his bed. But his hart did faile him that should have given fire to that mercilesse pistol. So, not finding that course to be the best they joined togither to usurp the government, thereby to escape their punishment, and excuse themselves by accusing him. The President, had notice of their projects: the which to withstand, though his old souldiers importuned him but permit them to take of their heads that would resist his commaund, yet he would not permit them, But sent for the masters of the ships and tooke order with them for his returne for England. Seeing there was neither chirurgion, nor chirurgery in the fort to cure his hurt, and the ships to depart the next daie, his commission to be suppressed he knew not why, himselfe and souldiers to be rewarded he knew not how, and a new commission graunted they knew not to whom, the which so disabled that authority he had, as made them presume so oft to those mutinies and factions as they did. Besides so grievous were his wounds, and so cruell his torment, few expected he could live, nor was hee able to follow his businesse to regaine what they had lost, suppresse those factions and range the countries for provision as he intended, and well he knew in those affaires his owne actions and presence was as requisit as his experience, and directions, which now could not be; he went presently abord, resolving there to appoint them governours, and to take order for the mutiners and their confederates. Who seeing him gone, perswaded Master Persie (to stay) and be their President, and within lesse then an howre was this mutation begun and concluded. For when the company understood Smith would leave them, and see the rest in Armes called Presidents and councellors, divers began to fawne on those new commanders, that now bent all their wits to get him resigne them his commission, who after many salt and bitter repulses, that their confusion should not be attributed to him for leaving the country without government and authority; having taken order to bee free from danger of their malice; he was not unwilling they should steale it from him, but never consented to deliver it to any. But had that unhappy blast not hapned, he would quickly have quallified the heate of those humors and factions, had the ships but once left them and us to our fortunes, and have made that provision from among the Salvages, as we neither feared Spanyard, Salvage, nor famine: nor would have left Virginia, nor our lawfull authoritie, but at as deare a price as we had bought it, and paid for it. What shall I say? but thus we lost him, that in all his proceedings, made Justice his first guid, and experience his second; ever hating basenesse, sloth, pride, and indignitie, more then any dangers; that never allowed more for himselfe, then his souldiers with him; that upon no danger would send them where he would not lead them himselfe; that would never see us want what he either had, or could by any meanes get us; that would rather want then borrow, or starve then not pay; that loved actions more then wordes, and hated falshood and cousnage worse then death:[54] whose adventures were our lives, and whose losse our deathes. Leaving us thus with 3 ships, 7 boates, commodities ready to trade, the harvest newly gathered, 10 weekes provision in the store, 490 and odde persons, 24 peeces of ordinances, 300 muskets, snaphances and fire lockes, shot, powder, and match sufficient, curats, pikes, swords, and moryons more then men:[55] the Salvages their language and habitations wel knowne to 100 well trained and expert souldiers; nets for fishing, tooles of all sortes to worke, apparell to supply our wants, 6 mares and a horse, 5 or 600 swine, as many hens and chickens; some goates, some sheep; what was brought or bread there remained, but they regarded nothing but from hand to mouth, to consume that we had, tooke care for nothing but to perfit some colourable complaints against Captaine Smith, for effecting whereof, 3 weekes longer they stayed the 6 ships til they could produce them.[56] That time and charge might much better have beene spent, but it suted well with the rest of their discreations.

Now all those Smith had either whipped, punished, or any way disgraced, had free power and liberty to say or sweare any thing, and from a whole armefull of their examinations this was concluded.

The mutiners at the Falles, complained hee caused the Salvages assalt them, for that hee would not revenge their losse, they being but 120, and he 5 men and himselfe, and this they proved by the oath of

54. *Cousnage* for *cozenage*, meaning "cheating or deception."
55. Snaphances were an early form of flintlock, but most of the colonists' muskets were matchlocks; a lighted wick or match was necessary to light the powder in the pan. Curats are cuirasses, armor for the chest and back consisting of plates that buckle together, and moryons are helmets without beaver or visor.
56. "Perfit some colourable complaints" means that the colonists whom Smith had disciplined now perfected plausible accusations against him.

one hee had oft whipped for perjurie and pilfering. The dutch-men that he had appointed to bee stabd for their treacheries, swore he sent to poison them with rats baine. The prudent Councel, that he would not submit himselfe to their stolne authoritie. Coe and Dyer, that should have murdered him, were highly preferred for swearing, they heard one say, he heard Powhatan say, that he heard a man say: if the king would not send that corne he had, he should not long enjoy his copper crowne, nor those robes he had sent him: yet those also swore hee might have had corne for tooles but would not. The truth was, Smith had no such ingins as the king demanded, nor Powhatan any corne. Yet this argued he would starve them. Others complained hee would not let them rest in the fort (to starve) but forced them to the oyster bankes, to live or starve, as he lived himselfe. For though hee had of his owne private provisions sent from England, sufficient; yet hee gave it all away to the weake and sicke, causing the most untoward (by doing as he did) to gather their food from the unknowne parts of the rivers and woods, that they lived (though hardly) that otherwaies would have starved, ere they would have left their beds, or at most the sight of James Towne to have got their own victuall. Some propheticall spirit calculated hee had the Salvages in such subjection, hee would have made himselfe a king, by marrying Pocahontas, Powhatans daughter. It is true she was the very nomparell of his kingdome, and at most not past 13 or 14 yeares of age. Very oft shee came to our fort, with what shee could get for Captaine Smith, that ever loved and used all the Countrie well, but her especially he ever much respected: and she so well requited it, that when her father intended to have surprized him, shee by stealth in the darke night came through the wild woods and told him of it. But her marriage could no way have intitled him by any right to the kingdome, nor was it ever suspected hee had ever such a thought, or more regarded her, or any of them, then in honest reason, and discreation he might. If he would he might have married her, or have done what him listed. For there was none that could have hindred his determination. Some that knewe not any thing to say, the Councel instructed, and advised what to sweare. So diligent they were in this businesse, that what any could remember, hee had ever done, or said in mirth, or passion, by some circumstantiall oath, it was applied to their fittest use, yet not past 8 or 9 could say much and that nothing but circumstances, which all men did knowe was most false and un-true. Many got their passes by promising in England to say much against him. I have presumed to say this much in his behalfe for that I never heard such foule slaunders, so certainely beleeved, and urged for truthes by many a hundred, that doe still not spare to spread them, say them and sweare them, that I thinke doe scarse know him though they meet him, nor have they ether cause or reason, but their wills, or zeale to rumor or opinion. For the honorable and better sort of our Virginian adventurers I think they understand it as I have writ it. For instead of accusing him, I have never heard any give him a better report, then many of those witnesses themselves that were sent only home to testifie against him.

Richard Pots, W. P.

[*Proceedings:* I, 268–275]

Smith's catalog of the thriving colony he left, well equipped and strong, contrasted sharply with the picture of desolation that greeted the next ships; the colonists were reduced from several hundred to about sixty in the space of six months. Captain Smith felt this was all the endorsement his policies needed.

T HE DAY before Captaine Smith returned for England with the ships, Captaine Davis arrived in a small Pinace, with some sixteene proper men more: To these were added a company from James towne, under the command of Captaine John Sickelmore alias Ratliffe, to inhabit Point Comfort. Captaine Martin and Captaine West, having lost their boats and neere halfe their men among the Salvages, were returned to James towne; for the Salvages no sooner understood Smith was gone, but they all revolted, and did spoile and murther all they incountered. Now wee were all constrained to live onely on that Smith had onely for his owne Companie, for the rest had consumed their proportions, and now they had twentie Presidents with all their appurtenances: Master Piercie our new President, was so sicke hee could neither goe nor stand. But ere all was consumed, Captaine West and Captaine Sickelmore, each with a small ship and thirtie or fortie men well appointed, sought abroad to trade. Sickelmore upon the confidence of Powhatan, with about thirtie others as carelesse as himselfe, were all slaine, onely Jeffrey Shortridge escaped, and Pokahontas the Kings daughter saved a boy called Henry Spilman, that lived many yeeres after, by her meanes, amongst the Patawomekes. Powhatan still as he found meanes, cut off their Boats, denied them trade, so that Captaine West set saile for England. Now we all found the losse of

Captaine Smith, yea his greatest maligners could now curse his losse: as for corne, provision and contribution from the Salvages, we had nothing but mortall wounds, with clubs and arrowes; as for our Hogs, Hens, Goats, Sheepe, Horse, or what lived, our commanders, officers and Salvages daily consumed them, some small proportions sometimes we tasted, till all was devoured; then swords, armes, pieces, or any thing, wee traded with the Salvages, whose cruell fingers were so oft imbrewed in our blouds, that what by their crueltie, our Governours indiscretion, and the losse of our ships, of five hundred within six moneths after Captaine Smiths departure, there remained not past sixtie men, women and children, most miserable and poore creatures; and those were preserved for the most part, by roots, herbes, acornes, walnuts, berries, now and then a little fish: they that had startch in these extremities, made no small use of it;[57] yea, even the very skinnes of our horses. Nay, so great was our famine, that a Salvage we slew, and buried, the poorer sort tooke him up againe and eat him, and so did divers one another boyled and stewed with roots and herbs: And one amongst the rest did kill his wife, powdered her, and had eaten part of her before it was knowne, for which hee was executed, as hee well deserved; now whether shee was better roasted, boyled or car-bonado'd, I know not, but of such a dish as powdered wife I never heard of.[58] This was that time, which still to this day we called the starving time; it were too vile to say, and scarce to be beleeved, what we endured: but the occasion was our owne, for want of providence, industrie and government, and not the barrennesse and defect of the Countrie, as is generally supposed; for till then in three yeeres, for the numbers were landed us, we had never from England provision suffi-cient for six moneths, though it seemed by the bils of loading suffi-cient was sent us, such a glutton is the Sea, and such good fellowes the Mariners; we as little tasted of the great proportion sent us, as they of our want and miseries, yet notwithstanding they ever over-swayed and ruled the businesse, though we endured all that is said, and chiefly lived on what this good Countrie naturally afforded; yet had wee beene even in Paradice it selfe with these Governours, it would not have beene much better with us; yet there was amongst us, who had

57. "They that had startch" means that those who had brought starch for their ruffs now ate it.
58. To powder meat is to preserve it by salting or corning it. *Carbonado'd* means "grilled."

they had the government as Captaine Smith appointed, but that they could not maintaine it, would surely have kept us from those extremities of miseries. This in ten daies more, would have supplanted us all with death.

But God that would not this Countrie should be unplanted, sent Sir Thomas Gates, and Sir George Sommers with one hundred and fiftie people most happily preserved by the Bermudas to preserve us: strange it is to say how miraculously they were preserved in a leaking ship, as at large you may reade in the insuing Historie of those Ilands.[59]

The Government resigned to Sir Thomas Gates, *1610.*

WHEN THESE two Noble Knights did see our miseries, being but strangers in that Countrie, and could understand no more of the cause, but by conjecture of our clamours and complaints, of accusing and excusing one another: They embarked us with themselves, with the best meanes they could, and abandoning James towne, set saile for England, whereby you may see the event of the government of the former Commanders left to themselves; although they had lived there many yeeres as formerly hath beene spoken (who hindred now their proceedings, Captaine Smith being gone.)

At noone they fell to the Ile of Hogs, and the next morning to Mulbery point, at what time they descried the Long-boat of the Lord la Ware, for God would not have it so abandoned. For this honourable Lord, then Governour of the Countrie, met them with three ships exceedingly well furnished with all necessaries fitting, who againe returned them to the abandoned James towne.[60] [*Generall Historie:* II, 231–234]

59. Gates, Somers, and their men had built two ships of cedar on Bermuda after their shipwreck. Though Bermuda was uninhabited, it was plentifully supplied with pigs, possibly the descendants of a breeding pair that had been left behind by a Spanish ship.
60. Thomas West, Baron De La Warr, accepted the governorship of Virginia; the company thought the colony's problems might stem from lack of a leader whose rank was sufficient to overawe the settlers. He stayed a very short time before sickness forced his return to England, allowing Smith once again to make his point that experience was more important than status in such new ventures.

PART THREE

JOHN SMITH

AS ETHNOGRAPHER

HIS RELATIONS WITH

THE INDIANS

I

Thomas Harriot, a young scientist sent by Ralegh to his Roanoke colony in 1585, wrote the earliest report of the eastern Algonquian Indians. His excellent account was published in 1588 and was republished in 1590 accompanied by woodcuts of the paintings done by John White from life during their stay on the Carolina Outer Banks. John Smith knew Harriot's book and evidently aimed to write a similar account of the Chesapeake Bay Algonquians.

Lively debate in Europe centered on the origins of the Indians. Since orthodoxy demanded a single creation and the descent of all humanity from the known survivors of Noah's flood, the Indians must be the heirs of a people known to antiquity. A common answer was that they were the descendants of the Ten Lost Tribes of Israel. Language was thought to be the best evidence by which the question could be settled, so many early accounts, like Smith's, included Indian words and phrases.

Because many doe desire to knowe the maner of their
language, I have inserted these few words.

Ka ka torawincs yowo. What call you this.
Nemarough. a man.
Crenepo. a woman.
Marowanchesso. a boy.
Yehawkans. Houses.
Matchcores. Skins, or garments.
Mockasins. Shooes.
Tussan. Beds.
Pokatawer. Fire.
Attawp. A bowe.
Attonce. Arrowes.
Monacookes. Swords.
Aumoughhowgh. A Target.
Pawcussacks. Gunnes.
Tomahacks. Axes.
Tockahacks. Pickaxes.
Pamesacks. Knives.

Accowprets. Sheares.
Pawpecones. Pipes.
Mattassin. Copper.
Ussawassin. Iron, Brasse, Silver, or any white mettal.
Musses. Woods.
Attasskuss. Leaves, weeds, or grasse.
Chepsin. Land.
Shacquohocan. A stone.
Wepenter, a cookold.[1]
Suckahanna. Water.
Noughmass. Fish.
Copotone. Sturgion.
Weghshaughes. Flesh.
Sawwehone. Bloud.
Netoppew. Friends.
Marrapough. Enimies.

1. *Cookold* for *cuckold.*

Maskapow. The worst of the enimies.

Mawchick chammay. The best of friends.

Casacunnakack, peya quagh acquintan uttasantasough. In how many daies will there come hether any more English ships?

Their numbers.

Necut. 1.

Ningh. 2.

Nuss. 3.

Yowgh. 4.

Paranske. 5.

Comotinch. 6.

Toppawoss. 7.

Nusswash. 8.

Kekatawgh. 9.

Kaskeke.

They count no more but by tennes as followeth.

Case, how many.

Ninghsapooeksku. 20.

Nussapooeksku. 30.

Yowghapooeksku. 40.

Parankestassapooeksku. 50.

Comatinchtassapooeksku. 60.

Nusswashtassapooeksku. 80.

Toppawousstassapooeksku. 70.

Kekataughtassapooeksku. 90.

Necuttoughtysinough. 100.

Necuttweunquaough. 1000.

Rawcosowghs. Daies.

Keskowghes. Sunnes.

Toppquough. Nights.

Nepawweshowghs. Moones.

Pawpaxsoughes. Yeares.

Pummahumps. Starres.

Osies. Heavens.

Okes. Gods.

Quiyoughcosucks. Pettie Gods, and their affinities.

Righcomoughes. Deaths.

Kekughes. Lives.

Mowchick woyawgh tawgh noeragh kaquere mecher. I am verie hungrie, what shall I eate?

Tawnor nehiegh Powhatan. where dwels Powwahtan.

Mache, nehiegh yowrowgh, orapaks. Now he dwels a great way hence at Orapaks.

Uttapitchewayne anpechitchs nehawper werowacomoco. You lie, he staide ever at Werowocomoco.

Kator nehiegh mattagh neer uttapitchewayne. Truely he is there I doe not lie.

Spaughtynere keragh werowance mawmarinough kekaten wawgh peyaquaugh. Run you then to the king mawmarynough and bid him come hither.

Utteke, e peya weyack wighwhip. Get you gone, and come againe quickly.

Kekaten pokahontas patiaquagh ningh tanks manotyens neer mowchick rawrenock audowgh. Bid Pokahontas bring hither two little Baskets, and I wil give her white beads to make her a chaine.

FINIS.

[*Map of Virginia:* I, 136–139]

Smith's description of Indian agriculture served a double purpose: knowledge of Indian crops and techniques would help English colonists during the early years when they could not transplant their own agriculture successfully.

THEY DIVIDE the yeare into 5. seasons. Their winter some call *Popanow*, the spring *Cattapeuk*, the sommer *Cohattayough*, the earing of their Corne *Nepinough*, the harvest and fall of leafe *Taquitock*. From September untill the midst of November are the chiefe Feasts and sacrifice. Then have they plenty of fruits as well planted as naturall, as corne, greene and ripe, fish, fowle, and wilde beastes exceeding fat.

The greatest labour they take, is in planting their corne, for the country naturally is overgrowne with wood. To prepare the ground they bruise the barke of the trees neare the root, then do they scortch the roots with fire that they grow no more. The next yeare with a crooked peece of wood, they beat up the woodes by the rootes, and in that moulde they plant their corne. Their manner is this. They make a hole in the earth with a sticke, and into it they put 4 graines of wheate, and 2 of beanes. These holes they make 4 foote one from another; Their women and children do continually keepe it with weeding, and when it is growne midle high, they hill it about like a hop-yard.

In Aprill they begin to plant, but their chiefe plantation is in May, and so they continue till the midst of June. What they plant in Aprill they reape in August, for May in September, for June in October; Every stalke of their corne commonly beareth two eares, some 3, seldome any 4, many but one and some none. Every eare ordinarily hath betwixt 200 and 500 graines. The stalke being green hath a sweet juice in it, somewhat like a suger Cane, which is the cause that when they gather their corne greene, they sucke the stalkes: for as wee gather greene pease, so doe they their corne being greene, which excelleth their old. They plant also pease they cal *Assentamens*, which are the same they cal in Italy, *Fagioli*. Their Beanes are the same the Turkes cal *Garnanses*, but these they much esteeme for dainties.[2]

Their corne they rost in the eare greene, and bruising it in a morter of wood with a Polt, lappe it in rowles in the leaves of their corne, and so boyle it for a daintie.[3] They also reserve that corne late planted that will not ripe, by roasting it in hot ashes, the heat thereof drying it. In winter they esteeme it being boyled with beans for a rare dish, they call *Pausarowmena*. Their old wheat they first steep a night in hot water, in the morning pounding it in a morter. They use a small basket for their Temmes, then pound againe the grout, and so separating by dashing their hand in the basket, receave the flower in a platter made of wood scraped to that forme with burning and shels. Tempering this flower with water, they make it either in cakes covering them with ashes till they bee baked, and then washing them in faire water they drie presently with their owne heat: or else boyle them in water eating the broth with the bread which they call *Ponap*. The grouts and peeces of the cornes remaining, by fanning in a Platter or in the wind, away, the branne they boile 3 or 4 houres with water, which is an ordinary food

---

2. *Garnanses:* Smith is comparing American beans to chick-peas, or garbanzos. He and the other colonists, thinking of corn as comparable to European grains like wheat or barley, were surprised when the Indians brought some varieties to them to eat fresh; the colonists thought it was not yet ripe.

3. A polt is a pestle.

they call *Ustatahamen*.[4] But some more thrifty then cleanly, doe burne the core of the eare to powder which they call *Pungnough*, mingling that in their meale, but it never tasted well in bread, nor broth. Their fish and flesh they boyle either very tenderly, or broyle it so long on hurdles over the fire, or else after the Spanish fashion, putting it on a spit, they turne first the one side, then the other, til it be as drie as their jerkin beefe in the west Indies, that they may keepe it a month or more without putrifying. The broth of fish or flesh they eate as commonly as the meat.

In May also amongst their corne they plant Pumpeons, and a fruit like unto a muske millen, but lesse and worse, which they call *Macocks*. These increase exceedingly, and ripen in the beginning of July, and continue until September. They plant also *Maracocks* a wild fruit like a lemmon, which also increase infinitely.[5] They begin to ripe in September and continue till the end of October. When all their fruits be gathered, little els they plant, and this is done by their women and children; neither doth this long suffice them, for neere 3 parts of the yeare, they only observe times and seasons, and live of what the Country naturally affordeth from hand to mouth, etc. [*Map of Virginia:* I, 156–159]

In the following long section, Smith aimed to present a complete picture of Indian life. When he compared Indian practices to those of the Irish, the Tartars, or the Turks, he was both making them more readily understandable and displaying his own experience and learning.

---

4. *Pausarowmena* would later become known generally by the Narragansett word *succotash*. Smith is describing the process of making corn bread or pone (ponap). The dried corn (old wheat) is steeped and pounded, then sifted through a small basket, the meal (grout) is repounded and resifted, and the flour caught underneath. The modern word *hominy* is derived from *ustatahamen*.

5. Pumpeons are pumpkins. *Maracocks*, later called maypops, are the fruits of the passion vine.

Of the naturall Inhabitants of Virginia.

THE LAND is not populous, for the men be few; their far greater number is of women and children. Within 60 myles of James Towne, there are about some 5000 people, but of able men fit for their warres scarce 1500. To nourish so many together they have yet no meanes, because they make so small a benefit of their land, be it never so fertile. Six or seaven hundred have beene the most hath beene seene together, when they gathered themselves to have surprised mee at Pamaunkee, having but fifteene to withstand the worst of their fury. As small as the proportion of ground that hath yet beene discovered, is in comparison of that yet unknowne: the people differ very much in stature, especially in language, as before is expressed. Some being very great as the Sasquesahanocks; others very little, as the Wighcocomocoes: but generally tall and straight, of a comely proportion, and of a colour browne when they are of any age, but they are borne white. Their hayre is generally blacke, but few have any beards. The men weare halfe their heads shaven, the other halfe long; for Barbers they use their women, who with two shels will grate away the hayre, of any fashion they please. The women are cut in many fashions, agreeable to their yeares, but ever some part remaineth long. They are very strong, of an able body and full of agilitie, able to endure to lie in the woods under a tree by the fire, in the worst of winter, or in the weedes and grasse, in Ambuscado in the Sommer.[6] They are inconstant in every thing, but what feare constraineth them to keepe. Craftie, timerous, quicke of apprehension, and very ingenuous. Some are of disposition fearefull, some bold, most cautelous, all Savage. Generally covetous of Copper, Beads, and such like trash.[7] They are soone moved to anger, and so malicious, that they seldome forget an injury: they seldome steale one from another, least their conjurers should reveale it, and so they be pursued and punished. That they are thus feared is certaine, but that any can reveale their offences by conjuration I am doubtfull. Their women are carefull not to be suspected of dishonestie without the leave of their husbands. Each houshold knoweth their owne lands, and gardens, and most live of their owne labours. For their apparell, they are sometime covered with the skinnes of wilde beasts, which in Winter are dressed with the hayre, but in Sommer without. The better

6. *Ambuscado* means "ambush."
7. *Cautelous* means "cautious, wary." Trash is anything of little value.

sort use large mantels of Deare skins, not much differing in fashion from the Irish mantels. Some imbrodered with white beads, some with Copper, other painted after their manner. But the common sort have scarce to cover their nakednesse, but with grasse, the leaves of trees, or such like. We have seene some use mantels made of Turky feathers, so prettily wrought and woven with threads that nothing could be discerned but the feathers. That was exceeding warme and very handsome. But the women are alwayes covered about their middles with a skin, and very shamefast to be seene bare. They adorne themselves most with copper beads and paintings. Their women, some have their legs, hands, breasts and face cunningly imbrodered with divers workes, as beasts, serpents, artificially wrought into their flesh with blacke spots. In each eare commonly they have 3 great holes, whereat they hang chaines, bracelets, or copper. Some of their men weare in those holes, a small greene and yellow coloured snake, neare halfe a yard in length, which crawling and lapping her selfe about his necke oftentimes familiarly would kisse his lips. Others weare a dead Rat tyed by the taile. Some on their heads weare the wing of a bird, or some large feather with a Rattell. Those Rattels are somewhat like the chape of a Rapier, but lesse, which they take from the taile of a snake. Many have the whole skinne of a Hawke or some strange foule, stuffed with the wings abroad. Others a broad peece of Copper, and some the hand of their enemy dryed. Their heads and shoulders are painted red with the roote *Pocone* brayed to powder, mixed with oyle, this they hold in sommer to preserve them from the heate, and in winter from the cold. Many other formes of paintings they use, but he is the most gallant that is the most monstrous to behold.

Their buildings and habitations are for the most part by the rivers, or not farre distant from some fresh spring. Their houses are built like our Arbors, of small young springs bowed and tyed, and so close covered with Mats, or the barkes of trees very handsomely, that notwithstanding either winde, raine, or weather, they are as warme as stooves, but very smoaky, yet at the toppe of the house there is a hole made for the smoake to goe into right over the fire.

Against the fire they lie on little hurdles of Reeds covered with a Mat, borne from the ground a foote and more by a hurdle of wood.[8] On these round about the house they lie heads and points one by th'other against the fire, some covered with Mats, some with skins,

8. Hurdles are wooden frames; Smith is describing sleeping benches.

and some starke naked lie on the ground, from 6 to 20 in a house. Their houses are in the midst of their fields or gardens, which are small plots of ground. Some 20 acres, some 40. some 100. some 200. some more, some lesse. In some places from 2 to 50 of those houses together, or but a little separated by groves of trees. Neare their habitations is little small wood or old trees on the ground by reason of their burning of them for fire. So that a man may gallop a horse amongst these woods any way, but where the creekes or Rivers shall hinder.[9]

Men, women, and children have their severall names according to the severall humor of their Parents. Their women (they say) are easily delivered of childe, yet doe they love children very dearely. To make them hardie, in the coldest mornings they wash them in the rivers, and by painting and oyntments so tanne their skinnes, that after a yeare or two, no weather will hurt them.

The men bestow their times in fishing, hunting, warres, and such manlike exercises, scorning to be seene in any woman-like exercise, which is the cause that the women be very painefull, and the men often idle.[10] The women and children doe the rest of the worke. They make mats, baskets, pots, morters, pound their corne, make their bread, prepare their victuals, plant their corne, gather their corne, beare all kind of burdens, and such like.

Their fire they kindle presently by chafing a dry pointed sticke in a hole of a little square peece of wood, that firing it selfe, will so fire mosse, leaves, or any such like dry thing, that will quickly burne. In March and Aprill they live much upon their fishing wires;[11] and feed on fish, Turkies, and Squirrels. In May and June they plant their fields, and live most of Acornes, Walnuts, and fish. But to mend their dyet, some disperse themselves in small companies, and live upon fish, beasts, crabs, oysters, land Tortoises, strawberries, mulberries, and such like. In June, July, and August, they feed upon the rootes of *Tockwough* berries, fish, and greene wheat.[12] It is strange to see how their bodies alter with their dyet, even as the deere and wilde beasts they seeme fat and leane, strong and weake. Powhatan their great

9. Smith here refers to the Indian practice of burning the underbrush in the woods to facilitate travel and hunting.

10. *Painful* here means "hardworking or diligent, taking pains." Smith, like most Europeans, viewed the hunting and ceremonial duties of the men as recreation or idleness.

11. By *wires*, he means *weirs*, fish traps.

12. *Tockwough* (tuckahoe) is green arrow arum. Green wheat is fresh corn.

King, and some others that are provident, rost their fish and flesh upon hurdles as before is expressed, and keepe it till scarce times.

For fishing, hunting, and warres they use much their bow and arrowes. They bring their bowes to the forme of ours by the scraping of a shell. Their arrowes are made some of straight young sprigs, which they head with bone, some 2 or 3 ynches long. These they use to shoot at Squirrels on trees. Another sort of arrowes they use made of Reeds. These are peeced with wood, headed with splinters of christall, or some sharpe stone, the spurres of a Turkey, or the bill of some bird. For his knife he hath the splinter of a Reed to cut his feathers in forme. With this knife also, he will joynt a Deere, or any beast, shape his shooes, buskins, mantels, etc.[13] To make the nock of his arrow he hath the tooth of a Beaver, set in a sticke, wherewith he grateth it by degrees. His arrow head he quickly maketh with a little bone, which he ever weareth at his bracer, of any splint of a stone, or glasse in the forme of a heart, and these they glew to the end of their arrowes. With the sinewes of Deere, and the tops of Deeres hornes boyled to a jelly, they make a glew that will not dissolve in cold water.

For their warres also they use Targets that are round and made of the barkes of trees, and a sword of wood at their backes, but oftentimes they use for swords the horne of a Deere put through a peece of wood in forme of a Pickaxe. Some a long stone sharpned at both ends, used in the same manner. This they were wont to use also for hatchets, but now by trucking they have plentie of the same forme of yron.[14] And those are their chiefe instruments and armes.

Their fishing is much in Boats. These they make of one tree by burning and scratching away the coales with stones and shels, till they have made it in forme of a Trough. Some of them are an elne deepe,[15] and fortie or fiftie foote in length, and some will beare 40 men, but the most ordinary are smaller, and will beare 10, 20, or 30. according to their bignesse. In stead of Oares, they use Paddles and stickes, with which they will row faster then our Barges. Betwixt their hands and thighes, their women use to spin, the barkes of trees, Deere sinewes, or a kind of grasse they call *Pemmenaw*, of these they make a thread very even and readily. This thread serveth for many uses. As about their housing, apparell, as also they make nets for fishing, for the quantitie

13. A buskin is a short boot.
14. Targets are shields. *Trucking* means "trading," in this case with the English.
15. *Elne* is an old form of *ell*, a measurement of about 45 inches.

as formally braded as ours. They make also with it lines for angles.[16] Their hookes are either a bone grated as they nock their arrowes in the forme of a crooked pinne or fish-hooke, or of the splinter of a bone tyed to the clift of a little sticke, and with the end of the line, they tie on the bait. They use also long arrowes tyed in a line, wherewith they shoote at fish in the rivers. But they of Accawmack use staves like unto Javelins headed with bone. With these they dart fish swimming in the water. They have also many artificiall wires, in which they get abundance of fish.

In their hunting and fishing they take extreame paines; yet it being their ordinary exercise from their infancy, they esteeme it a pleasure and are very proud to be expert therein. And by their continuall ranging, and travell, they know all the advantages and places most frequented with Deere, Beasts, Fish, Foule, Roots, and Berries. At their huntings they leave their habitations, and reduce themselves into companies, as the Tartars doe, and goe to the most desert places with their families, where they spend their time in hunting and fowling up towards the mountaines, by the heads of their rivers, where there is plentie of game. For betwixt the rivers the grounds are so narrowe, that little commeth here which they devoure not. It is a marvell they can so directly passe these deserts, some 3 or 4 dayes journey without habitation.[17] Their hunting houses are like unto Arbours covered with Mats. These their women beare after them, with Corne, Acornes, Morters, and all bag and baggage they use. When they come to the place of exercise, every man doth his best to shew his dexteritie, for by their excelling in those qualities, they get their wives. Fortie yards will they shoot levell, or very neare the marke, and 120 is their best at Random.[18] At their huntings in the deserts they are commonly two or three hundred together. Having found the Deere, they environ them with many fires, and betwixt the fires they place themselves. And some take their stands in the midsts. The Deere being thus feared by the fires, and their voyces, they chase them so long within that circle, that many times they kill 6, 8, 10, or 15 at a hunting. They use also to drive them into some narrow poynt of land, when they find that advantage; and so force them into the river, where with their boats they have

---

16. *Angles* here means "fishhooks," which survives in the modern term *angler*.
17. *Desert* means "wild, uninhabited." A dense wood could be called a desert.
18. Archers could get much greater range by shooting on an elevated trajectory rather than straight at the target, but with reduced accuracy.

Ambuscadoes to kill them. When they have shot a Deere by land, they follow him like bloud-hounds by the bloud, and straine, and often-times so take them.[19] Hares, Partridges, Turkies, or Egges, fat or leane, young or old, they devoure all they can catch in their power. In one of these huntings they found me in the discovery of the head of the river of Chickahamania, where they slew my men, and tooke me prisoner in a Bogmire, where I saw those exercises, and gathered these Obser-vations.

One Salvage hunting alone, useth the skinne of a Deere slit on the one side, and so put on his arme, through the neck, so that his hand comes to the head which is stuffed, and the hornes, head, eyes, eares, and every part as artificially counterfeited as they can devise. Thus shrowding his body in the skinne by stalking, he approacheth the Deere, creeping on the ground from one tree to another. If the Deere chance to find fault, or stand at gaze, he turneth the head with his hand to his best advantage to seeme like a Deere, also gazing and licking himselfe. So watching his best advantage to approach, having shot him, he chaseth him by his bloud and straine till he get him.

When they intend any warres, the Werowances usually have the advice of their Priests and Conjurers, and their allies, and ancient friends, but chiefely the Priests determine their resolution.[20] Every Werowance, or some lustie fellow, they appoint Captaine over every nation. They seldome make warre for lands or goods, but for women and children, and principally for revenge. They have many enemies, namely, all their westernly Countries beyond the mountaines, and the heads of the rivers. Upon the head of the Powhatans are the Mona-cans, whose chiefe habitation is at Rasauweak, unto whom the Mow-hemenchughes, the Massinnacacks, the Monahassanughs, the Mona-sickapanoughs, and other nations pay tributes. Upon the head of the river of Toppahanock is a people called Mannahoacks. To these are contributers the Tauxanias, the Shackaconias, the Ontponeas, the Teg-ninateos, the Whonkenteaes, the Stegarakes, the Hassinnungaes, and divers others, all confederates with the Monacans, though many differ-ent in language, and be very barbarous, living for the most part of wild beasts and fruits. Beyond the mountaines from whence is the head of the river Patawomeke, the Salvages report inhabit their most mortall

---

19. *Strain* refers to the deer's track.
20. Werowances were subchiefs under Powhatan; they were both administrative and military leaders at the village level.

enemies, the Massawomekes, upon a great salt water, which by all likelihood is either some part of Cannada, some great lake, or some inlet of some sea that falleth into the South sea. These Massawomekes are a great nation and very populous. For the heads of all those rivers, especially the Pattawomekes, the Pautuxuntes, the Sasquesahanocks, the Tockwoughes are continually tormented by them: of whose crueltie, they generally complained, and very importunate they were with me, and my company to free them from these tormentors. To this purpose they offered food, conduct, assistance, and continuall subjection. Which I concluded to effect. But the councell then present emulating my successe,[21] would not thinke it fit to spare me fortie men to be hazzarded in those unknowne regions, having passed (as before was spoken of) but with 12, and so was lost that opportunitie. Seaven boats full of these Massawomekes wee encountred at the head of the Bay; whose Targets, Baskets, Swords, Tobacco pipes, Platters, Bowes, and Arrowes, and every thing shewed, they much exceeded them of our parts, and their dexteritie in their small boats, made of the barkes of trees, sowed with barke and well luted with gumme, argueth that they are seated upon some great water.[22]

Against all these enemies the Powhatans are constrained sometimes to fight. Their chiefe attempts are by Stratagems, trecheries, or surprisals. Yet the Werowances women and children they put not to death, but keepe them Captives. They have a method in warre, and for our pleasures they shewed it us, and it was in this manner performed at Mattapanient.

Having painted and disguised themselves in the fiercest manner they could devise. They divided themselves into two Companies, neare a hundred in a company. The one company called Monacans, the other Powhatans. Either army had their Captaine. These as enemies tooke their stands a musket shot one from another; ranked themselves 15 a breast, and each ranke from another 4 or 5 yards, not in fyle, but in the opening betwixt their fyles. So as the Reare could shoot as conveniently as the Front. Having thus pitched the fields: from either part

21. By "emulating my successe," Smith means that the council in Jamestown was jealous of him.
22. The Massawomecks had birchbark canoes instead of the dugouts whose manufacture Smith describes above. *Luted* means that the joints were sealed to make them watertight.

went a messenger with these conditions, that whosoever were vanquished, such as escape upon their submission in two dayes after should live, but their wives and children should be prize for the Conquerours. The messengers were no sooner returned, but they approached in their orders; On each flanke a Serjeant, and in the Reare an Officer for Lieutenant, all duly keeping their orders, yet leaping and singing after their accustomed tune, which they use onely in Warres. Upon the first flight of arrowes they gave such horrible shouts and screeches, as so many infernall hell hounds could not have made them more terrible. When they had spent their arrowes, they joyned together prettily, charging and retyring, every ranke seconding other. As they got advantage they catched their enemies by the hayre of the head, and downe he came that was taken. His enemy with his wooden sword seemed to beat out his braines, and still they crept to the Reare, to maintaine the skirmish. The Monacans decreasing, the Powhatans charged them in the forme of a halfe Moone; they unwilling to be inclosed, fled all in a troope to their Ambuscadoes, on whom they led them very cunningly. The Monacans disperse themselves among the fresh men, whereupon the Powhatans retired, with all speed to their seconds; which the Monacans seeing, tooke that advantage to retire againe to their owne battell, and so each returned to their owne quarter. All their actions, voyces, and gestures, both in charging and retiring were so strained to the height of their qualitie and nature, that the strangenesse thereof made it seeme very delightfull.

For their Musicke they use a thicke Cane, on which they pipe as on a Recorder. For their warres they have a great deepe platter of wood. They cover the mouth thereof with a skin, at each corner they tie a walnut, which meeting on the backside neere the bottome, with a small rope they twitch them together till it be so tought and stiffe, that they may beat upon it as upon a drumme. But their chiefe instruments are Rattles made of small gourds, or Pumpeons shels. Of these they have Base, Tenor, Countertenor, Meane, and Treble.[23] These mingled with their voyces sometimes twenty or thirtie together, make such a terrible noise as would rather affright, then delight any man. If any great commander arrive at the habitation of a Werowance, they spread a Mat as the Turkes doe a Carpet for him to sit upon. Upon another right opposite they sit themselves. Then doe all with a tunable voice of

23. The meane is the alto recorder.

shouting bid him welcome.[24] After this doe two or more of their chiefest men make an Oration, testifying their love. Which they doe with such vehemency, and so great passions, that they sweat till they drop, and are so out of breath they can scarce speake. So that a man would take them to be exceeding angry, or stark mad. Such victuall as they have, they spend freely, and at night where his lodging is appointed, they set a woman fresh painted red with *Pocones* and oyle, to be his bed-fellow.

Their manner of trading is for copper, beads, and such like, for which they give such commodities as they have, as skins, foule, fish, flesh, and their Country Corne. But their victualls are their chiefest riches.

Every spring they make themselves sicke with drinking the juyce of a roote they call *Wighsacan*, and water; whereof they powre so great a quantitie, that it purgeth them in a very violent manner; so that in three or foure dayes after, they scarce recover their former health.[25] Sometimes they are troubled with dropsies, swellings, aches, and such like diseases; for cure whereof they build a Stove in the forme of a Dove-house with mats, so close that a few coales therein covered with a pot, will make the patient sweat extreamely. For swellings also they use small peeces of touchwood, in the forme of cloves, which pricking on the griefe they burne close to the flesh, and from thence draw the corruption with their mouth. With this roote *Wighsacan* they ordinarily heale greene wounds. But to scarrifie a swelling, or make incision, their best instruments are some splinted stone. Old ulcers, or putrified hurts are seldome seene cured amongst them. They have many professed Phisicians, who with their charmes and Rattles, with an infernall rout of words and actions, will seeme to sucke their inward griefe from their navels, or their grieved places; but of our Chirurgians they were so conceited, that they beleeved any Plaister would heale any hurt.[26]

24. *Tunable* means "harmonious, sweet sounding."

25. The drink made from *wighsacan* was an emetic; that is, excessive intake of it caused violent vomiting. It was drunk as part of a solemn ritual intended to purify the participants. As European medicine made extensive use of emetics, such purging would not have seemed unduly strange to the colonists. The root Smith saw used was probably from the milkweed plant, but the word *wighsacan* may have been used for all medicine.

26. A plaister is a bandage, probably spread with an ointment.

But 'tis not alwayes in Phisicians skill,
To heale the Patient that is sicke and ill:
For sometimes sicknesse on the Patients part,
Proves stronger farre then all Phisicians art.

Of their Religion.

THERE IS yet in Virginia no place discovered to be so Savage, in which they have not a Religion, Deere, and Bow, and Arrowes. All things that are able to doe them hurt beyond their prevention, they adore with their kinde of divine worship; as the fire, water, lightning, thunder, our Ordnance, peeces, horses, etc. But their chiefe God they worship is the Devill. Him they call *Okee*, and serve him more of feare then love. They say they have conference with him, and fashion themselves as neare to his shape as they can imagine. In their Temples they have his image evill favouredly carved, and then painted and adorned with chaines of copper, and beads, and covered with a skin, in such manner as the deformitie may well suit with such a God.[27] By him is commonly the sepulcher of their Kings. Their bodies are first bowelled,[28] then dried upon hurdles till they be very dry, and so about the most of their joynts and necke they hang bracelets, or chaines of copper, pearle, and such like, as they use to weare, their inwards they stuffe with copper beads, hatchets, and such trash. Then lappe they them very carefully in white skins, and so rowle them in mats for their winding sheets. And in the Tombe which is an arch made of mats, they lay them orderly. What remaineth of this kinde of wealth their Kings have, they set at their feet in baskets. These Temples and bodies are kept by their Priests.

For their ordinary burials, they dig a deepe hole in the earth with

27. The Powhatans believed in a benevolent, but remote creator, Ahone, who did not take an active role in human affairs, and Okee, a much more problematical figure. Okee could act to help or harm; he was worshipped in order to appease or cajole him and to solicit his aid. Worship of Okee reinforced the ceremonial round associated with the agricultural calendar. It was natural for Smith to associate Okee with the devil; as a Christian, he was familiar with the concept of two great supernatural powers, one wholly good and the other wholly evil. He could not discern the complexity of Okee's role.

28. *Bowelled* means "disemboweled."

These paintings of Virginia Indian religious life are all based on the paintings of John White from Roanoke. Robert Vaughan here portrayed Okee as an idol, using the same carved figure that William Hole had adapted into a picture of Powhatan (p. 88). Vaughan inserted a picture of Smith into his rendition of White's drawing of a religious ceremony and used it to illustrate Smith's story of the Indians' conjuration about his fate. Neither Hole nor Vaughan had been to America; their reliance on White, who was in America several times, is understandable.
Courtesy of the Princeton University Library.

sharpe stakes, and the corpse being lapped in skins and mats with their jewels, they lay them upon stickes in the ground, and so cover them with earth. The buriall ended, the women being painted all their faces with blacke cole and oyle, doe sit twenty foure houres in the houses mourning and lamenting by turnes, with such yelling and howling, as may expresse their great passions.

In every Territory of a Werowance is a Temple and a Priest, two or three or more. Their principall Temple or place of superstition is at Uttamussack at Pamaunkee, neare unto which is a house, Temple, or place of Powhatans.

Upon the top of certaine red sandy hils in the woods, there are three great houses filled with images of their Kings, and Devils, and Tombes of their Predecessors. Those houses are neare sixtie foot in length built arbour-wise, after their building. This place they count so holy as that but the Priests and Kings dare come into them; nor the Salvages dare not goe up the river in boats by it, but they solemnly cast some peece of copper, white beads, or *Pocones* into the river, for feare their *Okee* should be offended and revenged of them.[29]

Thus,

Feare was the first their Gods begot:
Till feare began, their Gods were not.

In this place commonly are resident seaven Priests. The chiefe differed from the rest in his ornaments, but inferior Priests could hardly be knowne from the common people, but that they had not so many holes in their eares to hang their jewels at. The ornaments of the chiefe Priest were certaine attires for his head made thus. They tooke a dosen, or 16, or more snakes skins and stuffed them with mosse, and of Weesels and other Vermines skins a good many. All these they tie by their tailes, so as all their tailes meete in the toppe of their head like a great Tassell. Round about this Tassell is as it were a crowne of feathers, the skins hang round about his head, necke, and shoulders, and in a manner cover his face. The faces of all their Priests are painted as ugly as they can devise, in their hands they had every one his Rattle, some base, some smaller. Their devotion was most in songs, which the chiefe Priest beginneth and the rest followed him, sometimes he

29. *Pocones* is a root that in addition to producing a red dye had medicinal properties, as a salve for swellings and painful joints.

maketh invocations with broken sentences by starts and strange passions, and at every pause, the rest give a short groane.

> *Thus seeke they in deepe foolishnesse,*
> *To climbe the height of happinesse.*

It could not be perceived that they keepe any day as more holy then
other; But onely in some great distresse of want, feare of enemies,
times of triumph and gathering together their fruits, the whole Country of men, women, and children come together to solemnities. The
manner of their devotion is, sometimes to make a great fire, in the
house or fields, and all to sing and dance about it with Rattles and
shouts together, foure or five houres. Sometimes they set a man in the
midst, and about him they dance and sing, he all the while clapping his
hands, as if he would keepe time, and after their songs and dauncings
ended they goe to their Feasts.

> *Through God begetting feare,*
> *Mans blinded minde did reare*
> *A hell-god to the ghosts;*
> *A heaven-god to the hoasts;*
> *Yea God unto the Seas:*
> *Feare did create all these.*

They have also divers conjurations, one they made when I was their
prisoner; of which hereafter you shall reade at large.[30]

They have also certaine Altar stones they call *Pawcorances*, but these
stand from their Temples, some by their houses, others in the woods
and wildernesses, where they have had any extraordinary accident, or
incounter. And as you travell, at those stones they will tell you the
cause why they were there erected, which from age to age they instruct
their children, as their best records of antiquities. Upon these they
offer bloud, Deere suet, and Tobacco. This they doe when they returne
from the Warres, from hunting, and upon many other occasions. They
have also another superstition that they use in stormes, when the waters are rough in the Rivers and Sea coasts. Their Conjurers runne to
the water sides, or passing in their boats, after many hellish outcryes
and invocations, they cast Tobacco, Copper, *Pocones*, or such trash into
the water, to pacifie that God whom they thinke to be very angry in
those stormes. Before their dinners and suppers the better sort will

---

30. For this description, see pp. 61–65, above.

take the first bit, and cast it in the fire, which is all the grace they are knowne to use.

In some part of the Country they have yearely a sacrifice of children. Such a one was at Quiyoughcohanock some ten myles from James Towne, and thus performed. Fifteene of the properest young boyes, betweene ten and fifteene yeares of age they painted white. Having brought them forth, the people spent the forenoone in dancing and singing about them with Rattles. In the afternoone they put those children to the roote of a tree. By them all the men stood in a guard, every one having a Bastinado in his hand, made of reeds bound together. This made a lane betweene them all along, through which there were appointed five young men to fetch these children: so every one of the five went through the guard to fetch a childe each after other by turnes, the guard fiercely beating them with their Bastinadoes, and they patiently enduring and receiving all defending the children with their naked bodies from the unmercifull blowes, that pay them soundly, though the children escape. All this while the women weepe and cry out very passionately, providing mats, skins, mosse, and dry wood, as things fitting their childrens funerals. After the children were thus passed the guard, the guard tore down the trees, branches and boughs, with such violence that they rent the body, and made wreaths for their heads, or bedecked their hayre with the leaves. What els was done with the children, was not seene, but they were all cast on a heape, in a valley as dead, where they made a great feast for all the company. The Werowance being demanded the meaning of this sacrifice, answered that the children were not all dead, but that the *Okee* or Divell did sucke the bloud from their left breast, who chanced to be his by lot, till they were dead, but the rest were kept in the wildernesse by the young men till nine moneths were expired, during which time they must not converse with any, and of these were made their Priests and Conjurers.[31] This sacrifice they held to be so necessary, that if they should omit it, their *Okee* or Devill, and all their other *Quiyoughcosughes*, which are their other Gods, would let them have no Deere,

31. This black-boy ceremony, as Smith calls it in a marginal note, or *huskenaw*, was a puberty rite that involved a symbolic death of the child, who emerged as an adult member; the mothers mourned the loss of their children as children. The children were carried through two lines of men who attempted to beat them with *bastinadoes* made of reeds tied together; Smith had passed through such a line, his *bissone*, before he was put through a similar symbolic death and rebirth during his captivity. See the account on p. 61, above.

Turkies, Corne, nor fish, and yet besides, he would make a great slaughter amongst them.

They thinke that their Werowances and Priests which they also esteeme *Quiyoughcosughes*, when they are dead, doe goe beyond the mountaines towards the setting of the sunne, and ever remaine there in forme of their *Okee*, with their heads painted with oyle and *Pocones*, finely trimmed with feathers, and shall have beads, hatchets, copper, and Tobacco, doing nothing but dance and sing, with all their Predecessors. But the common people they suppose shall not live after death, but rot in their graves like dead dogs.

To divert them from this blind Idolatry, we did our best endevours, chiefly with the Werowance of Quiyoughcohanock, whose devotion, apprehension, and good disposition, much exceeded any in those Countries, who although we could not as yet prevaile, to forsake his false Gods, yet this he did beleeve that our God as much exceeded theirs, as our Gunnes did their Bowes and Arrowes,[32] and many times did send to me to James Towne, intreating me to pray to my God for raine, for their Gods would not send them any. And in this lamentable ignorance doe these poore soules sacrifice themselves to the Devill, not knowing their Creator; and we had not language sufficient, so plainly to expresse it as make them understand it; which God grant they may. For,

> *Religion 'tis that doth distinguish us,*
> *From their bruit humor, well we may it know;*
> *That can with understanding argue thus,*
> *Our God is truth, but they cannot doe so.*

Of the manner of the Virginians Government.

ALTHOUGH THE Country people be very barbarous, yet have they amongst them such government, as that their Magistrates for good commanding, and their people for due subjection, and obeying, excell many places that would be counted very civill. The forme of their Common-wealth is a Monarchicall government, one as Emperour ruleth over many Kings or Governours. Their chiefe ruler is called Powhatan, and taketh his name of his principall place of dwelling

32. Because the Powhatans were polytheists, they could attempt to add the powers of the Christian god to their arsenal without disloyalty to their own gods.

called Powhatan. But his proper name is Wahunsonacock. Some Countries he hath which have beene his ancestors, and came unto him by inheritance, as the Country called Powhatan, Arrohateck, Appama-tuck, Pamaunkee, Youghtanund, and Mattapanient. All the rest of his Territories expressed in the Mappe, they report have beene his severall Conquests. In all his ancient inheritances, he hath houses built after their manner like arbours, some 30. some 40. yards long, and at every house provision for his entertainement according to the time. At Werowcomoco on the Northside of the river Pamaunkee, was his resi-dence, when I was delivered him prisoner, some 14 myles from James Towne, where for the most part, he was resident, but at last he tooke so little pleasure in our neare neighbourhood, that he retired himselfe to Orapakes, in the desert betwixt Chickahamania and Youghtanund.[33] He is of personage a tall well proportioned man, with a sower looke, his head somwhat gray, his beard so thinne, that it seemeth none at all, his age neare sixtie; of a very able and hardy body to endure any labour. About his person ordinarily attendeth a guard of 40 or 50 of the tallest men his Country doth afford. Every night upon the foure quarters of his house are foure Sentinels, each from other a flight shoot, and at every halfe houre one from the Corps du guard doth hollow, shaking his lips with his finger betweene them; unto whom every Sentinell doth answer round from his stand: if any faile, they presently send forth an officer that beateth him extreamely.[34]

A myle from Orapakes in a thicket of wood, he hath a house in which he keepeth his kinde of Treasure, as skinnes, copper, pearle, and beads, which he storeth up against the time of his death and buriall. Here also is his store of red paint for oyntment, bowes and arrowes, Targets and clubs. This house is fiftie or sixtie yards in length, fre-quented onely by Priests. At the foure corners of this house stand foure Images as Sentinels, one of a Dragon, another a Beare, the third like a Leopard, and the fourth like a giantlike man, all made evill favouredly, according to their best workemanship.

He hath as many women as he will, whereof when he lieth on his bed, one sitteth at his head, and another at his feet, but when he sitteth, one sitteth on his right hand and another on his left. As he is

33. Having the English colonists as near neighbors meant constant pressure on the Indians' food supply; Powhatan's way of dealing with the problem was to move away into the interior.
34. The English colonists had extreme difficulty posting and maintaining reliable watches.

weary of his women, he bestoweth them on those that best deserve them at his hands. When he dineth or suppeth, one of his women before and after meat, bringeth him water in a wooden platter to wash his hands. Another waiteth with a bunch of feathers to wipe them in stead of a Towell, and the feathers when he hath wiped are dryed againe. His kingdomes descend not to his sonnes nor children, but first to his brethren, whereof he hath 3. namely, Opitchapan, Opechan-canough, and Catataugh, and after their decease to his sisters. First to the eldest sister, then to the rest, and after them to the heires male or female of the eldest sister, but never to the heires of the males.

He nor any of his people understand any letters, whereby to write or reade, onely the lawes whereby he ruleth is custome. Yet when he listeth his will is a law and must be obeyed: not onely as a King, but as halfe a God they esteeme him. His inferiour Kings whom they call Werowances, are tyed to rule by customes, and have power of life and death at their command in that nature. But this word Werowance, which we call and construe for a King, is a common word, whereby they call all commanders: for they have but few words in their language, and but few occasions to use any officers more then one commander, which commonly they call Werowance, or *Caucorouse*, which is Captaine. They all know their severall lands, and habitations, and limits, to fish, foule, or hunt in,[35] but they hold all of their great Werowance Powhatan, unto whom they pay tribute of skinnes, beads, copper, pearle, deere, turkies, wild beasts, and corne. What he commandeth they dare not disobey in the least thing. It is strange to see with what great feare and adoration, all these people doe obey this Powhatan. For at his feet they present whatsoever he commandeth, and at the least frowne of his brow, their greatest spirits will tremble with feare: and no marvell, for he is very terrible and tyrannous in punishing such as offend him. For example, he caused certaine male-factors to be bound hand and foot, then having of many fires gathered great store of burning coales, they rake these coales round in the forme of a cockpit, and in the midst they cast the offenders to broyle to death. Sometimes he causeth the heads of them that offend him, to be laid upon the altar or sacrificing stone, and one with clubbes beats out their braines. When he would punish any notorious enemy or malefac-

35. This was an extremely important point. Theorists in England held that the Indians merely ranged over the land like the deer and therefore did not own it in a European sense. Smith is saying that each village had recognized territories and boundaries, all held in a feudal tenure from Powhatan.

tor, he causeth him to be tyed to a tree, and with Mussell shels or reeds, the executioner cutteth off his joynts one after another, ever casting what they cut of into the fire; then doth he proceed with shels and reeds to case the skinne from his head and face; then doe they rip his belly and so burne him with the tree and all. Thus themselves reported they executed George Cassen. Their ordinary correction is to beate them with cudgels. We have seene a man kneeling on his knees, and at Powhatans command, two men have beate him on the bare skin, till he hath fallen senselesse in a sound, and yet never cry nor complained. And he made a woman for playing the whore, sit upon a great stone, on her bare breech twenty-foure houres, onely with corne and water, every three dayes, till nine dayes were past, yet he loved her exceedingly: notwithstanding there are common whores by profession.

In the yeare 1608, he surprised the people of Payankatank his neare neighbours and subjects. The occasion was to us unknowne, but the manner was thus. First he sent divers of his men as to lodge amongst them that night, then the Ambuscadoes environed all their houses, and at the houre appointed, they all fell to the spoyle, twenty-foure men they slew, the long haire of the one side of their heads, with the skinne cased off with shels or reeds, they brought away. They surprised also the women, and the children, and the Werowance. All these they presented to Powhatan. The Werowance, women and children became his prisoners, and doe him service. The lockes of haire with their skinnes he hanged on a line betwixt two trees. And thus he made ostentation of his triumph at Werowocomoco, where he intended to have done as much to mee and my company. [*Generall Historie:* II, 114–128]

Captain Smith never forgot his primary purpose in describing Indian culture: to aid the English in settling among the Indians and in defending themselves against the Indians' natural resistance to such encroachment. One of his earliest reports on the tribes of Chesapeake Bay gives population figures always in terms of the number of fighting men the various villages could muster.

ON THE west side of the Bay, wee said were 5. faire and delightfull navigable rivers, of which wee will nowe proceed to report. . . . The most of these rivers are inhabited by severall nations, or rather families, of the name of the rivers. They have also in every of those places some Governour, as their king, which they call *Werowances*. In a Peninsula on the North side of this river are the English planted in a place by them called James Towne, in honour of the Kings most excellent Majestie, upon which side are also many places under the Werowances.

The first and next the rivers mouth are the Kecoughtans, who besides their women and children, have not past 20. fighting men. The Paspaheghes on whose land is seated the English Colony, some 40. miles from the Bay have not past 40. The river called Chickahamania neere 200. The Weanocks 100. The Arrowhatocks 30. The place called Powhatan, some 40. On the South side this river the Appamatucks have 60 fighting men. The Quiyougcohanocks, 25. The Warraskoyacks 40. The Nandsamunds 200. The Chesapeacks are able to make 100. Of this last place the Bay beareth the name. In all these places is a severall commander, which they call Werowance, except the Chickhamanians, who are governed by the Priestes and their Assistants or their Elders called *Caw-cawwassoughes*. . . .

Foureteene miles Northward from the river Powhatan, is the river Pamaunke, which is navigable 60 or 70 myles, but with Catches and small Barkes 30 or 40 myles farther. At the ordinary flowing of the salt water, it divideth it selfe into two gallant branches. On the South side inhabit the people of Youghtanund, who have about 60 men for warres. On the North branch Mattapament, who have 30 men. Where this river is divided the Country is called Pamaunke, and nourisheth neere 300 able men. About 25 miles lower on the North side of this river is Werawocomoco, where their great King inhabited when Captain Smith was delivered him prisoner; yet there are not past 40 able men. But now he hath abandoned that, and liveth at Orapakes by Youghtanund in the wildernesse; 10 or 12 myles lower, on the South side of this river is Chiskiack, which hath some 40 or 50 men. These, as also Apamatuck, Arrohatock, and Powhatan, are their great kings chiefe alliance and inhabitance. The rest (as they report) his Conquests.

Before we come to the third river that falleth from the mountaines, there is another river (some 30 myles navigable) that commeth from the Inland, the river is called Payankatanke, the Inhabitants are about some 40 serviceable men.

The third navigable river is called Toppahanock. (This is navigable some 130 myles). At the top of it inhabit the people called Manna-hoackes amongst the mountaines, but they are above the place we describe. Upon this river on the North side are seated a people called Cuttatawomen, with 30 fighting men. Higher on the river are the Moraughtacunds, with 80 able men. Beyond them Toppahanock with 100 men. Far above is another Cuttatawomen with 20 men. On the South, far within the river is Nantaughtacund having 150 men. This river also as the two former, is replenished with fish and foule.

The fourth river is called Patawomeke and is 6 or 7 miles in breadth. It is navigable 140 miles, and fed as the rest with many sweet rivers and springs, which fall from the bordering hils. These hils many of them are planted, and yeelde no lesse plenty and variety of fruit then the river exceedeth with abundance of fish. This river is inhabited on both sides. First on the South side at the very entrance is Wighcocomoco and hath some 130 men, beyond them Sekacawone with 30. The Onawmanient with 100. Then Patawomeke with 160 able men. Here doth the river divide it selfe into 3 or 4 convenient rivers; The greatest of the last is called Quiyough treadeth north west, but the river it selfe turneth North east and is stil a navigable streame. On the westerne side of this bought is Tauxenent with 40 men. On the north of this river is Secowocomoco with 40 men. Some what further Potapaco with 20. In the East part of the bought of the river,[36] is Pamacacack with 60 men, After Moyowances with 100. And lastly Nacotchtanke with 80 able men. The river 10 miles above this place maketh his passage downe a low pleasant vally overshaddowed in manie places with high rocky mountaines; from whence distill innumerable sweet and pleasant springs.

The fifth river is called Pawtuxunt, and is of a lesse proportion then the rest; but the channell is 16 or 18 fadome deepe in some places. Here are infinit skuls of divers kinds of fish more then elsewhere.[37] Upon this river dwell the people called Acquintanacksuak, Pawtuxunt and Mattapanient. 200 men was the greatest strength that could bee there perceived. But they inhabit togither, and not so dispersed as the rest. These of al other were found the most civill to give intertainement.

Thirty leagues Northward is a river not inhabited, yet navigable; for the red earth or clay resembling bole Armoniack the English called it

36. A bought is a bend or curve; the more familiar *bight* is another form.
37. *Skuls* for *schools.*

Bolus.[38] At the end of the Bay where it is 6 or 7 miles in breadth, there fall into it 4 small rivers, 3 of them issuing from diverse bogges invironed with high mountaines. There is one that commeth du north 3 or 4. daies journy from the head of the Bay and fals from rocks and mountaines, upon this river inhabit a people called Sasquesahanock. They are seated 2 daies higher then was passage for the discoverers Barge, which was hardly 2 toons,[39] and had in it but 12 men to perform this discovery. . . . But to proceed, 60 of those Sasquesahanocks, came to the discoverers with skins, Bowes, Arrowes, Targets, Beads, Swords, and Tobacco pipes for presents. Such great and well proportioned men, are seldome seene, for they seemed like Giants to the English, yea and to the neighbours, yet seemed of an honest and simple disposition, with much adoe restrained from adoring the discoverers as Gods. Those are the most strange people of all those Countries, both in language and attire; for their language it may well beseeme their proportions, sounding from them, as it were a great voice in a vault, or cave, as an Eccho. Their attire is the skinnes of Beares, and Woolves, some have Cassacks made of Beares heades and skinnes that a mans necke goes through the skinnes neck, and the eares of the beare fastned to his shoulders behind, the nose and teeth hanging downe his breast, and at the end of the nose hung a Beares Pawe, the halfe sleeves comming to the elbowes were the neckes of Beares and the armes through the mouth with pawes hanging at their noses. One had the head of a Woolfe hanging in a chaine for a Jewell, his Tobacco pipe 3 quarters of a yard long, prettily carved with a Bird, a Beare, a Deare, or some such devise at the great end, sufficient to beat out the braines of a man, with bowes, and arrowes, and clubs, sutable to their greatnesse and conditions. These are scarse knowne to Powhatan. They can make neere 600 able and mighty men and are pallisadoed in their Townes to defend them from the Massawomekes their mortall enimies. 5 of their chiefe Werowances came aboard the discoverers and crossed the Bay in their Barge. The picture of the greatest of them is signified in the Mappe. The calfe of whose leg was 3 quarters of a yard about, and all the rest of his limbes so answerable to that proportion, that he seemed the goodliest man that ever we beheld. His haire, the one side was long, the other shore close with a ridge over his crown like a cocks

38. Bole Armoniack is a clay with astringent properties that was used in medicine, a valuable commodity.
39. *Toons* for *tons*.

combe. His arrowes were five quarters long, headed with flints or splinters of stones, in forme like a heart, an inch broad, and an inch and a halfe or more long. These hee wore in a woolves skinne at his backe for his quiver, his bow in the one hand and his clubbe in the other, as is described.

On the East side the Bay is the river of Tockwhogh, and upon it a people that can make 100 men, seated some 7 miles within the river: where they have a Fort very wel pallisadoed and mantelled with the barke of trees. Next to them is Ozinies with 60 men. More to the South of that East side of the Bay, the river of Rapahanock, neere unto which is the river of Kuskarawaock. Upon which is seated a people with 200 men. After that is the river of Tants Wighcocomoco, and on it a people with 100 men. The people of those rivers are of little stature, of another language from the rest, and very rude. But they on the river of Acohanock with 40 men, and they of Accomack 80 men doth equalize any of the Territories of Powhatan and speake his language, who over all those doth rule as king.[40] [*Map of Virginia:* I, 145–150]

II

John Smith's greatest continuing struggle with his fellow colonists and with the company in London was over Indian policy. The timely arrival of Capt. Christopher Newport in January 1608 with the first supplies for the colony saved Captain Smith from the vengeance of the council when he returned from his captivity with Powhatan. While he was in the colony, Newport, the direct representative of the Virginia Company, took precedence over the council and president; he wanted to impress Powhatan with the importance and grandeur of the Virginia Company. Though Newport was a veteran of many expeditions, especially against the Spanish, Smith considered him a novice at dealing with the Indians; Captain Smith demonstrated that there was always damage to be repaired when the Virginia Company, without understanding the situation, tried to intervene directly in American affairs.

40. The Powhatans' language was of the Algonquian group. Smith was in contact with Indians of other language families; for example, the Susquehannocks spoke an Iroquoian language.

B UT N E W P O R T got in and arrived at James Towne, not long after the redemption of Captaine Smith. To whom the Salvages, as is sayd, every other day repaired, with such provisions that sufficiently did serve them from hand to mouth: part alwayes they brought him as Presents from their Kings, or Pocahontas; the rest he as their Market Clarke set the price himselfe, how they should sell: so he had inchanted these poore soules being their prisoner; and now Newport, whom he called his Father arriving, neare as directly as he foretold, they esteemed him as an Oracle, and had them at that submission he might command them what he listed. That God that created all things they knew he adored for his God: they would also in their discourses tearme the God of Captaine Smith.[41]

> *Thus the Almightie was the bringer on,*
> *The guide, path, terme, all which was God alone.*

But the President and Councell so much envied his estimation among the Salvages, (though we all in generall equally participated with him of the good thereof,) that they wrought it into the Salvages understandings (by their great bounty in giving foure times more for their commodities then Smith appointed) that their greatnesse and authoritie as much exceeded his, as their bountie and liberalitie. Now the arrivall of this first supply so overjoyed us, that wee could not devise too much to please the Marriners. We gave them libertie to trucke or trade at their pleasures. But in a short time it followed, that could not be had for a pound of Copper, which before was sould us for an ounce: thus ambition and sufferance cut the throat of our trade, but confirmed their opinion of the greatnesse of Captaine Newport, (wherewith Smith had possessed Powhatan) especially by the great presents Newport often sent him, before he could prepare the Pinnace to goe and visit him: so that this great Savage desired also to see him. A great coyle there was to set him forward.[42] When he went he was accompanied with Captaine Smith, and Master Scrivener, a very wise understanding Gentleman, newly arrived and admitted of the Councell, with thirtie or fortie chosen men for their guard. Arriving at Werowocomoco, Newports conceit of this great Savage bred many

---

41. See p. 154, above.
42. *Coyle* means "bustle, stir," with the implication of hurriedness and confusion.

doubts and suspitions of trecheries.[43] . . . But finding all things well, by two or three hundred Salvages they were kindly conducted to their towne. Where Powhatan strained himselfe to the utmost of his greatnesse to entertaine them, with great shouts of joy, Orations of protestations; and with the most plenty of victualls he could provide to feast them. Sitting upon his bed of mats, his pillow of leather imbrodered (after their rude manner with pearle and white Beads) his attyre a faire robe of skinnes as large as an Irish mantell: at his head and feete a handsome young woman: on each side his house sat twentie of his Concubines, their heads and shoulders painted red, with a great chaine of white beads about each of their neckes. Before those sat his chiefest men in like order in his arbour-like house, and more then fortie platters of fine bread stood as a guard in two fyles on each side the doore. Foure or five hundred people made a guard behinde them for our passage; and Proclamation was made, none upon paine of death to presume to doe us any wrong or discourtesie. With many pretty Discourses to renew their old acquaintance, this great King and our Captaine spent the time, till the ebbe left our Barge aground. Then renewing their feasts with feates, dauncing and singing, and such like mirth, we quartered that night with Powhatan. The next day Newport came a shore and received as much content as those people could give him: a boy named Thomas Salvage was then given unto Powhatan, whom Newport called his sonne; for whom Powhatan gave him Namontack his trustie servant, and one of a shrewd, subtill capacitie. Three or foure dayes more we spent in feasting, dauncing, and trading, wherein Powhatan carried himselfe so proudly, yet discreetly (in his salvage manner) as made us all admire his naturall gifts, considering his education. As scorning to trade as his subjects did; he bespake Newport in this manner.

> Captaine Newport it is not agreeable to my greatnesse, in this pedling manner to trade for trifles; and I esteeme you also a great Werowance. Therefore lay me downe all your commodities together; what I like I will take, and in recompence give you what I thinke fitting their value.

Captaine Smith being our interpreter, regarding Newport as his father, knowing best the disposition of Powhatan, tould us his intent

43. *Conceit* means "conception"; *doubts* means "fears" or "apprehensions."

was but onely to cheate us; yet Captaine Newport thinking to out brave this Salvage in ostentation of greatnesse,[44] and so to bewitch him with his bountie, as to have what he listed, it so hapned, that Powhatan having his desire, valued his corne at such a rate, that I thinke it better cheape in Spaine: for we had not foure bushells for that we expected to have twentie hogsheads. This bred some unkindnesse betweene our two Captaines; Newport seeking to please the unsatiable desire of the Salvage, Smith to cause the Salvage to please him; but smothering his distast to avoyd the Salvages suspition, glanced in the eyes of Powhatan many trifles, who fixed his humor upon a few blew beades.[45] A long time he importunately desired them, but Smith seemed so much the more to affect them, as being composed of a most rare substance of the coulour of the skyes, and not to be worne but by the greatest kings in the world. This made him halfe madde to be the owner of such strange Jewells: so that ere we departed, for a pound or two of blew beades, he brought over my king for 2. or 300. Bushells of corne; yet parted good friends. The like entertainment we found of Opechankanough king of Pamaunkee, whom also he in like manner fitted (at the like rates) with blew beads, which grew by this meanes, of that estimation, that none durst weare any of them but their great kings, their wives and children. [*Generall Historie:* II, 154–157]

POWHATAN (to expresse his love to Newport) when he departed, presented him with twentie Turkies, conditionally to returne him twentie swords, which immediately was sent him; now after his departure he presented Captaine Smith with the like luggage, but not finding his humor obeyed in not sending such weapons as he desired, he caused his people with twentie devices to obtaine them. At last by ambuscadoes at our very Ports they would take them perforce, surprise us at worke, or any way; which was so long permitted, they became so insolent there was no rule; the command from England was so strait not to offend them, as our authoritie-bearers (keeping their houses) would rather be any thing then peace-breakers. This charitable humor

---

44. *To out brave* here means "to challenge by making a show of splendor or greatness."

45. When Smith says he glanced trifles in the eyes of Powhatan, he means that he cast his "jewels" before him in such a way that they produced flashes of light. He used Powhatan's desire for blue beads to repair the trading balance.

prevailed, till well it chanced they medled with Captaine Smith, who without farther deliberation gave them such an incounter, as some he so hunted up and downe the Isle, some he so terrified with whipping, beating, and imprisonment, as for revenge they surprised two of our forraging disorderly souldiers, and having assembled their forces, boldly threatned at our Ports to force Smith to redeliver seven Salvages, which for their villanies he detained prisoners, or we were all but dead men. But to try their furies he sallied out amongst them, and in lesse then an houre, he so hampred their insolencies, they brought them his two men, desiring peace without any further composition for their prisoners. Those he examined, and caused them all beleeve, by severall vollies of shot one of their companions was shot to death, because they would not confesse their intents and plotters of those villanies. And thus they all agreed in one point, they were directed onely by Powhatan to obtaine him our weapons, to cut our owne throats, with the manner where, how, and when, which we plainly found most true and apparant: yet he sent his messengers, and his dearest daughter Pocahontas with presents to excuse him of the injuries done by some rash untoward Captaines his subjects, desiring their liberties for this time, with the assurance of his love for ever. After Smith had given the prisoners what correction he thought fit, used them well a day or two after, and then delivered them Pocahontas, for whose sake onely he fayned to have saved their lives, and gave them libertie.[46] The patient Councell that nothing would move to warre with the Salvages, would gladly have wrangled with Captaine Smith for his crueltie, yet none was slaine to any mans knowledge, but it brought them in such feare and obedience, as his very name would sufficiently affright them; where before, wee had sometime peace and warre twice in a day, and very seldome a weeke, but we had some trecherous villany or other. [*Generall Historie:* II, 159–160]

Captain Newport was back in Jamestown with the second supply in September 1608, shortly after Smith had assumed the presidency. Newport was expected to find gold, the passage to the South Sea (the Pacific), or the Roa-

---

46. *Fayned* means "pretended or claimed"; Smith claimed that it was the appearance of Pocahontas as intermediary that caused him to spare the lives of his Indian captives.

noke colonists left by Ralegh twenty years previously before he returned to England, which diverted the colonists from the more pressing tasks of preparing for the winter. Moreover, he brought presents for Powhatan, who was to be crowned as a vassal of the king of England. Newport insisted on carrying out the coronation despite Smith's resistance.

How or why Captaine Newport obtained such a private Commission, as not to returne without a lumpe of gold, a certaintie of the South sea, or one of the lost company sent out by Sir Walter Raleigh, I know not; nor why he brought such a five peeced Barge, not to beare us to that South sea, till we had borne her over the mountaines, which how farre they extend is yet unknowne.[47] As for the Coronation of Powhatan, and his presents of Bason and Ewer, Bed, Bedstead, Clothes, and such costly novelties, they had beene much better well spared then so ill spent, for wee had his favour much better onely for a playne peece of Copper, till this stately kinde of soliciting, made him so much overvalue himselfe, that he respected us as much as nothing at all. As for the hyring of the Poles and Dutchmen, to make Pitch, Tar, Glasse, Milles,[48] and Sope ashes when the Country is replenished with people, and necessaries, would have done well, but to send them and seaventie more without victualls to worke, was not so well advised nor considered of, as it should have beene. Yet this could not have hurt us had they beene 200. though then we were 130 that wanted for our selves. For we had the Salvages in that decorum (their harvest being newly gathered) that we feared not to get victuals for 500. Now was there no way to make us miserable, but to neglect that time to make provision whilst it was to be had, the which was done by the direction from England to performe this strange discovery, but a more strange Coronation to loose that time, spend that victualls we had, tyre and starve our men, having no meanes to carry victuals, munition, the hurt or sicke, but on their owne backes. How or by whom they were invented I know not: but Captaine Newport we onely accounted the Author, who to effect these projects, had

47. "Five peeced Barge": Since the colonists had reported that they could not navigate the river beyond the fall line, the Virginia Company sent a boat in pieces that they hoped could be carried over the mountains and there assembled for the continued journey upriver.

48. Despite the comma between *Glasse* and *Milles*, Smith probably means glass mills, buildings in which the manufacture of glass was carried on.

so guilded mens hopes with great promises, that both Company and Councell concluded his resolution for the most part:[49] God doth know they little knew what they did, nor understood their owne estates to conclude his conclusions, against all the inconveniences the foreseeing President alledged. Of this Supply there was added to the Councell, one Captaine Richard Waldo, and Captaine Wynne, two auncient Souldiers, and valiant Gentlemen, but yet ignorant of the busines, (being but newly arrived.) Ratliffe was also permitted to have his voyce, and Master Scrivener, desirous to see strange Countries: so that although Smith was President, yet the Major part of the Councell had the authoritie and ruled it as they listed. As for clearing Smiths objections, how Pitch and Tarre, Wainscot, Clapbord, Glasse, and Sope ashes, could be provided, to relade the ship, or provision got to live withall, when none was in the Country, and that we had, spent, before the ship departed to effect these projects. The answer was, Captaine Newport undertooke to fraught the Pinnace of twentie tunnes with Corne in going and returning in his Discovery, and to refraught her againe from Werowocomoco of Powhatan. Also promising a great proportion of victualls from the Ship; inferring that Smiths propositions were onely devices to hinder his journey, to effect it himselfe; and that the crueltie he had used to the Salvages, might well be the occasion to hinder these Designes, and seeke revenge on him. For which taxation all workes were left, and 120 chosen men were appointed for Newports guard in this Discovery. But Captaine Smith to make cleare all those seeming suspitions, that the Salvages were not so desperate as was pretended by Captaine Newport, and how willing (since by their authoritie they would have it so) he was to assist them what he could, because the Coronation would consume much time, he undertooke himselfe their message to Powhatan, to intreat him to come to James Towne to receive his presents. And where Newport durst not goe with lesse then 120. he onely tooke with him Captaine Waldo, Master Andrew Buckler, Edward Brinton, and Samuel Collier: with these foure he went over land to Werowocomoco, some 12 myles; there he passed the river of Pamaunkee in a Salvage Canow. Powhatan being 30 myles of, was presently sent for: in the meane time, Pocahontas and her women entertained Captaine Smith in this manner.

In a fayre plaine field they made a fire, before which, he sitting upon a mat, suddainly amongst the woods was heard such a hydeous noise

49. *Guilded* for *gilded.*

and shreeking, that the English betooke themselves to their armes, and seized on two or three old men by them, supposing Powhatan with all his power was come to surprise them. But presently Pocahontas came, willing him to kill her if any hurt were intended, and the beholders, which were men, women, and children, satisfied the Captaine there was no such matter. Then presently they were presented with this anticke;[50] thirtie young women came naked out of the woods, onely covered behind and before with a few greene leaves, their bodies all painted, some of one colour, some of another, but all differing, their leader had a fayre payre of Bucks hornes on her head, and an Otters skinne at her girdle, and another at her arme, a quiver of arrowes at her backe, a bow and arrowes in her hand; the next had in her hand a sword, another a club, another a pot-sticke; all horned alike: the rest every one with their severall devises. These fiends with most hellish shouts and cryes, rushing from among the trees, cast themselves in a ring about the fire, singing and dauncing with most excellent ill varietie, oft falling into their infernall passions, and solemnly againe to sing and daunce; having spent neare an houre in this Mascarado, as they entred in like manner they departed.

Having reaccommodated themselves, they solemnly invited him to their lodgings, where he was no sooner within the house, but all these Nymphes more tormented him then ever, with crowding, pressing, and hanging about him, most tediously crying, Love you not me? love you not me? This salutation ended, the feast was set, consisting of all the Salvage dainties they could devise: some attending, others singing and dauncing about them; which mirth being ended, with fire-brands in stead of Torches they conducted him to his lodging.

Thus did they shew their feats of armes, and others art in dauncing:
Some other us'd there oaten pipe, and others voyces chanting.

The next day came Powhatan. Smith delivered his message of the presents sent him, and redelivered him Namontack he had sent for England, desiring him to come to his Father Newport, to accept those presents, and conclude their revenge against the Monacans. Whereunto this subtile Savage thus replyed.

If your King have sent me Presents, I also am a King, and this is my land: eight dayes I will stay to receive them. Your Father is to

---

50. An anticke is a grotesque theatrical.

come to me, not I to him, nor yet to your Fort, neither will I bite at such a bait: as for the Monacans I can revenge my owne injuries, and as for Atquanachuk, where you say your brother was slaine, it is a contrary way from those parts you suppose it; but for any salt water beyond the mountaines, the Relations you have had from my people are false.

Whereupon he began to draw plots upon the ground (according to his discourse) of all those Regions. Many other discourses they had (yet both content to give each other content in complementall Courtesies) and so Captaine Smith returned with this Answer.

Upon this the Presents were sent by water which is neare an hundred myles, and the Captains went by land with fiftie good shot. All being met at Werowocomoco, the next day was appointed for his Coronation, then the presents were brought him, his Bason and Ewer, Bed and furniture set up, his scarlet Cloke and apparell with much adoe put on him, being perswaded by Namontack they would not hurt him: but a foule trouble there was to make him kneele to receive his Crowne, he neither knowing the majesty nor meaning of a Crowne, nor bending of the knee, endured so many perswasions, examples, and instructions, as tyred them all; at last by leaning hard on his shoulders, he a little stooped, and three having the crowne in their hands put it on his head, when by the warning of a Pistoll the Boats were prepared with such a volley of shot, that the King start up in a horrible feare, till he saw all was well. Then remembring himselfe, to congratulate their kindnesse, he gave his old shooes and his mantell to Captaine Newport: but perceiving his purpose was to discover the Monacans, he laboured to divert his resolution, refusing to lend him either men or guides more then Namontack; and so after some small complementall kindnesse on both sides, in requitall of his presents he presented Newport with a heape of wheat eares that might containe some 7 or 8 Bushels, and as much more we bought in the Towne, wherewith we returned to the Fort. [*Generall Historie:* II, 181–184]

After Newport had left again, Smith began preparing the colony to survive the winter. Through his descriptions of his encounters with Powhatan and his brother Opechancanough, Smith presented his Indian policy: in every confrontation, the English must seize and maintain the upper hand, instilling fear by every means, but they must always focus on the main goal of

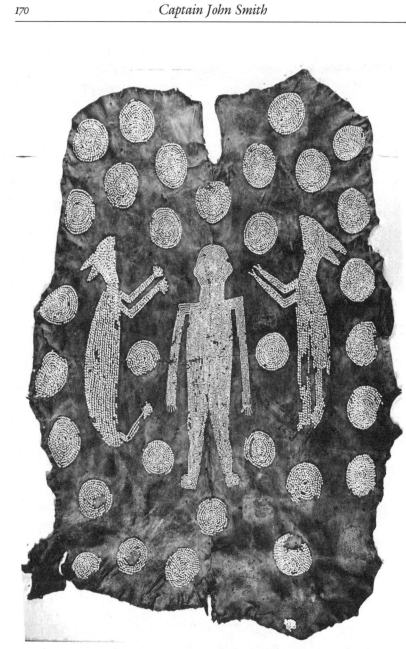

This deerskin robe, decorated with shells, is thought to be the mantle that Powhatan gave to Capt. Christopher Newport (see the earlier description of Powhatan's clothing on p. 163). Courtesy of the Ashmolean Museum, Oxford, England.

obtaining necessary supplies and never give in to the desire for simple vengeance. Smith presented his arguments in the form of speeches exchanged in a kind of verbal fencing match between him and the Indian leaders. In these passages, Captain Smith aimed to produce work of real literary value.

T HE PRESIDENT seeing this procrastinating of time, was no course to live, resolved with Captaine Waldo, (whom he knew to be sure in time of need) to surprise Powhatan, and al his provision, but the unwillingnes of Captaine Winne, and Master Scrivener (for some private respects) did their best to hinder their project: But the President whom no perswasions could perswade to starve, being invited by Powhatan to come unto him, and if he would send him but men to build him a house, bring him a grinstone, 50. swords, some peeces, a cock and a hen, with copper and beads, he would loade his shippe with corne.[51] The President not ignoraunt of his devises, yet unwilling to neglect any opportunity, presently sent 3. Dutch-men and 2. English (having no victuals to imploy them, all for want therof being idle) knowing there needed no better castel, then that house to surprize Powhatan, to effect this project he took order with Captaine Waldo to second him if need required; Scrivener he left his substitute; and set forth with the Pinnas 2. barges and six and forty men which only were such as voluntarily offered themselves for his journy, the which (by reason of Master Scriveners ill successe) was censured very desperate, they all knowing Smith would not returne empty howsoever, caused many of those that he had appointed, to finde excuses to stay behinde. . . .

This company being victualled but for 3. or 4. daies lodged the first night at Weraskoyack, where the President tooke sufficient provision. This kind Salvage did his best to divert him from seeing Powhatan, but perceiving he could not prevaile, he advised in this maner.

Captaine Smith, you shall finde Powhatan to use you kindly, but trust him not, and bee sure hee hath no opportunitie to seaze on your armes, for hee hath sent for you only to cut your throats.

The Captaine thanked him for his good counsell, yet the better to try his love, desired guides to Chowanoke, for he would send a present to that king to bind him his friend. To performe this journey, was sent

51. Pieces are guns.

Michael Sicklemore, a very honest, valiant, and painefull souldier, with him two guids, and directions howe to search for the lost company of Sir Walter Rawley, and silke grasse:[52] then wee departed thence, the President assuring the king his perpetuall love, and left with him Samuell Collier his page to learne the language.

The next night being lodged at Kecoughtan 6 or 7 daies, the extreame wind, raine, frost, and snowe, caused us to keepe Christmas amongst the Salvages, where wee were never more merrie, nor fedde on more plentie of good oysters, fish, flesh, wild foule, and good bread, nor never had better fires in England then in the drie warme smokie houses of Kecoughtan. But departing thence, when we found no houses, we were not curious in any weather, to lie 3 or 4 nights together upon any shore under the trees by a good fire.[53] 148 fowles the President, Anthony Bagly, and Edward Pising, did kill at 3 shoots. At Kiskiack the frost forced us 3 or 4 daies also to suppresse the insolencie of those proud Salvages; to quarter in their houses, and guard our barge, and cause them give us what wee wanted, yet were we but 12 with the President, and yet we never wanted harbour where we found any houses. The 12 of Januarie we arrived at Werawocomoco, where the river was frozen neare halfe a mile from the shore; but to neglect no time, the President with his barge, so farre had approached by breaking the Ice as the eb left him amongst those oozie shoules, yet rather then to lie there frozen to death, by his owne example hee taught them to march middle deepe, more then a flight shot through this muddie frore ooze;[54] when the barge floted he appointed 2 or 3 to returne her abord the Pinnace, where for want of water in melting the salt Ice they made fresh water, but in this march Master Russell (whome none could perswade to stay behind) being somewhat ill, and exceeding heavie, so overtoiled him selfe, as the rest had much adoe (ere he got a shore) to regaine life, into his dead benummed spirits. Quartering in the next houses we found, we sent to Powhatan for provision, who sent us plentie of bread, Turkies, and Venison. The next day having feasted us after his ordinarie manner, he began to aske, when we would bee gon, faining hee sent not for us, neither had hee

52. Silk grass is a plant, possibly yucca, whose fibers it was hoped would produce a silklike thread. It was discovered by the Roanoke colonists and publicized by Thomas Harriot.
53. *Curious* means "difficult to satisfy, fastidious."
54. Ooze is slimy, marshy terrain; *shoules* is for *shoals*; *frore* means "frozen or extremely cold."

any corne, and his people much lesse, yet for 40 swords he would procure us 40 bushels. The President shewing him the men there present, that brought him the message and conditions, asked him how it chaunced he became so forgetful, threat the king concluded the matter with a merry laughter, asking for our commodities, but none he liked without gunnes and swords, valuing a basket of corne more pretious then a basket of copper, saying he could eate his corne, but not his copper.

Captaine Smith seeing the intent of this subtil Salvage began to deale with him after this manner,[55]

Powhatan, though I had many courses to have made my provision, yet beleeving your promises to supply my wants, I neglected all, to satisfie your desire, and to testifie my love, I sent you my men for your building, neglecting my owne: what your people had you have engrossed, forbidding them our trade, and nowe you thinke by consuming the time, wee shall consume for want, not having to fulfill your strange demandes. As for swords, and gunnes, I told you long agoe, I had none to spare. And you shall knowe, those I have, can keepe me from want, yet steale, or wrong you I will not, nor dissolve that friendship, wee have mutually promised, except you constraine mee by your bad usage.

The king having attentively listned to this discourse; promised, that both hee and his Country would spare him what they could, the which within 2 daies, they should receave.

Yet Captaine Smith, (saith the king) some doubt I have of your comming hither, that makes me not so kindly seeke to relieve you as I would; for many do informe me, your comming is not for trade, but to invade my people and possesse my Country, who dare not come to bring you corne, seeing you thus armed with your men. To cleere us of this feare, leave abord your weapons, for here they are needlesse we being all friends and for ever Powhatans.

With many such discourses they spent the day, quartring that night in the kings houses. The next day he reviewed his building, which hee little intended should proceed; for the Dutchmen finding his plenty, and knowing our want, and perceived his preparation to surprise us,

55. *Subtil* can mean "wise" or "clever, crafty, cunning."

little thinking wee could escape both him and famine, (to obtaine his favour) revealed to him as much as they knew of our estates and projects, and how to prevent them; one of them being of so good a judgement, spirit, and resolution, and a hireling that was certaine of wages for his labour, and ever well used, both he and his countrimen, that the President knewe not whome better to trust, and not knowing any fitter for that imploiment, had sent him as a spie to discover Powhatans intent, then little doubting his honestie, nor could ever be certaine of his villany, till neare halfe a yeare after.

Whilst we expected the comming in of the countrie, we wrangled out of the king 10 quarters of corne for a copper kettle, the which the President perceived him much to affect, valued it at a much greater rate, but (in regard of his scarcety) hee would accept of as much more the next yeare, or else the country of Monacan, the king exceeding liberall of that hee had not yeelded him Monacan. Wherewith each seeming well contented; Powhatan began to expostulate the difference betwixt peace and war, after this manner.

Captaine Smith you may understand, that I, having seene the death of all my people thrice, and not one living of those 3 generations, but my selfe, I knowe the difference of peace and warre, better then any in my Countrie.[56] But now I am old, and ere long must die, my brethren, namely Opichapam, Opechankanough, and Kekataugh, my two sisters, and their two daughters, are distinctly each others successours, I wish their experiences no lesse then mine, and your love to them, no lesse then mine to you; but this brute[57] from Nansamund that you are come to destroy my Countrie, so much affrighteth all my people, as they dare not visit you; what will it availe you, to take that perforce, you may quietly have with love, or to destroy them that provide you food? what can you get by war, when we can hide our provision and flie to the woodes, whereby you must famish by wronging us your friends; and whie are you thus jealous of our loves, seeing us

56. Powhatan may be referring to the devastating effects of European diseases on the Virginia Algonquians. These epidemics would have occurred as a result of exposure to some exploring or fishing voyage and therefore would have preceded colonization. The Jamestown colonists were not, thus, venturing into a population that had heretofore been untouched by Europeans.

57. *Brute* for *bruit*, report.

unarmed, and both doe, and are willing still to feed you with that you cannot get but by our labours? think you I am so simple not to knowe, it is better to eate good meate, lie well, and sleepe quietly with my women and children, laugh and be merrie with you, have copper, hatchets, or what I want, being your friend; then bee forced to flie from al, to lie cold in the woods, feed upon acorns, roots, and such trash, and be so hunted by you, that I can neither rest, eate, nor sleepe; but my tired men must watch, and if a twig but breake, everie one crie there comes Captaine Smith, then must I flie I knowe not whether, and thus with miserable feare end my miserable life; leaving my pleasures to such youths as you, which through your rash unadvisednesse, may quickly as miserably ende, for want of that you never knowe how to find? Let this therefore assure you of our loves and everie yeare our friendly trade shall furnish you with corne, and now also if you would come in friendly manner to see us, and not thus with your gunnes and swords, as to invade your foes.[58]

To this subtil discourse the President thus replied.

Seeing you will not rightly conceave of our words, wee strive to make you knowe our thoughts by our deeds. The vow I made you of my love, both my selfe and my men have kept. As for your promise I finde it everie daie violated, by some of your subjects, yet wee finding your love and kindnesse (our custome is so far from being ungratefull) that for your sake only, wee have curbed our thirsting desire of revenge, else had they knowne as wel the crueltie we use to our enimies as our true love and curtesie to our friendes. And I thinke your judgement sufficient to conceive as well by the adventures we have undertaken, as by the advantage we have by our armes of yours: that had wee intended you anie hurt, long ere this wee coulde have effected it; your people comming to me at James towne, are entertained with their bowes and arrowes without exception; we esteeming it with you, as it is with us, to weare our armes as our apparell. As for the dangers of our enimies, in such warres consist our chiefest pleasure, for your riches we have no use, as for the hiding your provision, or by your

58. Powhatan's "subtil discourse" shows that he was keenly aware of English weakness and dependence on the Indians for food.

flying to the woods, we shall so unadvisedly starve as you conclude, your friendly care in that behalfe is needlesse; for we have a rule to finde beyond your knowledge.

Manie other discourses they had, til at last they began to trade, but the king seing his will would not bee admitted as a lawe, our gard dispersed, nor our men disarmed, he (sighing) breathed his mind, once more in this manner.

Captaine Smith, I never used anie of Werowances, so kindlie as your selfe; yet from you I receave the least kindnesse of anie. Captaine Newport gave me swords, copper, cloths, a bed, tooles, or what I desired, ever taking what I offered him, and would send awaie his gunnes when I intreated him: none doth denie to laie at my feet (or do) what I desire, but onelie you, of whom I can have nothing, but what you regard not, and yet you wil have whatsoever you demand. Captain Newport you call father, and so you call me, but I see for all us both, you will doe what you list, and wee must both seeke to content you: but if you intend so friendlie as you saie, sende hence your armes that I may beleeve you, for you see the love I beare you, doth cause mee thus nakedlie forget my selfe.

Smith seeing this Salvage but trifled the time to cut his throat: procured the Salvages to breake the ice, (that his boat might come to fetch both him and his corne) and gave order for his men to come ashore, to have surprised the king, with whom also he but trifled the time till his men landed, and to keepe him from suspition, entertained the time with this reply.

Powhatan, you must knowe as I have but one God, I honour but one king; and I live not here as your subject, but as your friend, to pleasure you with what I can: by the gifts you bestowe on me, you gaine more then by trade; yet would you visite mee as I doe you, you should knowe it is not our customes to sell our curtesie as a vendible commoditie. Bring all your Country with you for your gard, I will not dislike of it as being over jealous. But to content you, to morrow I will leave my armes, and trust to your promise. I call you father indeed, and as a father you shall see I will love you, but the smal care you had of such a child, caused my men perswade me to shift for my selfe.

By this time Powhatan having knowledge, his men were readie: whilst the ice was breaking, his luggage women, and children fledde, and to avoid suspition, left 2 or 3 of his women talking with the Captaine, whilst he secretly fled, and his men as secretlie beset the house, which being at the instant discovered to Captaine Smith, with his Pistol, Sword and Target, he made such a passage amongst those naked divels, that they fled before him some one waie some another, so that without hurt he obtained the Corps du-guard; when they perceived him so well escaped, and with his 8 men (for he had no more with him), to the uttermost of their skill, they sought by excuses to dissemble the matter, and Powhatan to excuse his flight, and the suddaine comming of this multitude, sent our Captaine a greate bracelet, and a chaine of pearle, by an ancient Orator that bespoke us to this purpose, (perceiving them from our Pinnace, a barge and men departing and comming unto us.)

> Captaine Smith, our Werowans is fled, fearing your guns, and knowing when the ice was broken there would come more men, sent those of his to guard his corne from the pilfrie,[59] that might happen without your knowledge: now though some bee hurt by your misprision,[60] yet he is your friend, and so wil continue: and since the ice is open hee would have you send awaie your corne; and if you would have his companie send also your armes, which so affrighteth his people, that they dare not come to you, as he hath promised they should.

Nowe having provided baskets for our men to carrie the corne, they kindlie offered their service to gard our armes, that none should steale them. A great manie they were, of goodlie well appointed fellowes as grim as divels; yet the verie sight of cocking our matches against them, and a few words, caused them to leave their bowes and arrowes to our gard, and beare downe our corne on their own backes; wee needed not importune them to make quick dispatch. But our own barge being left by the ebb, caused us to staie, till the midnight tide carried us safe abord, having spent that halfe night with such mirth, as though we never had suspected or intended any thing, we left the Dutchmen to

59. Pilfrie is pilfering, stealing.
60. *Misprision* can mean "wrongful action," but Smith probably has Powhatan's "ancient Orator" use it in the sense of an unjust suspicion.

build, Brinton to kil fowle for Powhatan (as by his messengers he importunately desired) and left directions with our men to give Powhatan all the content they could, that we might injoy his company at our returne from Pamaunke.

How we escaped surprising at Pamaunke.

WEE HAD no sooner set saile, but Powhatan returned, and sent Adam and Francis (2. stout Dutch men) to the fort, who faining to Captaine Winne that al things were well, and that Captaine Smith had use for their armes, wherefore they requested newe (the which were given them) they told him their comming was for some extraordinary tooles and shift of apparell; by this colourable excuse, they obtained 6. or 7. more to their confederacie, such expert theefes, that presently furnished them with a great many swords, pike-heads, peeces, shot, powder and such like. They had Salvages at hand ready to carry it away, the next day they returned unsuspected, leaving their confederates to follow, and in the interim, to convay them a competencie of all things they could, for which service they should live with Powhatan as his chiefe affected: free from those miseries that would happen the Colony. Samuell their other consort, Powhatan kept for their pledge, whose diligence had provided them, 300. of their kinde of hatchets, the rest, 50. swords, 8. peeces, and 8. pikes: Brinton, and Richard Salvage seeing the Dutch-men so strangly diligent to accommodate the Salvages these weapons attempted to have got to James Towne, but they were apprehended; within 2. or 3. daies we arrived at Pamaunke: the king as many daies, entertained us with feasting and much mirth: and the day he appointed to begin our trade, the President, with Master Persie, Master West, Master Russell, Master Beheathland, Master Powell, Master Crashaw, Master Ford, and some others to the number of 15. went up to Opechancanougs house (near a quarter of a mile from the river,) where we founde nothing, but a lame fellow and a boy, and all the houses about, of all things abandoned; not long we staide ere the king arrived, and after him came divers of his people loaded with bowes and arrowes, but such pinching commodities, and those esteemed at such a value, as our Captaine beganne with him in this manner.

Opechancanough the great love you professe with your tongue, seemes meere deceipt by your actions; last yeare you kindly fraughted our ship, but now you have invited me to starve with hunger. You know my want, and I your plenty, of which by some meanes I must have part, remember it is fit for kings to keepe their promise. Here are my commodities, wherof take your choice; the rest I will proportion, fit bargaines for your people.

The king seemed kindly to accept his offer; and the better to colour his project, sold us what they had to our own content; promising the next day, more company, better provided; (the barges, and Pinnas being committed to the charge of Master Phetiplace) the President with his old 15 marched up to the kings house, where we found 4 or 5 men newly come with great baskets, not long after came the king, who with a strained cheerefulnes held us with discourse, what paines he had taken to keepe his promise; til Master Russell brought us in news that we were all betraied: for at least 6. or 700. of well appointed Indians had invironed the house and beset the fields. The king conjecturing what Russell related, we could wel perceive how the extremity of his feare bewrayed his intent: whereat some of our companie seeming dismaide with the thought of such a multitude; the Captaine incouraged us after this manner.

Worthy countrymen were the mischiefes of my seeming friends, no more then the danger of these enemies, I little cared, were they as many more, if you dare do, but as I. But this is my torment, that if I escape them, our malicious councell with their open mouthed minions, will make mee such a peace-breaker (in their opinions) in England, as wil break my neck; I could wish those here, that make these seeme Saints, and me an oppressor. But this is the worst of all, wherin I pray aide me with your opinions; should wee begin with them and surprize this king, we cannot keep him and defend well our selves. If we should each kill our man and so proceede with al in this house; the rest will all fly, then shall we get no more, then the bodies that are slaine, and then starve for victuall: as for their fury it is the least danger; for well you know, (being alone assaulted with 2 or 300 of them) I made them compound to save my life, and we are now 16 and they but 700. at the most, and assure your selves God wil so assist us, that if you dare but to stande to discharge your peeces, the very smoake will bee sufficient to affright them; yet howsoever (if there be occasion) let us fight like men, and not die like sheep; but first I will deale with them, to bring it to passe, we may fight for some thing and draw them to it by conditions. If you like this motion, promise me youle be valiant.

The time not permitting any argument, all vowed to execute whatso-ever he attempted, or die; whereupon the captaine, approaching the king bespoke him in this manner.

I see Opechancanough your plot to murder me, but I feare it not, as yet your men and mine, have done no harme, but by our directions. Take therefore your arms; you see mine; my body shalbe as naked as yours; the Ile in your river is a fit place, if you be contented: and the conqueror (of us two) shalbe Lord and Master over all our men; otherwaies drawe all your men into the field; if you have not enough take time to fetch more, and bring what number you will, so everie one bring a basket of corne, against all which I will stake the value in copper; you see I have but 15 men, and our game shalbe the conquerer take all.

The king, being guarded with 50 or 60 of his chiefe men, seemed kindly to appease Smiths suspition of unkindnesse, by a great present at the dore, they intreated him to receive. This was to draw him with-out the dore where the present was garded with at the least 200 men and 30 lying under a greate tree (that lay thwart as a Barricado) each his arrow nocked ready to shoot; some the President commanded to go and see what kinde of deceit this was, and to receive the present, but they refused to do it, yet divers offered whom he would not permit; but commanding Master Persie and Master West to make good the house, tooke Master Powell and Master Beheathland to guard the dore, and in such a rage snatched the king by his vambrace in the midst of his men, with his pistoll ready bent against his brest:[61] thus he led the trembling king, (neare dead with feare) amongst all his people, who delivering the Captaine his bow and arrowes, all his men were easily intreated to cast downe their armes, little dreaming anie durst in that manner have used their king; who then to escape him-selfe, bestowed his presents in goodsadnesse.[62] And having caused all his multitude to approach disarmed; the President argued with them to this effect.

61. A vambrace is protective armor for the forearm.
62. *In goodsadness* means "with ample seriousness."

John Smith takes the king of Pamaunke prisoner, 1608. Here again, Robert Vaughan adapts a John White image for the central Indian figure. William Hole used the same source for the "gyant-like" Susquehannock in his map of Virginia (pp. 88–89). Courtesy of the Princeton University Library.

I see you Pamaunkies the great desire you have to cut my throat; and my long suffering your injuries, have inboldened you to this presumption. The cause I have forborne your insolencies, is the promise I made you (before the God I serve) to be your friend, till you give me just cause to bee your enimie. If I keepe this vow, my God will keepe me, you cannot hurt me; if I breake it he will destroie me. But if you shoot but one arrow, to shed one drop of blood of any of my men, or steale the least of these beades, or copper, (I spurne before me with my foot) you shall see, I wil not cease revenge, (if once I begin) so long as I can heare where to find one of your nation that will not deny the name of Pamaunke; I am not now at Rasseweac (halfe drownd with mire) where you tooke me prisoner, yet then for keeping your promise, and your good usage, and saving my life, I so affect you, that your denials of your treacherie, doth half perswade me to mistake my selfe. But if I be the marke you aime at, here I stand, shoote hee that dare. You promised to fraught my ship ere I departed, and so you shall, or I meane to load her with your dead carkases; yet if as friends you wil come and trade, I once more promise not to trouble you, except you give me the first occasion.

Upon this awaie went their bowes and arrowes, and men, women, and children brought in their commodities, but 2 or three houres they so thronged about the President, and so overwearied him, as he retired himself to rest, leaving Master Beheathland and Master Powel to accept their presents; but some Salvage perceiving him fast asleepe, and the guard carelesly dispersed, 40 or 50 of their choice men each with an English sword in his hand, began to enter the house, with 2 or 300 others that pressed to second them. The noise and hast they made in, did so shake the house, as they awoke him from his sleep, and being halfe amazed with this suddaine sight,[63] betooke him straight to his sword and target, Master Crashaw and some other charging in like manner, they thronged faster backe, then before forward. The house thus clensed, the king and his ancients, with a long oration came to excuse this intrusion. The rest of the day was spent with much kindnesse, the company againe renuing their presents of their best provi-

---

63. *Amazed* means "confused," or even "terrified."

sion. And what soever we gave them, they seemed well contented with it.

Now in the meane while since our departure, this hapned at the fort, Master Scrivener willing to crosse the surprizing of Powhatan; 9 daies after the Presidents departure, would needs visit the Ile of hogges, and took with him Captaine Waldo (though the President had appointed him to bee readie to second his occasions) with Master Anthony Gosnoll and eight others;[64] but so violent was the wind (that extreame frozen time) that the boat sunke, but where or how, none doth knowe, for they were all drowned; onlie this was knowne, that the Skiffe was much overloaded, and would scarse have lived in that extreame tempest, had she beene emptie; but by no perswasion hee could bee diverted, though both Waldo and 100 others doubted as it hapned. The Salvages were the first that found their bodies, which so much the more encouraged them to effect their projects. To advertise the President of this heavie newes, none could bee found would undertake it, but the journey was often refused of all in the fort, untill Master Wiffin undertooke alone the performance thereof; wherein he was encountred with many dangers and difficulties, and in all parts as hee passed (as also that night he lodged with Powhatan) perceived such preparation for warre, that assured him, some mischiefe was intended, but with extraordinarie bribes, and much trouble, in three daies travell at length hee found us in the midst of these turmoiles. This unhappie newes, the President swore him to conceale from the rest, and so dissembling his sorrow, with the best countenance he could, when the night approached, went safely abord with all his companie.

Now so extreamely Powhatan had threatned the death of his men, if they did not by some meanes kill Captaine Smith, that the next day they appointed the Countrie should come to trade unarmed: yet unwilling to be treacherous, but that they were constrained, hating fighting almost as ill as hanging, such feare they had of bad successe. The next morning the sunne had not long appeared, but the fieldes appeared covered with people, and baskets to tempt us ashore. The President determined to keepe abord, but nothing was to bee had without his presence, nor they would not indure the sight of a gun;

---

64. *To cross* means "to thwart or oppose." Captain Waldo was to be ready to "second his occasions," to back Smith up. Below, in "doubted as it hapned," *doubted* means "feared or expected."

then the President seeing many depart, and being unwilling to lose such a booty, so well contrived the Pinnace, and his barges with Ambuscadoes, as only with Master Persie, Master West, and Master Russell armed, he went ashore, others unarmed he appointed to receive what was brought; the Salvages flocked before him in heapes, and (the bancke serving as a trench for retreat) hee drewe them faire open to his ambuscadoes, for he not being to be perswaded to go to visit their king, the King came to visit him with 2 or 300 men, in the forme of two halfe moons, with some 20 men, and many women loaded with great painted baskets; but when they approached somewhat neare us, their women and children fled; for when they had environed and beset the fieldes in this manner, they thought their purpose sure; yet so trembled with fear as they were scarse able to nock their arrowes: Smith standing with his 3 men readie bent beholding them, till they were within danger of our ambuscado, who, upon the word discovered themselves, and he retiring to the banke; which the Salvages no sooner perceived but away they fled, esteeming their heeles for their best advantage.

That night we sent to the fort Master Crashaw and Master Foard, who (in the mid-way betweene Werawocomoco and the fort) met 4 or 5. of the Dutch mens confederates going to Powhatan, the which (to excuse those gentlemens Suspition of their running to the Salvages) returned to the fort and there continued.

The Salvages hearing our barge depart in the night were so terriblie affraide, that we sent for more men, (we having so much threatned their ruine, and the rasing of their houses, boats, and canowes) that the next day the king sent our Captaine a chaine of pearle to alter his purpose; and stay his men, promising (though they wanted themselves) to fraught our ship, and bring it abord to avoid suspition, so that 5 or 6 daies after, from al parts of the countrie within 10 or 12 miles, in the extreame cold frost, and snow, they brought us provision on their naked backes.

Yet notwithstanding this kindnesse and trade; had their art and poison bin sufficient, the President with Master West and some others had been poysoned; it made them sicke, but expelled it selfe; Wecuttanow a stout yong fellow, knowing hee was suspected for bringing this present of poison, with 40 or 50. of his choice companions (seeing the President but with a few men at Potauncac) so prowdlie braved it, as though he expected to incounter a revenge; which the President perceiving in the midst of his companie did not onlie beat, but spurned him like a dogge, as scorning to doe him anie worse mischiefe; whereupon all of them fled into the woods, thinking they had done a great matter, to have so well escaped; and the townsmen remaining, presentlie fraughted our barge, to bee rid of our companies, framing manie excuses to excuse Wecuttanow (being son to their chiefe king but Powhatan) and told us if we would shew them him that brought the poyson, they would deliver him to us to punish as wee pleased.

Men maie thinke it strange there should be this stir for a little corne, but had it been gold with more ease we might have got it; and had it wanted, the whole collonie had starved. We maie be thought verie patient, to indure all those injuries; yet onlie with fearing them, we got what they had. Whereas if we had taken revenge, then by their losse we should have lost our selvs. We searched also the countries of Youghtanund and Mattapamient, where the people imparted that little they had, with such complaints and tears from women and children; as he had bin too cruell to be a Christian that would not have bin satisfied, and moved with compassion. But had this happened in October, November, and December, when that unhappie discoverie of Monacan was made, we might have fraughted a ship of 40 tuns, and twice as much might have bin had from the rivers of Toppahannock, Patawomeck, and Pawtuxunt. The maine occasion of our temporizing with the Salvages was to part friends, (as we did) to give the lesse cause of suspition to Powhatan to fly; by whom we now returned, with a purpose, to have surprised him and his provision. For effecting whereof, (when we came against the towne) the President sent Master Wiffin and Master Coe ashore to discover and make waie for his intended project. But they found that those damned Dutch-men had caused Powhatan to abandon his new house, and Werawocomoco, and to carrie awaie all his corne and provision;[65] and the people, they found (by their means so ill affected), that had they not stood well upon their guard, they had hardlie escaped with their lives. So the President finding his intention thus frustrated, and that there was nothing now to be had, and therefore an unfit time to revenge their abuses, helde on his course for James Towne; we having in this Jornie (for 25[l] of copper 50[l]

---

65. Though the Indians produced an agricultural surplus, they were not prepared to keep the colonists alive through the winter as well as themselves. In the extremely cold conditions, Smith and his men were pressing hard on available food supplies.

of Iron and beads) kept 40 men 6. weekes, and dailie feasted with bread, corne, flesh, fish, and fowle, everie man having for his reward (and in consideration of his commodities) a months provision; (no trade being allowed but for the store,) and we delivered at James Towne to the Cape-Marchant 279 bushels of corne.[66] [*Proceedings:* I, 242–257]

Smith summed up his accomplishments in Indian relations in this section. The title notwithstanding, what he described was in fact a mutually benefi-cial truce; his inclusion of Okaning's speech asserting the dependence of the English on the Indians made that clear. Smith used a combination of physi-cal and psychological pressure to achieve his goals; he cleverly made use of surprises such as the recovery of the Indian suffering from smoke inhalation. This short section also includes another major theme of all Smith's work: the Europeans he had to deal with were often more troublesome than the sup-posed savages.

How the Salvages became subject to the English.

WHEN THE Ships departed, all the provision of the Store (but that the President had gotten) was so rotten with the last Sum-mers rayne, and eaten with Rats and Wormes, as the Hogges would scarcely eate it. Yet it was the Souldiers dyet till our returnes, so that we found nothing done, but our victuals spent, and the most part of our tooles, and a good part of our Armes conveyed to the Salvages. But now casting up the Store, and finding sufficient till the next harvest, the feare of starving was abandoned, and the company divided into tens, fifteens, or as the businesse required; six houres each day was spent in worke, the rest in Pastime and merry exercises, but the un-towardnesse of the greatest number caused the President advise as followeth.

Countrymen, the long experience of our late miseries, I hope is sufficient to perswade every one to a present correction of him-selfe, and thinke not that either my pains, nor the Adventurers

---

66. The cape merchant was in charge of supplies.

purses, will ever maintaine you in idlenesse and sloath. I speake not this to you all, for divers of you I know deserve both honour and reward, better then is yet here to be had: but the greater part must be more industrious, or starve, how ever you have beene heretofore tollerated by the authoritie of the Councell, from that I have often commanded you. You see now that power resteth wholly in my selfe: you must obey this now for a Law, that he that will not worke shall not eate[67] (except by sicknesse he be disabled) for the labours of thirtie or fortie honest and industrious men shall not be consumed to maintaine an hundred and fiftie idle loyterers. And though you presume the authoritie here is but a shadow, and that I dare not touch the lives of any but my owne must answer it: the Letters patents shall each weeke be read to you, whose Contents will tell you the contrary. I would wish you therefore without contempt seek to observe these orders set downe, for there are now no more Counsellers to protect you, nor curbe my endevours. Therefore he that offendeth, let him assuredly expect his due punishment.

He made also a Table, as a publicke memoriall of every mans deserts, to incourage the good, and with shame to spurre on the rest to amendment. By this many became very industrious, yet more by punishment performed their businesse, for all were so tasked, that there was no excuse could prevaile to deceive him: yet the Dutch-mens consorts so closely convayed them powder, shot, swords, and tooles, that though we could find the defect, we could not finde by whom, till it was too late.

All this time the Dutch men remaining with Powhatan, (who kindly entertained them to instruct the Salvages the use of our Armes) and their consorts not following them as they expected; to know the cause, they sent Francis their companion, a stout young fellow, disguised like a Salvage, to the Glasse-house, a place in the woods neare a myle from James Towne; where was their Rendezvous for all their unsuspected villany. Fortie men they procured to lie in Ambuscado for Captaine Smith, who no sooner heard of this Dutch-man, but he sent to apprehend him (but he was gone) yet to crosse his returne to Powhatan, the Captaine presently dispatched 20. shot after him, himselfe returning from the Glasse-house alone. By the way he incountred the King of

---

67. This phrase is a reference to 2 Thessalonians 3:10.

Paspahegh, a most strong stout Salvage, whose perswasions not being able to perswade him to his Ambush, seeing him onely armed but with a faucheon,[68] attempted to have shot him, but the President prevented his shoot by grapling with him, and the Salvage as well prevented him for drawing his faucheon, and perforce bore him into the River to have drowned him. Long they strugled in the water, till the President got such hold on his throat, he had neare strangled the King; but having drawne his faucheon to cut off his head, seeing how pittifully he begged his life, he led him prisoner to James Towne, and put him in chaynes.

The Dutch-man ere long was also brought in, whose villany though all this time it was suspected, yet he fayned such a formall excuse, that for want of language Captaine Winne understood him not rightly, and for their dealings with Powhatan, that to save their lives they were constrained to accommodate his armes, of whom he extreamely complained to have detained them perforce, and that he made this escape with the hazard of his life, and meant not to have returned, but was onely walking in the woods to gather Walnuts. Yet for all this faire tale, there was so small appearance of truth, and the plaine confession of Paspahegh of his trechery, he went by the heeles: Smith purposing to regaine the Dutch-men, by the saving his life.[69] The poore Salvage did his best by his daily messengers to Powhatan, but all returned that the Dutch-men would not returne, neither did Powhatan stay them; and to bring them fiftie myles on his mens backes they were not able. Daily this Kings wives, children, and people came to visit him with presents, which he liberally bestowed to make his peace. Much trust they had in the Presidents promise: but the King finding his guard negligent, though fettered yet escaped. Captaine Winne thinking to pursue him found such troupes of Salvages to hinder his passage, as they exchanged many vollies of shot for flights of Arrowes. Captaine Smith hearing of this in returning to the Fort, tooke two Salvages prisoners, called Kemps and Tussore, the two most exact villaines in all the Country.[70] With these he sent Captaine Winne and fiftie choise men, and

68. Wowinchopunk was werowance of the Paspaheghs, the closest Indians to Jamestown. A faucheon, or falchion, is a broad sword, slightly curved.

69. To set by the heels is to put someone in irons. Smith proposed to hold Wowinchopunk as ransom for the Dutchmen, but they stayed with Powhatan voluntarily and could not be forced to return.

70. *Most exact* means "most perfect or accomplished."

John Smith's capture of the king of Paspahegh, engraved by Robert Vaughan.
Courtesy of the Princeton University Library.

Lieutenant Percie, to have regained the King, and revenged this injury, and so had done, if they had followed his directions, or beene advised with those two villaines, that would have betrayed both King and kindred for a peece of Copper, but he trifling away the night, the Salvages the next morning by the rising of the Sunne, braved him to come ashore to fight: a good time both sides let fly at other, but we heard of no hurt, onely they tooke two Canowes, burnt the Kings house, and so returned to James towne.

The President fearing those Bravado's would but incourage the Salvages, began againe himselfe to try his conclusions; whereby six or seaven were slaine, as many made prisoners. He burnt their houses, tooke their Boats, with all their fishing wires, and planted some of them at James towne for his owne use, and now resolved not to cease till he had revenged himselfe of all them had injured him. But in his journey passing by Paspahegh towards Chickahamania, the Salvages did their best to draw him to their Ambuscadoes; but seeing him regardlesly passe their Country, all shewed themselves in their bravest manner. To try their valours he could not but let fly, and ere he could land, they no sooner knew him, but they threw downe their armes and desired peace. Their Orator was a lustie young fellow called Okaning, whose worthy discourse deserveth to be remembred. And thus it was:

> Captaine Smith, my Master is here present in the company, thinking it Captaine Winne, and not you, (of him he intended to have beene revenged) having never offended him. If he hath offended you in escaping your imprisonment, the fishes swim, the foules fly, and the very beasts strive to escape the snare and live. Then blame not him being a man. He would intreat you remember, you being a prisoner, what paines he tooke to save your life. If since he hath injured you he was compelled to it: but howsoever, you have revenged it with our too great losse. We perceive and well know you intend to destroy us, that are here to intreat and desire your friendship, and to enjoy our houses and plant our fields, of whose fruit you shall participate: otherwise you will have the worse by our absence; for we can plant any where, though with more labour, and we know you cannot live if you want our harvest, and that reliefe we bring you. If you promise us peace, we will beleeve you; if you proceed in revenge we will abandon the Country.

Upon these tearmes the President promised them peace, till they did us injury, upon condition they should bring in provision. Thus all departed good friends, and so continued till Smith left the Countrey.

Arriving at James Towne, complaint was made to the President, that the Chickahamanians, who all this while continued trade and seemed our friends, by colour thereof were the onely theeves.[71] And amongst other things a Pistoll being stolne and the theefe fled, there was apprehended two proper young fellowes, that were brothers, knowne to be his confederates. Now to regaine this Pistoll, the one was imprisoned, the other was sent to returne the Pistoll againe within twelve houres, or his brother to be hanged. Yet the President pittying the poore naked Salvage in the dungeon, sent him victuall and some Char-coale for a fire: ere midnight his brother returned with the Pistoll, but the poore Salvage in the dungeon was so smoothered with the smoake he had made, and so pittiously burnt, that wee found him dead. The other most lamentably bewayled his death, and broke forth into such bitter agonies, that the President to quiet him, told him that if hereafter they would not steale, he would make him alive againe: but he little thought he could be recovered. Yet we doing our best with Aqua vitæ and Vineger,[72] it pleased God to restore him againe to life, but so drunke and affrighted, that he seemed Lunaticke, the which as much tormented and grieved the other, as before to see him dead. Of which maladie upon promise of their good behaviour, the President promised to recover him: and so caused him to be layd by a fire to sleepe, who in the morning having well slept, had recovered his perfect senses, and then being dressed of his burning, and each a peece of Copper given them, they went away so well contented, that this was spread among all the Salvages for a miracle, that Captaine Smith could make a man alive that was dead.

Another ingenuous Salvage of Powhatans, having gotten a great bag of Powder, and the backe of an Armour, at Werowocomoco amongst a many of his companions, to shew his extraordinary skill, he did dry it on the backe as he had seene the Souldiers at James Towne. But he dryed it so long, they peeping over it to see his skill, it tooke fire, and blew him to death, and one or two more, and the rest so scorched, they had little pleasure to meddle any more with powder.

71. The Chickahominies were a strong tribe that had maintained its independence of Powhatan.
72. Aquavitae is brandy or other strong alcoholic drink.

These and many other such pretty Accidents,[73] so amazed and affrighted both Powhatan, and all his people, that from all parts with
presents they desired peace; returning many stolne things which we
never demanded nor thought of; and after that, those that were taken
stealing, both Powhatan and his people have sent them backe to James
towne, to receive their punishment; and all the Country became absolute as free for us, as for themselves. [*Generall Historie:* II, 208–212]

III

*After he had been back in England for some years, Smith reflected on the
later history of Virginia and on what he had learned of the Indians of New
England. He grew increasingly embittered over his rejection by colonial
promoters, as he saw the same mistakes being made over and over again.
The devastating Indian attack of 1622, led by Powhatan's successor Opechancanough, was in response to the insatiable land hunger of the colonists
once tobacco had been established as a cash crop. Smith thought the attack
could have been avoided if the colonists had continued to pursue his policy of
overawing the Indians; though warfare had followed Smith's departure,
peace had been achieved after Pocahontas's marriage to John Rolfe and the
settlers had become careless.*

*Smith was contemptuous of tobacco as a crop and of the planters' ignoring
all good order and prudence in their pursuit of it. By quoting chunks of
Virginia reports and letters and adding his own analysis, he put together an
indictment of the colonists, showing how they heedlessly went down the path
of greedy neglect. His documents for 1617–1618 and then for 1621 present a
community courting disaster.*

The government devolved to Captaine Samuel Argall, 1617.

THE TREASURER, Councell and Companie, having well furnished Captaine Samuel Argall, the Lady Pocahontas alias Rebecca, with her husband and others, in the good ship called the *George*,
it pleased God at Gravesend to take this young Lady to his mercie,

---

73. *Pretty accident* means "agreeable or satisfactory event or incident."

where shee made not more sorrow for her unexpected death, than joy to the beholders, to heare and see her make so religious and godly an end. Her little childe Thomas Rolfe therefore was left at Plimoth with Sir Lewis Stukly, that desired the keeping of it. Captaine Hamar his vice-Admirall was gone before, but hee found him at Plimoth. In March they set saile 1617. and in May he arrived at James towne, where hee was kindly entertained by Captaine Yearley and his Companie in a martiall order, whose right hand file was led by an Indian. In James towne he found but five or six houses, the Church downe, the Palizado's broken, the Bridge in pieces, the Well of fresh water spoiled; the Store-house they used for the Church, the market-place, and streets, and all other spare places planted with Tobacco, the Salvages as frequent in their houses as themselves, whereby they were become expert in our armes, and had a great many in their custodie and possession, the Colonie dispersed all about, planting Tobacco. Captaine Argall not liking those proceedings, altered them agreeable to his owne minde, taking the best order he could for repairing those defects which did exceedingly trouble us; we were constrained every yeere to build and repaire our old Cottages, which were alwaies a decaying in all places of the Countrie, yea, the very Courts of Guard built by Sir Thomas Dale, was ready to fall, and the Palizado's not sufficient to keepe out Hogs. Their number of people were about 400. but not past 200. fit for husbandry and tillage: we found there in all one hundred twentie eight cattell, and fourescore and eight Goats, besides innumerable numbers of Swine, and good plentie of Corne in some places, yet the next yeere the Captaine sent out a Frigat and a Pinnace, that brought us neere six hundred bushels more, which did greatly relieve the whole Colonie: For from the tenants wee seldome had above foure hundred bushels of rent Corne to the store, and there was not remaining of the Companies companie, past foure and fiftie men, women and Children.[74]

This yeere having planted our fields, came a great drought, and such a cruell storme of haile, which did such spoile both to the Corne and Tobacco, that wee reaped but small profit, the Magazine that came in the *George*, being five moneths in her passage, proved very badly conditioned,[75] but ere she arrived, we had gathered and made up our

74. The *Companies companie* refers to the servants who were sent out by the Virginia Company as paid employees.
75. *Magazine* refers to the supplies sent by the company for sale to the colonists.

Tobacco, the best at three shillings the pound, the rest at eighteene pence.

To supply us, the Councell and Company with all possible care and diligence, furnished a good ship of some two hundred and fiftie tunne, with two hundred people and the Lord la Ware. They set saile in Aprill, and tooke their course by the westerne Iles, where the Governour of the Ile of Saint Michael received the Lord la Ware, and honourably feasted him, with all the content hee could give him.[76] Going from thence, they were long troubled with contrary winds, in which time many of them fell very sicke, thirtie died, one of which number was that most honourable Lord Governour the Lord la Ware, whose most noble and generous disposition, is well knowne to his great cost, had beene most forward in this businesse for his Countries good: Yet this tender state of Virginia was not growne to that maturitie, to maintaine such state and pleasure as was fit for such a personage, with so brave and great attendance:[77] for some small number of adventrous Gentlemen to make discoveries, and lie in Garrison, ready upon any occasion to keepe in feare the inconstant Salvages, nothing were more requisite; but to have more to wait and play than worke, or more commanders and officers than industrious labourers was not so necessarie: for in Virginia, a plaine Souldier that can use a Pick-axe and spade, is better than five Knights, although they were Knights that could breake a Lance; for men of great place, not inured to those incounters; when they finde things not sutable, grow many times so discontented, they forget themselves, and oft become so carelesse, that a discontented melancholy brings them to much sorrow, and to others much miserie. [*Generall Historie:* II, 262–263]

THE INSTRUCTIONS and advertisements for this yeere were both from England and Virginia, much like the last: only whereas before they had ever a suspicion of Opechankanough, and all the rest of the Salvages, they had an eye over him more then any, but now they all write so confidently of their assured peace with the Salvages, there

76. The "westerne Iles" are the Azores; São Miguel is in the southeastern part of the group.
77. *Brave and great attendance* refers to the large company of finely dressed men that would be expected to attend a lord such as Baron De La Warr. Smith argues that such men were useless in a new settlement, which could not afford them.

is now no more feare nor danger either of their power or trechery, so that every man planteth himselfe where he pleaseth, and followeth his businesse securely. But the time of Sir George Yearley being neere expired, the Councel here made choise of a worthy young Gentleman Sir Francis Wyat to succeed him, whom they forthwith furnished and provided, as they had done his Predecessors, with all the necessary instructions all these times had acquainted them for the conversion of the Salvages, the suppressing of planting Tobacco, and planting of Corne, not depending continually to be supplied by the Salvages, but in case of necessity to trade with them, whom long ere this, it hath beene promised and expected should have beene fed and relieved by the English, not the English by them; and carefully to redresse all the complaints of the needlesse mortality of their people, and by all diligence seeke to send something home to satisfie the Adventurers, that all this time had only lived upon hopes, grew so weary and discouraged, that it must now be substance that must maintaine their proceedings, and not letters, excuses and promises; seeing they could get so much and such great estates for themselves, as to spend after the rate of 100. pounds, 2, 3, 4, 5, 6, 7, 8, 9, 10. nay some 2000. or 3000. pounds yearely, that were not worth so many pence when they went to Virginia, can scarce containe themselves either in diet, apparell, gaming, and all manner of such superfluity, within a lesse compasse than our curious, costly, and consuming Gallants here in England, which cannot possibly be there supported, but either by oppressing the Comminalty there, or deceiving the generality here (or both.)

Extracted out of the Councels Letters for Virginia.

From Virginia, by the relations of the Chieftains there, and many I have conferred with, that came from thence hither, I have much admired to heare of the incredible pleasure, profit and plenty this Plantation doth abound in, and yet could never heare of any returne but Tobacco, but it hath oft amazed me to understand how strangely the Salvages hath beene taught the use of our armes, and imploied in hunting and fowling with our fowling peeces, and our men rooting in the ground about Tobacco like Swine; besides that, the Salvages that doe little but continually exercise their bow and arrowes, should dwell and lie so familiarly amongst our men that practised little but the Spade, being so farre asunder, and in such small parties dispersed, and neither Fort, exercise of armes used, Ordnances mounted, Courts of guard, nor any preparation nor provision to prevent a forraine enemy, much more the Salvages howsoever.[78] [*Generall Historie:* II, 284–285]

In the aftermath of the great attack of 1622 that killed about 350 colonists, everyone interested in America analyzed the situation and presented reasons and recommendations. A royal inquiry set up in 1624 ultimately resulted in the loss of the Virginia Company charter, so badly was the company thought to have carried out its responsibilities. Though his attention had shifted to New England by this time, Smith included a section in his New Englands Trials *giving his immediate response to the news. His swaggering at this distance was far removed from his understanding of the complex interrelationship between the Indians and the English when he had actually been in the colony.*

H ERE I MUST intreate a little your favours to digresse. They did not kill the English because they were Christians, but for their weapons and commodities, that were rare novelties; but now they feare we may beate them out of their dens, which Lions and Tygers would not admit but by force. But must this be an argument for an English man, or discourage any either in Virginia or New England? No: for I have tried them both. For Virginia, I kept that country with 38, and had not to eate but what we had from the savages. When I had ten men able to go abroad, our common wealth was very strong: with such a number I ranged that unknown country 14 weeks; I had but 18 to subdue them all, with which great army I stayed six weekes before their greatest Kings habitations, till they had gathered together all the power they could; and yet the Dutch-men sent at a needlesse excessive charge did helpe Powhatan how to betray me.

Of their numbers we were uncertaine; but them two honorable Gentlemen (Captaine George Percie and Captaine Francis West), two of the Phittiplaces, and some other such noble gentlemen and resolute spirits bore their shares with me, and now living in England, did see me take this murdering Opechankanough now their great King by the long locke on his head, with my pistole at his breast, I led him among his greatest forces, and before we parted made him fill our Bark of

---

78. "Forraine enemy": The planters always feared an attack by Spanish forces.

twenty Tuns with corne. When their owne wants was such, I have given them part againe in pittie, and others have bought it againe to plant their fields.

For wronging a souldier but the value of a peny, I have caused Powhatan send his owne men to James Towne to receive their punishment at my discretion. It is true in our greatest extremitie they shot me, slue three of my men, and by the folly of them that fled tooke me prisoner; yet God made Pocahontas the Kings daughter the meanes to deliver me: and thereby taught me to know their trecheries to preserve the rest. It was also my chance in single combat to take the King of Paspahegh prisoner, and by keeping him, forced his subjects to worke in chaines, till I made all the country pay contribution, having little else whereon to live.[79]

Twise in this time I was their President, and none can say in all that time I had a man slaine: but for keeping them in that feare I was much blamed both there and here: yet I left 500 behind me that through their confidence in six months came most to confusion,[80] as you may reade at large in the description of Virginia. When I went first to those desperate designes, it cost me many a forgotten pound to hire men to go; and procrastination caused more run away then went. But after the ice was broken, came many brave voluntaries: notwithstanding since I came from thence, the honorable Company have bin humble suiters to his Majestie to get vagabonds and condemned men to go thither; nay so much scorned was the name of Virginia, some did chuse to be hanged ere they would go thither, and were: yet for all the worst of spite, detraction and discouragement, and this lamentable massacre, there is more honest men now suters to go, then ever hath bin constrained knaves;[81] and it is not unknown to most men of understanding, how happie many of those Collumners doe thinke themselves, that they might be admitted, and yet pay for their passage to go now to Virginia:[82] and had I but meanes to transport as many as would go, I might have choise of 10000 that would gladly be in any of those new places, which were so basely contemned by ungratefull base minds. [*New Englands Trials* (1622): I, 432–433]

79. He seems to have forgotten that the king of Paspahegh escaped very quickly.
80. *Confidence* seems to mean "overconfidence."
81. *Suters* is for *suitors*, men asking to go to Virginia.
82. *Collumner* means "slanderer."

Smith offered his services to the company in order to restore the Virginia colonists to safety. When that tender was ignored, he continued to offer his advice in print, publishing descriptions of events in the colony with his commentaries and analysis. Smith's suggestion for a "running army" was meant to deal with the major problem: the Indians were most stationary and therefore easier to fight while they were tending their crops, but planters could not leave their own fields to hunt the enemy at that season. At other times of the year, settlers were unwilling to leave their own plantations unguarded. An army paid to do nothing but protect the settlements was the obvious solution in Smith's view, but the company, having seen little return for years of investment, was unwilling.

The passage of time and Smith's own bitterness had dimmed his memory of the formidable fighting qualities of the Chesapeake Indians, of the colonists' dependence on them for food and knowledge, and of the tenuousness of his control of the situation while president. In aggrandizing his own accomplishments, Smith also belittled them by making them seem easier than they were. Now, a decade and a half later, he envisioned harnessing the Indians as a labor force and simply taking their land. Had his policy been what he later said it was, he would have been as unsuccessful as those he criticized.

The project and offer of Captaine John Smith, to the Right Honourable, and Right Worshipfull Company of Virginia.

IF YOU PLEASE I may be transported with a hundred Souldiers and thirty Sailers by the next Michaelmas,[83] with victuall, munition, and such necessary provision, by Gods assistance, we would endevour to inforce the Salvages to leave their Country, or bring them in that feare and subjection that every man should follow their businesse securely, whereas now halfe their times and labours are spent in watching and warding, onely to defend, but altogether unable to suppresse the Salvages, because every man now being for himselfe will be unwilling

---

83. Michaelmas was celebrated on September 29; it was the beginning of the fall quarter of the year.

to be drawne from their particular labours, to be made as pack-horses for all the rest, without any certainty of some better reward and preferment then I can understand any there can or will yet give them.

These I would imploy onely in ranging the Countries, and tormenting the Salvages, and that they should be as a running Army till this were effected, and then settle themselves in some such convenient place, that should ever remaine a garison of that strength, ready upon any occasion against the Salvages, or any other for the defence of the Countrey, and to see all the English well armed, and instruct them their use. But I would have a Barke of one hundred tunnes, and meanes to build sixe or seven Shalops, to transport them where there should bee occasion.

Towards the charge, because it is for the generall good, and what by the massacre and other accidents, Virginia is disparaged, and many men and their purses much discouraged, how ever a great many doe hasten to goe, thinking to bee next heires to all the former losses, I feare they will not finde all things as they doe imagine; therefore leaving those gilded conceits, and dive into the true estate of the Colony; I thinke if his Majestie were truly informed of their necessitie, and the benefit of this project, he would be pleased to give the custome of Virginia,[84] and the Planters also according to their abilities would adde thereto such a contribution, as would be fit to maintaine this garison till they be able to subsist, or cause some such other collections to be made, as may put it with all expedition in practice; otherwise it is much to be doubted, there will neither come custome, nor any thing from thence to England within these few yeares.

Now if this should be thought an imploiment more fit for ancient Souldiers there bred, then such new commers as may goe with me;[85] you may please to leave that to my discretion, to accept or refuse such voluntaries, that will hazard their fortunes in the trialls of these events, and discharge such of my company that had rather labour the ground then subdue their enemies: what releefe I should have from your Colony I would satisfie and spare them (when I could) the like courtesie. Notwithstanding these doubts, I hope to feede them as well as defend them, and yet discover you more land unknowne then they all yet

84. "Custome of Virginia": The king would donate the customs revenues received from Virginia.
85. *Ancient* here means "with many years' experience."

know, if you will grant me such priviledges as of necessity must be used.

For against any enemy we must be ready to execute the best can be devised by your state there, but not that they shall either take away my men, or any thing else to imploy as they please by vertue of their authority, and in that I have done somewhat for New-England as well as Virginia, so I would desire liberty and authority to make the best use I can of my best experiences,[86] within the limits of those two Patents, and to bring them both in one Map, and the Countries betwixt them, giving alwaies that respect to the Governors and government, as an Englishman doth in Scotland, or a Scotchman in England, or as the regiments in the Low-countries doe to the Governors of the Townes and Cities where they are billited, or in Garrison, where though they live with them, and are as their servants to defend them, yet not to be disposed on at their pleasure, but as the Prince and State doth command them, and for my owne paines in particular I aske not any thing but what I can produce from the proper labour of the Salvages.

Their Answer.

I CANNOT SAY, it was generally from the Company, for being published in their Court,[87] the most that heard it liked exceeding well of the motion, and some would have been very large Adventurers in it, especially Sir John Brookes and Master David Wyffin, but there were such divisions amongst them, I could obtaine no answer but this, the charge would be too great; their stocke was decayed, and they did thinke the Planters should doe that of themselves if I could finde meanes to effect it; they did thinke I might have leave of the Company, provided they might have halfe the pillage, but I thinke there are not many will much strive for that imploiment, for except it be a little Corne at some time of the yeere is to be had, I would not give twenty pound for all the pillage is to be got amongst the Salvages in twenty

86. Smith here asks for the kind of independence from the local authorities in Virginia that he had so greatly resented when he was president and Christopher Newport had intruded. Moreover, he did not want to be restricted to Virginia.
87. The Virginia Company held quarterly meetings, called courts, in London. Smith's proposal was published there, that is, it was read out to the stockholders.

yeeres: but because they supposed I spake only for my owne ends, it were good those understand providents for the Companies good they so much talke of, were sent thither to make triall of their profound wisdomes and long experiences.[88] [*Generall Historie:* II, 305–307]

WHAT OTHER passages or impediments hapned in their proceedings, that they were not fully revenged of the Salvages before they returned, I know not; nor could ever heare more, but that they supposed they slew two, and how it was impossible for any men to doe more then they did: yet worthy Ferdinando Courtus had scarce three hundred Spaniards to conquer the great Citie of Mexico, where thousands of Salvages dwelled in strong houses:[89] but because they were a civilized people, had wealth, and those meere Barbarians as wilde as beasts have nothing; I intreat your patience to tell you my opinion, which if it be Gods pleasure I shall not live to put in practice, yet it may be hereafter usefull for some, but howsoever I hope not hurtfull to any, and this it is.

Had these three hundred men beene at my disposing, I would have sent first one hundred to Captaine Rawley Chroshaw to Patawomek, with some small Ordnance for the Fort, the which but with daily exercising them, would have struck that love and admiration into the Patowomeks, and terror and amazement into his enemies, which are not farre off, and most seated upon the other side the River, they would willingly have beene friends, or have given any composition they could, before they would be tormented with such a visible feare.

Now though they be generally perfidious, yet necessity constraines those to a kinde of constancy because of their enemies, and neither my selfe that first found them, Captaine Argall, Chroshow, nor Hamar, never found themselves in fifteene yeares trials: nor is it likely now they would have so hostaged their men, suffer the building of a Fort, and their women and children amongst them, had they intended any villany; but suppose they had, who would have desired a better advantage then such an advertisement, to have prepared the Fort for such an assault, and surely it must be a poore Fort they could hurt, much more take, if there were but five men in it durst discharge a peece: Therefore

88. "Understand providents": Here in a garbled way Smith ridicules those in the London company who suspected his motives, and he suggests that they see how well they would do in the field.
89. Courtus is Cortés.

a man not well knowing their conditions, may be as wel too jealous as too carelesse; Such another Lope Skonce would I have had at Onawmanient,[90] and one hundred men more to have made such another at Atquacke upon the River of Toppahanock, which is not past thirteene miles distant from Onawmanient: each of which twelve men would keepe, as well as twelve thousand, and spare all the rest to bee imploied as there should be occasion. And all this with these numbers might easily have beene done, if not by courtesie, yet by compulsion, especially at that time of September when all their fruits were ripe, their beasts fat, and infinite numbers of wilde Fowle began to repaire to every creeke, that men if they would doe any thing, could not want victuall. This done, there remained yet one hundred who should have done the like at Ozinieke, upon the River of Chickahamania, not past six miles from the chiefe habitations of Opechankanough. These small Forts had beene cause sufficient to cause all the Inhabitants of each of those Rivers to looke to themselves. Then having so many Ships, Barks, and Boats in Virginia as there was at that present, with what facility might you have landed two hundred and twentie men, if you had but onely five or six Boats in one night; forty to range the branch of Mattapanyent, fortie more that of Youghtanund, and fortie more to keepe their randivous at Pamaunke it selfe. All which places lie so neere, they might heare from each other within foure or five houres, and not any of those small parties, if there were any valour, discretion, or industry in them, but as sufficient as foure thousand, to force them all to contribution, or take or spoile all they had. For having thus so many convenient randevous to releeve each other, though all the whole Countries had beene our enemies, where could they rest, but in the depth of Winter we might burne all the houses upon all those Rivers in two or three daies? Then without fires they could not live, which they could not so hide but wee should finde, and quickly so tire them with watching and warding, they would be so weary of their lives, as either fly all their Countries, or give all they had to be released of such an hourely misery. Now if but a small number of the Salvages would assist us, as there is no question but divers of them would; And to suppose they could not be drawne to such faction, were to beleeve they are more vertuous then many Christians, and the best governed people in the world. All the Pamaunkes might have beene dispatched as well in a moneth as a yeare, and then to have dealt with any other

90. A lopeskonce is an entrenchment.

enemies at our pleasure, and yet made all this toile and danger but a recreation.

If you think this strange or impossible, 12 men with my selfe I found sufficient, to goe where I would adaies, and surprise a house with the people, if not a whole towne in a night, or incounter all the power they could make, as a whole Army, as formerly at large hath beene related: And it seemes by these small parties last amongst them, by Captaine Crashow, Hamar, and Madyson, they are not growne to that excellency in policy and courage but they might bee encountred, and their wives and children apprehended. I know I shall bee taxed for writing so much of my selfe, but I care not much, because the judiciall know there are few such Souldiers as are my examples, have writ their owne actions, nor know I who will or can tell my intents better then my selfe.

Some againe finde as much fault with the Company for medling with so many Plantations together, because they that have many Irons in the fire some must burne; but I thinke no if they have men enow know how to worke them, but howsoever, it were better some burne then have none at all. The King of Spaine regards but how many powerfull Kingdomes he keepes under his obedience, and for the Salvage Countries he hath subjected, they are more then enow for a good Cosmographer to nominate,[91] and is three Mole-hills so much to us; and so many Empires so little for him? For my owne part, I cannot chuse but grieve, that the actions of an Englishman should be inferior to any, and that the command of England should not be as great as any Monarchy that ever was since the world began, I meane not as a Tyrant to torment all Christendome, but to suppresse her disturbers, and conquer her enemies. [*Generall Historie:* II, 315–318]

91. A cosmographer is a geographer; *to nominate* means "to list or specify by name."

PART FOUR

JOHN SMITH AS

INTERPRETER OF

THE ENVIRONMENT

I

Though Captain Smith is most famous as a manager of men, both colonists and Indians, his contribution to colonization was much greater than that. He gathered information about the natural history and geography of both Virginia and New England to facilitate colonization, and in doing so, he provided a remarkable record. His map of Virginia, drawn at his direction by William Hole based on Smith's notes and on what he had gleaned from the Indians, reduces the intricate three-dimensional reality of Chesapeake Bay to a recognizable two-dimensional representation and added greatly to knowledge of the coast. Smith indicated the extent of his voyages on each river with a little cross, to show where his own knowledge ended and where reliance on Indian information began. His map of New England, engraved by Simon van de Passe, was translated entirely from his notes and observations.

Smith's descriptions of the land and fruits it bore were not primarily for scholars; they were meant to present the truth about American commodities that might draw investors. Unlike many others, he underplayed his picture, because he well knew that inflated expectations led to disappointment and withdrawal. He clearly did mean to be taken for an educated man, though, as can be seen from his general description of America in his Description of New England.

N EW ENGLAND is that part of America in the Ocean Sea opposite to Nova Albyon in the South Sea;[1] discovered by the most memorable Sir Francis Drake in his voyage about the worlde. In regarde whereto this is stiled New England, beeing in the same latitude. New France, off it, is Northward: Southwardes is Virginia, and all the adjoyning Continent, with New Granado, New Spain, New Andolosia and the West Indies. Now because I have beene so oft asked such strange questions, of the goodnesse and greatnesse of those spatious Tracts of land, how they can bee thus long unknown, or not possessed by the Spaniard, and many such like demands; I intreat your pardons, if I chance to be too plaine, or tedious in relating my knowledge for plaine mens satisfaction.

Florida is the next adjoyning to the Indes, which unprosperously was attempted to bee planted by the French. A Country farre bigger

---

1. Nova Albyon is California; the South Sea is the Pacific.

then England, Scotland, France and Ireland, yet little knowne to any Christian, but by the wonderful endevours of Ferdinando de Soto a valiant Spaniard: whose writings in this age is the best guide knowne to search those parts.

Virginia is no Ile (as many doe imagine) but part of the Continent adjoyning to Florida; whose bounds may be stretched to the magnitude thereof without offence to any Christian inhabitant. For from the degrees of 30. to 45. his Majestie hath granted his Letters patents, the Coast extending South-west and North-east aboute 1500 miles; but to follow it aboard, the shore may well be 2000. at the least: of which, 20. miles is the most gives entrance into the Bay of Chisapeak, where is the London plantation: within which is a Country (as you may perceive by the description in a Booke and Map printed in my name of that little I there discovered) may well suffice 300000 people to inhabit. And Southward adjoyneth that part discovered at the charge of Sir Walter Rawley, by Sir Ralph Lane, and that learned Mathematician Master Thomas Heryot. Northward six or seaven degrees is the River Sagadahock, where was planted the Westerne Colony, by that Honourable Patrone of vertue Sir John Poppham, Lord chief Justice of England.[2] Ther is also a relation printed by Captaine Bartholomew Gosnould, of Elizabeths Iles: and an other by Captaine Waymoth, of Pemmaquid. From all these diligent observers, posterity may be bettered by the fruits of their labours. But for divers others that long before and since have ranged those parts, within a kenning sometimes of the shore,[3] some touching in one place some in another, I must entreat them pardon me for omitting them; or if I offend in saying that their true descriptions are concealed, or never well observed, or died with the Authors: so that the Coast is yet still but even as a Coast unknowne and undiscovered. I have had six or seaven severall plots of those Northren parts, so unlike each to other, and most so differing from any true proportion, or resemblance of the Countrey, as they did mee no more good, then so much waste paper, though they cost me more. It may be it was not my chance to see the best; but least others may be

2. Two Virginia Companies were founded in 1607: the London company founded Jamestown and the western merchants' company (headquartered in Plymouth) founded a colony at Sagadahock in Maine. All the coast was called Virginia; New England was then distinguished as the North Part of Virginia. The Sagadahock colony lasted less than a year; reverses in England and the death of its chief sponsor combined with the extreme cold of that winter to end it.
3. *Kenning* means "range of sight."

deceived as I was, or throgh dangerous ignorance hazard themselves as I did, I have drawen a Map from Point to Point, Ile to Ile, and Harbour to Harbour, with the Soundings, Sands, Rocks, and Land-marks as I passed close aboard the Shore in a little Boat; although there be many things to bee observed which the haste of other affaires did cause me omit: for, being sent more to get present commodities, then knowledge by discoveries for any future good, I had not power to search as I would: yet it will serve to direct any shall goe that waies, to safe Harbours and the Salvages habitations: What marchandize and commodities for their labour they may finde, this following discourse shall plainely demonstrate.

Thus you may see, of this 2000. miles more then halfe is yet unknowne to any purpose: no not so much as the borders of the Sea are yet certainly discovered. As for the goodnes and true substances of the Land, wee are for most part yet altogether ignorant of them, unlesse it bee those parts about the Bay of Chisapeack and Sagadahock: but onely here and there wee touched or have seene a little the edges of those large dominions, which doe stretch themselves into the Maine, God doth know how many thousand miles; whereof we can yet no more judge, then a stranger that saileth betwixt England and France can describe the Harbors and dangers by landing here or there in some River or Bay, tell thereby the goodnesse and substances of Spaine, Italy, Germany, Bohemia, Hungaria and the rest. By this you may perceive how much they erre, that think every one which hath bin at Virginia understandeth or knowes what Virginia is: Or that the Spaniards know one halfe quarter of those Territories they possesse; no, not so much as the true circumference of Terra Incognita, whose large dominions may equalize the greatnesse and goodnes of America, for any thing yet known. It is strange with what small power hee hath raigned in the East Indes; and few will understand the truth of his strength in America: where he having so much to keepe with such a pampered force, they neede not greatly feare his furie, in the Bermudas, Virginia, New France, or New England;[4] beyond whose bounds America doth stretch many thousand miles: into the frozen partes whereof one Master Hutson an English Mariner did make the greatest discoverie of any Christian I knowe of, where he unfortunately died.

4. Smith argues that the power of Spain is not to be feared; the Spanish cannot even control the territory they claim and their soldiers are spoiled by the luxury of the Indies.

For Affrica, had not the industrious Portugales ranged her unknowne parts, who would have sought for wealth among those fryed Regions of blacke brutish Negers,[5] where notwithstanding all the wealth and admirable adventures and endeavours more then 140 yeares, they knowe not one third of those blacke habitations. But it is not a worke for every one, to manage such an affaire as makes a discoverie, and plants a Colony: It requires all the best parts of Art, Judgement, Courage, Honesty, Constancy, Diligence and Industrie, to doe but neere well. Some are more proper for one thing then another; and therein are to be imployed: and nothing breedes more confusion then misplacing and misimploying men in their undertakings. Columbus, Cortez, Pitzara, Soto, Magellanes, and the rest served more then a prentiship to learne how to begin their most memorable attempts in the West Indes: which to the wonder of all ages succesfully they effected, when many hundreds of others farre above them in the worlds opinion, beeing instructed but by relation, came to shame and confusion in actions of small moment, who doubtlesse in other matters, were both wise, discreet, generous, and couragious. I say not this to detract any thing from their incomparable merits, but to answer those questionlesse[6] questions that keep us back from imitating the worthinesse of their brave spirits that advanced themselves from poore Souldiers to great Captaines, their posterity to great Lords, their King to be one of the greatest Potentates on earth, and the fruites of their labours, his greatest glory, power and renowne. [*Description of New England:* I, 324–328]

II

John Smith began his Map of Virginia *with a description of the land, its climate and situation.*

The Description of Virginia By Captaine Smith.

VIRGINIA IS A Country in America that lyeth betweene the degrees of 34 and 44 of the north latitude. The bounds thereof

5. Smith had never been in black Africa and may never have seen black Africans.
6. *Questionless* here means "genuine, real."

on the East side are the great Ocean. On the South lyeth Florida: on the North nova Francia. As for the West thereof, the limits are unknowne. Of all this country wee purpose not to speake, but only of that part which was planted by the English men in the yeare of our Lord, 1606. And this is under the degrees 37. 38. and 39. The temperature of this countrie doth agree well with English constitutions being once seasoned to the country. Which appeared by this, that though by many occasions our people fell sicke; yet did they recover by very small meanes and continued in health, though there were other great causes, not only to have made them sicke, but even to end their daies, etc.

The sommer is hot as in Spaine; the winter colde as in Fraunce or England. The heat of sommer is in June, Julie, and August, but commonly the coole Breeses asswage the vehemencie of the heat. The chiefe of winter is halfe December, January, February, and halfe March. The colde is extreame sharpe, but here the proverbe is true that no extreame long continueth.

In the yeare 1607 was an extraordinary frost in most of Europe, and this frost was founde as extreame in Virginia. But the next yeare for 8. or 10. daies of ill weather, other 14 daies would be as Sommer.

The windes here are variable, but the like thunder and lightning to purifie the aire, I have seldome either seene or heard in Europe. From the Southwest came the greatest gustes with thunder and heat. The Northwest winde is commonly coole and bringeth faire weather with it. From the North is the greatest cold, and from the East and South-East as from the Bermudas, fogs and raines.

Some times there are great droughts other times much raine, yet great necessity of neither, by reason we see not but that all the variety of needfull fruits in Europe may be there in great plenty by the industry of men, as appeareth by those we there planted.

There is but one entraunce by sea into this country and that is at the mouth of a very goodly Bay the widenesse whereof is neare 18. or 20. miles. The cape on the Southside is called Cape Henry in honour of our most noble Prince. The shew of the land there is a white hilly sand like unto the Downes, and along the shores great plentie of Pines and Firres.

The north Cape is called Cape Charles in honour of the worthy Duke of Yorke.[7] Within is a country that may have the prerogative

---

7. Prince Henry, oldest son of James I, died suddenly in 1612 at the age of 18; the future Charles I, then duke of York, became heir to the throne.

over the most pleasant places of Europe, Asia, Africa, or America, for large and pleasant navigable rivers, heaven and earth never agreed better to frame a place for mans habitation being of our constitutions, were it fully manured and inhabited by industrious people.[8] here are mountaines, hils, plaines, valleyes, rivers and brookes, all running most pleasantly into a faire Bay compassed but for the mouth with fruitfull and delightsome land. In the Bay and rivers are many Isles both great and small, some woody, some plaine, most of them low and not inhabited.[9] This Bay lieth North and South in which the water floweth neare 200 miles and hath a channell for 140 miles, of depth betwixt 7 and 15 fadome, holding in breadth for the most part 10 or 14 miles. From the head of the Bay at the north, the land is mountanous, and so in a manner from thence by a Southwest line; So that the more Southward, the farther off from the Bay are those mounetaines. From which fall certaine brookes which after come to five principall navigable rivers. These run from the Northwest into the Southeast, and so into the west side of the Bay, where the fall of every River is within 20 or 15 miles one of an other.[10]

The mountaines are of diverse natures for at the head of the Bay the rockes are of a composition like milnstones.[11] Some of marble, etc. And many peeces of christall we found as throwne downe by water from the mountaines. For in winter these mountaines are covered with much snow, and when it dissolveth the waters fall with such violence, that it causeth great inundations in the narrow valleyes which yet is scarce perceived being once in the rivers. These waters wash from the rocks such glistering tinctures that the ground in some places seemeth as guilded, where both the rocks and the earth are so splendent to behold, that better judgements then ours might have beene perswaded, they contained more then probabilities.[12] The vesture of the earth in most places doeth manifestly prove the nature of the soile to be lusty and very rich. The colour of the earth we found in diverse places, resembleth *bole Armoniac, terra sigillata* and *lemnia*, Fullers

---

8. *Manured* simply means "cultivated."

9. *Plain* means "flat and open, not wooded."

10. *Fall* here means "opening into the bay."

11. "Milnstone": Millstone would be coarse rock.

12. *Guilded* for *gilded*. Smith, as usual, indicates some probability of precious minerals, but refuses to be definite.

earth marle and divers other such appearances.[13] But generally for the most part the earth is a black sandy mould, in some places a fat slimy clay, in other places a very barren gravell. But the best ground is knowne by the vesture it beareth, as by the greatnesse of trees or abundance of weedes, etc.

The country is not mountanous nor yet low but such pleasant plaine hils and fertle valleyes, one prettily crossing an other, and watered so conveniently with their sweete brookes and christall springs, as if art it selfe had devised them. By the rivers are many plaine marishes containing some 20 some 100 some 200 Acres, some more, some lesse.[14] Other plaines there are fewe, but only where the Savages inhabit: but all overgrowne with trees and weedes being a plaine wildernes as God first made it. [*Map of Virginia:* I, 143–145]

Of such things which are naturall in Virginia and how they use them.

VIRGINIA DOTH afford many excellent vegitables and living Creatures, yet grasse there is little or none, but what groweth in lowe Marishes: for all the Countrey is overgrowne with trees, whose droppings continually turneth their grasse to weedes, by reason of the rancknesse of the ground which would soone be amended by good husbandry.[15] The wood that is most common is Oke and Walnut, many of their Okes are so tall and straight, that they will beare two foote and a halfe square of good timber for 20 yards long; Of this wood there is 2 or 3 severall kinds. The Acornes of one kind, whose barke is more white, then the other, is somewhat sweetish, which being boyled halfe

13. *Bole Armoniac, terra sigillata* and *lemnia* are clays with astringent properties that were imported into England for medicinal uses. They would have great economic value if found in America. Fuller's earth is naturally occurring aluminosilicate, which was used in the manufacture of woolen cloth, and marl is clay with a heavy mixture of carbonate of lime that was valued as a fertilizer. The general point is that both from the look of the various soils and from their "vesture," the growing plants that "clothed" the land, Smith concluded that Virginia was a very good prospect for agriculture.

14. *Marish* for *marsh.*

15. Rankness is excessive fertility that produces uncontrolled and undesirable growth.

a day in severall waters, at last afford a sweete oyle, which they keep in goards to annoint their heads and joints. The fruit they eate made in bread or otherwise. There is also some Elme, some black walnut tree, and some Ash: of Ash and Elme they make sope Ashes. If the trees be very great, the ashes will be good, and melt to hard lumps, but if they be small, it will be but powder, and not so good as the other. Of walnuts there is 2 or 3 kindes; there is a kinde of wood we called Cypres, because both the wood, the fruit, and leafe did most resemble it, and of those trees there are some neere 3 fadome about at the root very straight, and 50, 60, or 80 foot without a braunch.[16] By the dwelling of the Savages are some great Mulbery trees, and in some parts of the Countrey, they are found growing naturally in prettie groves. There was an assay made to make silke, and surely the wormes prospered excellent well, till the master workeman fell sicke. During which time they were eaten with rats.[17]

In some parts were found some Chesnuts whose wild fruit equalize the best in France, Spaine, Germany, or Italy, to their tasts that had tasted them all. Plumbs there are of 3 sorts. The red and white are like our hedge plumbs, but the other which they call *Putchamins*, grow as high as a Palmeta: the fruit is like a medler;[18] it is first greene then yellow, and red when it is ripe; if it be not ripe it will drawe a mans mouth awrie, with much torment, but when it is ripe, it is as delicious as an Apricock.

They have Cherries and those are much like a Damsen, but for their tastes and colour we called them Cherries. we see some few Crabs, but very small and bitter.[19] Of vines great abundance in many parts that climbe the toppes of the highest trees in some places, but these beare

16. A fathom (fadome) was traditionally the length of both outstretched arms; it was usually taken to be six feet.

17. In this paragraph, Smith is holding out the promise of many commodities needed in England. Because of the severe wood shortage, timber and wood products, such as soap ash, were particularly valued. Oil was needed to make sweet-smelling soap essential to the manufacture of woolen cloth, England's major industry; fish oil, the domestic source, imparted its odor to the wool. The dream of silk manufacture died hard in the colonies. There were mulberries growing wild in Virginia, but they were of the red variety, whereas silkworms require white mulberry leaves.

18. *Putchamins* are persimmons; a medlar is a fruit resembling a small brown apple, best eaten when it is soft and decayed.

19. A damson is a small black plum; crabs are crab apples.

but fewe grapes. But by the rivers and Savage habitations where they are not overshadowed from the sunne, they are covered with fruit, though never pruined nor manured. Of those hedge grapes wee made neere 20 gallons of wine, which was neare as good as your French Brittish wine, but certainely they would prove good were they well manured.[20] There is another sort of grape neere as great as a Cherry, this they call *Messaminnes*, they bee fatte, and the juyce thicke. Neither doth the tast so well please when they are made in wine. They have a small fruit growing on little trees, husked like a Chesnut, but the fruit most like a very small acorne. This they call *Chechinquamins* which they esteeme a great daintie. They have a berry much like our gooseberry, in greatnesse, colour, and tast; those they call *Rawcomenes*, and doe eat them raw or boyled. Of these naturall fruits they live a great part of the yeare, which they use in this manner, The walnuts, Chesnuts, Acornes, and *Chechinquamens* are dryed to keepe. When they need them they breake them betweene two stones, yet some part of the walnut shels will cleave to the fruit. Then doe they dry them againe upon a mat over a hurdle.[21] After they put it into a morter of wood, and beat it very small: that done they mix it with water, that the shels may sinke to the bottome. This water will be coloured as milke, which they cal *Pawcohiscora*, and keepe it for their use. The fruit like medlers they call *Putchamins*, they cast uppon hurdles on a mat and preserve them as Pruines. Of their Chesnuts and *Chechinquamens* boyled 4 houres, they make both broath and bread for their chiefe men, or at their greatest feasts. Besides those fruit trees, there is a white populer, and another tree like unto it, that yeeldeth a very cleere and an odoriferous Gumme like Turpentine, which some called Balsom. There are also Cedars and Saxafras trees.[22] They also yeeld gummes in a small proportion of themselves. Wee tryed conclusions to extract it out of the wood, but nature afforded more then our arts.

In the watry valleyes groweth a berry which they call *Ocoughtanamins* very much like unto Capers. These they dry in sommer. When they will eat them they boile them neare halfe a day; for otherwise they

20. *Brittish* here refers to Brittany.
21. *Chechinquamins* are dwarf chestnuts, and *rawcomenes* refers to the prickly wild gooseberry. Hurdles are wooden frames.
22. "Saxafras": Smith confuses the sassafras native to America with the saxifrage known to the Old World; both were thought to have medicinal qualities, but sassafras was especially prized as a cure for syphilis.

differ not much from poyson. *Mattoume* groweth as our bents do in meddows.[23] The seede is not much unlike to rie, though much smaller. this they use for a dainty bread buttered with deare suet.

During Somer there are either strawberries which ripen in April; or mulberries which ripen in May and June. Raspises hurtes; or a fruit that the Inhabitants call *Maracocks*, which is a pleasant wholsome fruit much like a lemond. Many hearbes in the spring time there are commonly dispersed throughout the woods, good for brothes and sallets, as Violets, Purslin, Sorrell, etc.[24] Besides many we used whose names we know not.

The chiefe roote they have for foode is called *Tockawhoughe*, It groweth like a flagge in low muddy freshes.[25] In one day a Savage will gather sufficient for a weeke. These rootes are much of the greatnes and taste of Potatoes. They use to cover a great many of them with oke leaves and ferne, and then cover all with earth in the manner of a colepit; over it, on each side, they continue a great fire 24 houres before they dare eat it. Raw it is no better then poison, and being roasted, except it be tender and the heat abated, or sliced and dried in the sun, mixed with sorrell and meale or such like, it will prickle and torment the throat extremely, and yet in sommer they use this ordinarily for bread.

They have an other roote which they call *wighsacan*: as th'other feedeth the body, so this cureth their hurts and diseases. It is a small root which they bruise and apply to the wound. *Pocones*, is a small roote that groweth in the mountaines, which being dryed and beate in powder turneth red. And this they use for swellings, aches, annointing their joints, painting their heads and garments. They account it very pretious and of much worth. *Musquaspenne* is a roote of the bignesse of a finger, and as red as bloud.[26] In drying it will wither almost to nothing. This they use to paint their Mattes, Targets and such like.

23. *Ocoughtanamins* may be chokecherries. Bent is a stiff, rushlike grass; the Virginia grass may be cane grass.

24. *Raspises* was the contemporary word for *raspberries*, and hurts are hurtleberries, or huckleberries. Maracocks, later known as maypops, are the fruits of the passion vine. Purslane (purslin) is a member of the portulaca family.

25. *Tockawhoughe* (tuckahoe) is green arrow arum; flag is coarse reedy grass.

26. The *wighsacan* Smith saw used was probably milkweed root, but the word may have meant medicine in general. He also described the ritual use of *wighsacan* as an emetic (see Part Three, Section I). *Pocones*, a root used as both a dye and a medicine, has not been identified definitely. *Musquaspenne* is bloodroot.

There is also Pellitory of Spaine, Sasafrage, and divers other simples, which the Apothecaries gathered, and commended to be good, and medicinable.[27]

In the low Marishes growe plots of Onyons containing an acre of ground or more in many places; but they are small not past the bignesse of the Toppe of ones Thumbe.

Of beastes the chiefe are Deare, nothing differing from ours. In the deserts towards the heads of the rivers, ther are many, but amongst the rivers few. There is a beast they call *Aroughcun*, much like a badger, but useth to live on trees as Squirrels doe.[28] Their Squirrels some are neare as greate as our smallest sort of wilde rabbits, some blackish or blacke and white, but the most are gray.

A small beast they have, they call *Assapanick* but we call them flying squirrels, because spreading their legs, and so stretching the largenesse of their skins that they have bin seene to fly 30 or 40 yards. An Opassom hath a head like a Swine, and a taile like a Rat, and is of the bignes of a Cat. Under her belly shee hath a bagge, wherein shee lodgeth, carrieth, and suckleth her young. *Mussascus*, is a beast of the forme and nature of our water Rats, but many of them smell exceeding strongly of muske. Their Hares no bigger then our Conies, and few of them to be found.[29]

Their Beares are very little in comparison of those of Muscovia and Tartaria. The Beaver is as bigge as an ordinary water dogge, but his legges exceeding short. His fore feete like a dogs, his hinder feet like a Swans. His taile somewhat like the forme of a Racket bare without haire, which to eate the Savages esteeme a great delicate. They have many Otters which as the Beavers they take with snares, and esteeme the skinnes great ornaments, and of all those beasts they use to feede when they catch them.[30]

There is also a beast they call *Vetchunquoyes* in the forme of a wilde Cat. Their Foxes are like our silver haired Conies of a small proportion, and not smelling like those in England. Their Dogges of that

27. Simples are medicinal herbs. *Sasafrage* again confuses sassafras with saxifrage. Pellitory of Spain is pyrethrum, which was used as a cure for toothache.

28. *Desert* simply refers to a wild, uninhabited (deserted) place. *Aroughcun* is *raccoon*.

29. *Mussascus* is *muskrat*, and a cony is a rabbit.

30. "Of all those beasts they use to feede" means that the Indians would eat any of these animals when they caught them.

country are like their Wolves, and cannot barke but howle, and their wolves not much bigger then our English Foxes. Martins, Powlecats, weessels and Minkes we know they have, because we have seen many of their skinnes, though very seldome any of them alive. But one thing is strange that we could never perceive their vermine destroy our hennes, Egges nor Chickens nor do any hurt, nor their flyes nor serpents anie waie pernitious, where in the South parts of America they are alwaies dangerous and often deadly.[31]

Of birds the Eagle is the greatest devourer. Hawkes there be of diverse sorts, as our Falconers called them, Sparowhawkes, Lanarets, Goshawkes, Falcons and Osperayes, but they all pray most upon fish. Partridges there are little bigger then our Quailes, wilde Turkies are as bigge as our tame. There are woosels or blackbirds with red shoulders, thrushes and diverse sorts of small birds, some red, some blew, scarce so bigge as a wrenne, but few in Sommer. In winter there are great plenty of Swans, Craynes, gray and white with blacke wings, Herons, Geese, Brants, Ducke, Wigeon, Dotterell, Oxeies, Parrats and Pigeons. Of all those sorts great abundance, and some other strange kinds to us unknowne by name. But in sommer not any or a very few to be seene.

Of fish we were best acquainted with Sturgeon, Grampus, Porpus, Seales, Stingraies, whose tailes are very dangerous. Brettes, mullets, white Salmonds, Trowts, Soles, Plaice, Herrings, Conyfish, Rockfish, Eeles, Lampreyes, Catfish, Shades, Pearch of 3 sorts, Crabs, Shrimps, Crevises, Oysters, Cocles and Muscles. But the most strange fish is a smal one so like the picture of St. George his Dragon, as possible can be, except his legs and wings, and the Todefish which will swell till it be like to brust, when it commeth into the aire.[32]

Concerning the entrailes of the earth little can be saide for certainty. There wanted good Refiners, for these that tooke upon them to have skill this way, tooke up the washings from the mounetaines and some moskered shining stones and spangles which the waters brought down, flattering themselves in their own vaine conceits to have bin supposed what they were not, by the meanes of that ore, if it proved as their arts and judgements expected. Only this is certaine, that many

31. Vermin are objectionable animals, especially those that prey on pets and livestock. Smith implies that nature is benign and familiar in Virginia unlike in the colonies farther south.

32. Brettes are turbot, shades may be shad, crevises are crayfish, and the dragon may be the sea robin. The toadfish (todefish) is the puffer.

regions lying in the same latitude, afford mines very rich of diverse natures. The crust also of these rockes would easily perswade a man to beleeve there are other mines then yron and steele, if there were but meanes and men of experience that knew the mine from spare.[33] [*Map of Virginia:* I, 151–156]

III

John Smith's task in writing about the environment of New England differed from his self-appointed role in the Virginia experiment. After the disastrous experience of the Sagadahock colony, the north was considered too cold and barren ever to be a good prospect for transplanted English society. Smith's analysis of the land's possibilities was more systematic than earlier; he was more experienced and the need for powerful persuasion was greater. He was careful, though, to be sober and controlled in his praise of New England, and to stress the need for good management.

He began with a short description of the earlier experience, followed by an account of his own expedition.

NOW THIS PART of America hath formerly beene called Norumbega, Virginia, Nuskoncus, Penaquida, Cannada, and such other names as those that ranged the Coast pleased. But because it was so mountainous, rocky and full of Iles, few have adventured much to trouble it, but as is formerly related. Notwithstanding, that honourable Patron of vertue, Sir John Popham, Lord chiefe Justice of England, in the yeere 1606. procured meanes and men to possesse it, and sent Captaine George Popham for President, Captaine Rawley Gilbert for Admirall, Captaine Edward Harlow master of the Ordnance, Captaine Robert Davis, Sargeant-Major, Captaine Elis Best, Marshall, Master Seaman, Secretary, Captaine James Davis to be Captaine of the Fort, Master Gome Carew, chiefe Searcher: all those were of the Councell, who with some hundred more were to stay in the Country: they set saile from Plimoth the last of May, and fell with Monahigan the eleventh of August. At Sagadahock 9. or 10. leagues southward, they planted themselves at the mouth of a faire navigable River, but

33. *Moskered* means "crumbling," and *spar* (spare) refers to crystalline rock with a lustrous appearance.

the coast all thereabouts most extreme stony and rocky: that extreme frozen Winter was so cold they could not range nor search the Country, and their provision so small, they were glad to send all but 45. of their company backe againe: their noble President Captaine Popham died, and not long after arrived two ships well provided of all necessaries to supply them, and some small time after another, by whom understanding of the death of the Lord chiefe Justice, and also of Sir John Gilbert, whose lands there the President Rawley Gilbert was to possesse according to the adventurers directions, finding nothing but extreme extremities, they all returned for England in the yeere 1608. and thus this Plantation was begunne and ended in one yeere, and the Country esteemed as a cold, barren, mountainous, rocky Desart. . . .

In the month of Aprill 1614. at the charge of Captaine Marmaduke Roydon, Captaine George Langman, Master John Buley and Master William Skelton, with two ships from London, I chanced to arrive at Monahigan an Ile of America, in 43½ of Northerly latitude: our plot was there to take Whales, for which we had one Samuel Cramton and divers others expert in that faculty, and also to make trialls of a Mine of gold and copper; if those failed, Fish and Furs were then our refuge to make our selves savers howsoever:[34] we found this Whale-fishing a costly conclusion, we saw many and spent much time in chasing them, but could not kill any. They being a kinde of Jubartes, and not the Whale that yeelds Fins and Oile as we expected; for our gold it was rather the Masters device to get a voyage that projected it, then any knowledge he had at all of any such matter; Fish and Furs were now our guard, and by our late arrivall and long lingring about the Whale, the prime of both those seasons were past ere wee perceived it, wee thinking that their seasons served at all times, but we found it otherwise, for by the middest of June the fishing failed, yet in July and August some were taken, but not sufficient to defray so great a charge as our stay required: of dry fish we made about forty thousand, of Cor-fish about seven thousand.[35] Whilest the Sailers fished, my selfe

---

34. *Plot* means "project"; when Smith speaks of their plan to make themselves "savers," he means that they hoped thereby to break even on the voyage.

35. Cor-fish are salted fish. There were two ways to preserve fish caught in America for sale in Europe. Cor, or green, fish were cleaned and then laid down in layers in the ship's hold with salt thickly strewn between the layers. The English, who did not have access to good supplies of salt, often dried their fish in the sun and open air if they had time, which greatly reduced the amount of salt necessary.

with eight others of them might best bee spared, ranging the Coast in a small Boat, we got for trifles neere eleven thousand Bever skinnes, one hundred Martins, as many Otters, and the most of them within the distance of twenty leagues: we ranged the Coast both East and West much further, but Eastward our commodities were not esteemed, they were so neere the French who afforded them better, with whom the Salvages had such commerce that only by trade they made exceeding great voyages, though they were without the limits of our precincts;[36] during the time we tried those conclusions, not knowing the coast, nor Salvages habitations: with these Furres, the traine Oile and Cor-fish,[37] I returned for England in the Barke, where within six moneths after our departure from the Downes, wee safely arrived backe: the best of this fish was sold for 5. li. the hundred, the rest by ill usage betwixt three pounds and 50. shillings. The other ship stayed to fit her selfe for Spaine with the dry fish which was sold at Maligo at forty Rialls the Quintall, each hundred weighing two quintals and a halfe. But one Thomas Hunt the Master of this ship (when I was gone) thinking to prevent that intent I had to make there a Plantation, thereby to keepe this abounding Countrey still in obscuritie, that onely he and some few Merchants more might enjoy wholly the benefit of the Trade, and profit of this Countrey, betraied foure and twenty of those poore Salvages aboord his ship, and most dishonestly and inhumanely for their kinde usage of me and all our men, caried them with him to Maligo, and there for a little private gaine sold those silly Salvages for Rials of eight; but this vilde act kept him ever after from any more imploiment to those parts.[38] Now because at this time I had taken a draught of the Coast, and called it New England, yet so long he and his Consorts drowned that name with the Eccho of Cannaday,

36. There was already a French presence in Canada.
37. Train oil is whale oil or any oil extracted by pressure.
38. One of the Indians captured by Thomas Hunt was Squanto, who somehow escaped from slavery in Spain (Maligo is Málaga) and made his way to England, where he was brought into contact with promoters of Newfoundland colonization. After some time in Newfoundland, he was back in England living in the household of Sir Ferdinando Gorges, a New England backer. Squanto was finally returned to New England in 1619 where he found his entire village dead of European diseases. He eventually came to live with the Pilgrims who, in 1620, settled on the land of his tribe, the Patuxet, and became their interpreter and intermediary. *Silly* here means "defenseless, deserving of pity." *Vilde* is for *vile*. Squanto proved to be very sophisticated in his dealings with the English.

Map of New England drawn by Simon van de Passe from John Smith's notes; the quality of Smith's survey is demonstrated by the accuracy of the map's detail. It was first published in 1616. Courtesy of the Houghton Library, Harvard University.

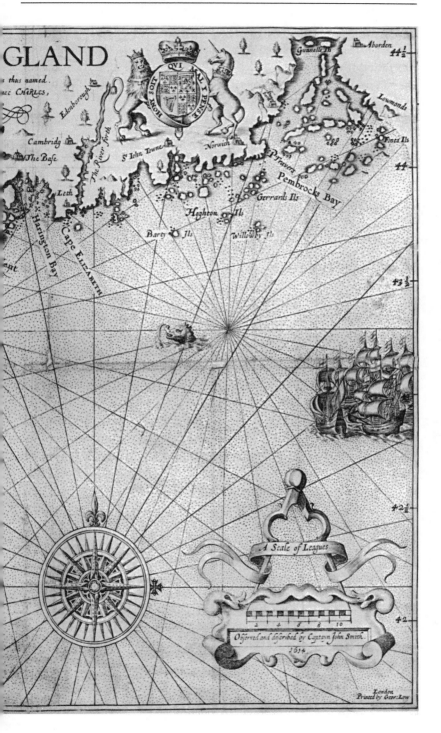

GLAND

s thus named .
acc CHARLES ,

Edenborough

Cambridg

The Bafe

Leth

HONI SOIT QVI MAL Y PENSE

Harrington Bay

Cape ElizAbeth

The River Forth

St. Iohn Towne

Norwich

Pyravers

Pembrocke Bay

Gerrards Ils

Heghton Ils

Barty Ils

Willowby Ils

Gunnells Ils

Aborden

Lowmonds

Fines Ils

44½

44

43½

42¾

42

A Scale of Leagues

Obferved and defcribed by Captayn Iohn Smith.
1614

London
Printed by Geor: Low

and some other ships from other parts also, that upon this good re-turne the next yeere went thither, that at last I presented this Discourse with the Map, to our most gracious Prince Charles, humbly intreating his Highnesse hee would please to change their barbarous names for such English, as posteritie might say Prince Charles was their God-father, which for your better understanding both of this Discourse and the Map, peruse this Schedule, which will plainly shew you the corre-spondency of the old names to the new, as his Highnesse named them. [*Generall Historie:* II, 398–401]

Captain Smith began his discussion of New England with the same kind of formal description found in his Virginia work.

The Description of New England.

THAT PART we call New England, is betwixt the degrees of fortie one and fortie five, the very meane betwixt the North pole and the line;[39] but that part this Discourse speaketh of, stretcheth but from Penobscot to Cape Cod, some seventie five leagues by a right line distant each from other; within which bounds I have seene at least fortie severall habitations upon the Sea Coast, and sounded about five and twentie excellent good Harbours, in many whereof there is an-chorage for five hundred saile of ships of any burden; in some of them for one thousand, and more then two hundred Iles over-growne with good Timber of divers sorts of wood, which doe make so many Har-bours, as required a longer time then I had to be well observed.

The principall habitation Northward we were at, was Pennobscot: Southward along the Coast and up the Rivers, we found Mecadacut, Segocket, Pemaquid, Nusconcus, Sagadahock, Aumoughcowgen, and Kenebeke; and to those Countries belong the people of Segotago, Paghhuntanuck, Pocopassum, Taughtanakagnet, Warbigganus, Nas-saque, Masherosqueck, Wawrigweck, Moshoquen, Wakcogo, Pashar-anack, etc. To these are alied in confederacy, the Countries of Auco-

39. The line is the equator. Many people thought that 45 degrees, exactly halfway between the most extreme heat and cold on earth, would be the most moderate of all places.

cisco, Accomynticus, Passataquack, Aggawom, and Naemkeck: All these for any thing I could perceive, differ little in language, fashion, or government, though most of them be Lords of themselves, yet they hold the Bashabes of Penobscot, the chiefe and greatest amongst them.[40]

The next I can remember by name, are Mattahunts, two pleasant Iles of Groves, Gardens, and Corne fields a league in the Sea from the maine: Then Totant, Massachuset, Topent, Secassaw, Totheet, Nasnocomacack, Accomack, Chawum, Patuxet, Massasoyts, Pakanokick: then Cape Cod, by which is Pawmet and the Ile Nawset, of the language and aliance of them of Chawum; the others are called Massachusets, and differ somewhat in language, custome, and condition: for their Trade and Merchandize, to each of their principall families or habitations, they have divers Townes and people belonging, and by their relations and descriptions, more then twentie severall habitations and rivers that stretch themselves farre into the Countrey, even to the Borders of divers great Lakes, where they kill and take most of their Otters. From Pennobscot to Sagadahoc, this Coast is mountainous, and Iles of huge Rockes, but over-growne for most part, with most sorts of excellent good woods, for building Houses, Boats, Barks or Ships, with an incredible abundance of most sorts of Fish, much Fowle, and sundry sorts of good Fruits for mans use.

Betwixt Sagadahock, and Sowocatuck, there is but two or three Sandy Bayes, but betwixt that and Cape James very many: especially the Coast of the Massachusets is so indifferently mixed with high Clay or Sandy clifts in one place, and the tracts of large long ledges of divers sorts, and Quaries of stones in other places, so strangely divided with tinctured veines of divers colours: as Free-stone for building, Slate for tyling, smooth stone to make Furnasses and Forges for Glasse and Iron, and Iron Ore sufficient conveniently to melt in them; but the most part so resembleth the Coast of Devonshire, I thinke most of the clifts would make such Lime-stone: if they bee not of these qualities, they are so like they may deceive a better judgement then mine: all which are so neere adjoyning to those other advantages I observed in these parts, that if the Ore prove as good Iron and Steele in those parts as I know it is within the bounds of the Countrey, I dare ingage my head (having but men skilfull to worke the Simples there growing) to

40. Bashabes was an Abenaki sachem who was overlord of a confederation that covered much of coastal Maine.

have all things belonging to the building and rigging of ships of any proportion and good Merchandise for their fraught, within a square of ten or foureteene leagues, and it were no hard matter to prove it within a lesse limitation.

And surely by reason of those sandy clifts, and clifts of rocks, both which we saw so planted with Gardens and Corne fields, and so well inhabited with a goodly, strong, and well proportioned people, besides the greatnesse of the Timber growing on them, the greatnesse of the Fish, and the moderate temper of the aire (for of five and forty not a man was sicke, but two that were many yeares diseased before they went, notwithstanding our bad lodging and accidentall diet) who can but approve this a most excellent place, both for health and fertilitie: and of all the foure parts of the world I have yet seene not inhabited, could I have but means to transport a Colony, I would rather live here then any where, and if it did not maintaine it selfe, were we but once indifferently well fitted, let us starve.

The maine staple from hence to bee extracted for the present, to produce the rest, is Fish, which howbeit may seeme a meane and a base Commoditie; yet who will but truly take the paines and consider the sequell, I thinke will allow it well worth the labour. It is strange to see, what great adventures the hopes of setting forth men of warre to rob the industrious innocent would procure, or such massie promises in grosse, though more are choaked then well fed with such hastie hopes. But who doth not know that the poore Hollanders chiefely by fishing at a great charge and labour in all weathers in the open Sea, are made a people so hardy and industrious, and by the venting this poore Commoditie to the Easterlings for as meane, which is Wood, Flax, Pitch, Tarre, Rozen, Cordage, and such like; which they exchange againe to the French, Spaniards, Portugals, and English, etc. for what they want, are made so mighty, strong, and rich, as no state but Venice of twice their magnitude is so well furnished, with so many faire Cities, goodly Townes, strong Fortresses, and that abundance of shipping, and all sorts of Merchandize, as well of Gold, Silver, Pearles, Diamonds, pretious Stones, Silkes, Velvets, and Cloth of Gold; as Fish, Pitch, Wood, or such grosse Commodities? What voiages and discoveries, East and West, North and South, yea about the world, make they? What an Army by Sea and Land have they long maintained, in despight of one of the greatest Princes of the world, and never could the Spaniard with all his Mines of Gold and Silver, pay his debts, his friends, and Army, halfe so truly as the Hollanders still have done by this contemptible Trade of Fish. Divers (I know) may alleage many other assistances; but this is the chiefest Mine, and the Sea the source of those silver streames of all their vertue, which hath made them now the very miracle of industry, the onely paterne of perfection for these affaires: and the benefit of fishing is that Primum Mobile that turnes all their spheares to this height, of plentie, strength, honor, and exceeding great admiration.

Herring, Cod, and Ling, is that triplicitie, that makes their wealth and shippings multiplicitie such as it is: and from which (few would thinke it) they should draw so many millions yeerely as they doe, as more in particular in the trials of New England you may see; and such an incredible number of ships, that breeds them so many Sailers, Mariners, Souldiers, and Merchants, never to be wrought out of that Trade, and fit for any other. I will not deny but others may gaine as well as they that will use it, though not so certainly, nor so much in quantitie, for want of experience: and this Herring they take upon the Coast of England and Scotland, their Cod and Ling upon the Coast of Izeland, and in the North seas.

If wee consider what gaines the Hamburgans, the Biskinners, and French make by fishing; nay, but how many thousands this fiftie or sixty yeeres have beene maintained by New found land, where they take nothing but small Cod, where of the greatest they make Cor-fish, and the rest is hard dried, which we call Poore-John, would amaze a man with wonder. If then from all those parts such paines is taken for this poore gaines of Fish, especially by the Hollanders, that hath but little of their owne, for building of ships and setting them to sea; but at the second, third, fourth, or fift hand, drawne from so many parts of the world ere they come together to be used in those voiages: If these (I say) can gaine, why should we more doubt then they; but doe much better, that may have most of all those things at our doores for taking and making, and here are no hard Landlords to racke us with high rents, or extorting fines, nor tedious pleas in Law to consume us with their many yeeres disputation for Justice; no multitudes to occasion such impediments to good orders as in popular States: so freely hath God and his Majestie bestowed those blessings on them will attempt to obtaine them, as here every man may be master of his owne labour and land, or the greatest part (if his Majesties royall meaning be not abused) and if he have nothing but his hands, he may set up his Trade; and by industry quickly grow rich, spending but halfe that time well, which in England we abuse in idlenesse, worse, or as ill. Here is ground as good as any lieth in the height of forty one, forty two, forty three, etc. which is as temperate, and as fruitfull as any other parallel in the world.

As for example, on this side the line, West of it in the South Sea, is Nova Albion, discovered as is said by Sir Francis Drake: East from it is the most temperate part of Portugall, the ancient Kingdomes of Galizia, Bisky, Navarre, Aragon, Cattilonia, Castillia the old, and the most moderatest of Castillia the new, and Valentia, which is the greatest part of Spaine; which if the Histories be true, in the Romans time abounded no lesse with gold and silver Mines, then now the West-Indies, the Romans then using the Spaniards to worke in those Mines, as now the Spaniards doe the Indians. In France the Provinces of Gascony, Langadocke, Avignon, Province, Dolphine, Pyamont, and Turyne, are in the same parallel, which are the best and richest parts of France. In Italy the Provinces of Genua, Lumbardy, and Verona, with a great part of the most famous state of Venice, the Dukedomes of Bononia, Mantua, Ferrara, Ravenna, Bolognia, Florence, Pisa, Sienna, Urbine, Ancona, and the ancient Citie and Countrey of Rome, with a great part of the Kingdome of Naples. In Slavonia, Istria, and Dalmatia, with the Kingdomes of Albania. In Grecia those famous Kingdomes of Macedonia, Bulgaria, Thessalia, Thracia, or Romania, where is seated the most pleasant and plentifull Citie in Europe, Constantinople.

In Asia in the same latitude, are the temperatest parts of Natolia, Armenia, Persia, and China; besides divers other large Countries and Kingdomes in those most milde and temperate Regions of Asia. Southward in the same height is the richest of Gold Mines, Chily, and Baldivia, and the mouth of the great River of Plate, etc. for all the rest of the world in that height is yet unknowne. Besides these reasons, mine owne eies that have seene a great part of those Cities and their Kingdomes (as well as it) can finde no advantage they have in Nature but this, they are beautified by the long labour and diligence of industrious people and art; This is onely as God made it when hee created the world: Therefore I conclude, if the heart and intrailes of those Regions were sought, if their Land were cultured, planted, and manured by men of industry, judgement, and experience; what hope is there, or what need they doubt, having the advantages of the Sea, but it might equalize any of these famous Kingdomes in all commodities, pleasures, and conditions, seeing even the very edges doe naturally affoord us such plentie, as no ship need returne away emptie: and onely use but the season of the Sea, Fish will returne an honest gaine, besides all other advantages, her treasures having yet never beene opened, nor her originals wasted, consumed, nor abused.

And whereas it is said the Hollanders serve the Easterlings themselves, and other parts that want with Herring, Ling, and wet Cod: The Easterlings, a great part of Europe, with Sturgion and Caviare, as the Blacke Sea doth Grecia, Podolia, Sagovia, Natolia, and the Hellespont. Cape Blanke, Spaine, Portugall, and the Levant, with Mulit and Puttargo. New found land, the most part of the chiefe Southerne Ports in Europe, with a thin Poore-John, which hath beene so long, so much over-laied with Fishers, as the fishing decaieth, so that many oft times are constrained to returne with a small fraught.[41] Norway and Poland affoords Pitch and Tarre, Masts and Yards. Sweathland and Russia, Iron and Ropes. France and Spaine, Canvase, Wine, Steele, Iron, and Oile. Italy and Greece, Silkes and Fruits. I dare boldly say, because I have seene naturally growing or breeding in those parts, the same materials that all these are made of, they may as well bee had here, or the most part of them within the distance of seventie leagues for some few ages, as from all those parts, using but the same meanes to have them that they doe; but surely in Virginia, their most tender and daintiest fruits or commodities, would be as perfit as theirs, by reason of the heat, if not in New England, and with all those advantages.

First, the ground is so fertill, that questionlesse it is capable of producing any Graine, Fruits, or Seeds, you will sow or plant, growing in the Regions aforenamed: But it may be not to that perfection of delicacy, because the Summer is not so hot, and the Winter is more cold in those parts we have yet tried neere the Sea side, then wee finde in the same height in Europe or Asia: yet I made a Garden upon the top of a Rocky Ile in three and forty degrees and an halfe, foure leagues from the maine in May, that grew so well, as it served us for Sallets in June and July.[42] All sorts of Cattle may here be bred and fed in the Iles or Peninsulaes securely for nothing. In the Interim, till they increase (if need be) observing the seasons, I durst undertake to have Corne enough from the Salvages for three hundred men, for a few trifles; and if they should be untowards, as it is most certaine they will, thirtie or fortie good men will be sufficient to bring them all in subjec-

41. Fraught is freight.
42. The maine is the mainland.

tion, and make this provision, if they understand what to doe; two hundred whereof may eight or nine moneths in the yeere be imploied in helping the Fisher-men, till the rest provide other necessaries, fit to furnish us with other Commodities.

In March, Aprill, May, and halfe June, heere is Cod in abundance; in May, June, July, and August, Mullit and Sturgion, whose Roes doe make Caviare and Puttargo;[43] Herring, if any desire them: I have taken many out of the bellies of Cods, some in nets; but the Salvages compare the store in the Sea with the haires of their heads: and surely there are an incredible abundance upon this Coast. In the end of August, September, October, and November, you may have Cod againe to make Core-fish or Poore-John: Hake you may have when the Cod failes in Summer, if you will fish in the night, which is better then Cod. Now each hundred you take here, is as good as two or three hundred in New found Land; so that halfe the labour in hooking, splitting and turning, is saved: And you may have your fish at what market you will, before they have any in New found land, where their fishing is chiefely but in June and July, where it is here in March, Aprill, May, September, October and November, as is said; so that by reason of this Plantation, the Merchants may have their fraught both out and home, which yeelds an advantage worth consideration. Your Core-fish you may in like manner transport as you see cause, to serve the Ports in Portugall, as Lisbone, Avera, Port Aport, and divers others, (or what market you please) before your Ilanders returne. They being tied to the season in the open Sea, and you having a double season, and fishing before your doores, may every night sleep quietly ashore with good cheere, and what fires you will, or when you please with your wives and family: they onely and their ships in the maine Ocean, that must carie and containe all they use, besides their fraught. The Mullits here are in that abundance, you may take them with nets sometimes by hundreds, where at Cape Blanke they hooke them; yet those are but a foot and a halfe in length; these two, three, or foure, as oft I have measured, which makes me suspect they are some other kinde of fish, though they seeme the same, both in fashion and goodnesse. Much Salmon some have found up the Rivers as they have passed, and here the aire is so temperate, as all these at any time may be preserved. Now, young Boies and Girles Salvages, or any other bee they never such idlers, may turne, carie or returne a fish, without

43. Botargo (puttargo) is a relish made from roe.

either shame or any great paine: He is very idle that is past twelve yeeres of age and cannot doe so much, and she is very old that cannot spin a threed to make Engins to catch a fish.

For their transportation, the ships that goe there to fish may transport the first: who for their passage will spare the charge of double manning their ships, which they must do in New found land to get their fraught; but one third part of that company are onely proper to serve a stage, carie a Barrow, and turne Poore-John;[44] notwithstanding, they must have meat, drinke, clothes, and passage so well as the rest. Now all I desire is but this, That those that voluntarily will send shipping, should make here the best choice they can, or accept such as shall bee presented them to serve them at that rate: and their ships returning leave such with me, with the value of that they should receive comming home, in such provisions and necessarie tooles, armes, bedding, apparell, salt, nets, hookes, lines, and such like, as they spare of the remainings; who till the next returne may keepe their Boats, and doe them many other profitable offices. Provided, I have men of abilitie to teach them their functions, and a company fit for Souldiers to be ready upon any occasion, because of the abuses that have beene offered the poore Salvages, and the libertie that both French and English, or any that will, have to deale with them as they please; whose disorders will be hard to reforme, and the longer the worse: Now such order with facilitie might be taken, with every Port, Towne, or Citie, with free power to convert the benefit of their fraughts to what advantage they please, and increase their numbers as they see occasion, who ever as they are able to subsist of themselves, may begin the new Townes in New England, in memory of their old: which freedome being confined but to the necessitie of the generall good, the event (with Gods helpe) might produce an honest, a noble, and a profitable emulation.[45]

Salt upon Salt may assuredly be made, if not at the first in ponds, yet till they be provided this may be used: then the ships may transport Kine, Horse, Goats, course Cloth, and such Commodities as we want; by whose arrivall may be made that provision of fish to fraught the ships that they stay not; and then if the Sailers goe for wages it matters not, it is hard if this returne defray not the charge: but care must be

44. A stage is a platform extending into the water on which the fish are processed.
45. "Emulation": Smith implies that the towns of New England will equal those of old.

had they arrive in the Spring, or else that provision be made for them against winter. Of certaine red berries called Kermes, which is worth ten shillings the pound, but of these have beene sold for thirty or forty shillings the pound, may yeerely be gathered a good quantity.[46] Of the Muskrat may be well raised gaines worth their labour, that will endevour to make triall of their goodnesse. Of Bevers, Otters and Martins, blacke Foxes, and Furres of price, may yeerely be had six or seven thousand, and if the trade of the French were prevented, many more: 25000. this yeere were brought from those northerne parts into France, of which trade we may have as good part as the French if we take good courses. Of Mines of Gold and Silver, Copper, and probabilities of Lead, Crystall and Allum, I could say much if relations were good assurances; it is true indeed, I made many trialls according to the instructions I had, which doth perswade me I need not despaire but that there are metals in the Country: but I am no Alcumist, nor will promise more then I know:[47] which is, who will undertake the rectifying of an iron Forge, if those that buy meat and drinke, coles, ore, and all necessaries at a deare rate, gaine, where all these things are to be had for taking up, in my opinion cannot lose.

Of woods, seeing there is such plenty of all sorts, if those that build ships and boats, buy wood at so great a price, as it is in England, Spaine, France and Holland, and all other provisions for the nourishment of mans life, live well by their trade; when labour is all required to take these necessaries without any other tax, what hazard will be here but to doe much better, and what commodity in Europe doth more decay then wood? for the goodnesse of the ground, let us take it fertill or barren, or as it is, seeing it is certaine it beares fruits to nourish and feed man and beast as well as England, and the Sea those severall sorts of fishes I have related: thus seeing all good things for mans sustenance may with this facility be had by a little extraordinary labour, till that transported be increased, and all necessaries for shipping onely for labour, to which may [be] added the assistance of the Salvages which may easily be had, if they be discreetly handled in their

46. Alkermes (*kermes*), thought to be a berry, is actually an insect; crushed, it was used to make a medicinal cordial. The insect feeds on a Mediterranean evergreen oak, so Smith was probably mistaken.

47. *Alcumist* for *alchemist*. Alchemy was part of the mix of early chemistry, physics, and mineralogy out of which the modern sciences grew. It was considered a legitimate science in Smith's day, so no insult is implied here.

kinds, towards fishing, planting, and destroying woods. What gaines might be raised if this were followed (when there is but once men to fill your store houses dwelling there, you may serve all Europe better and farre cheaper then can the Iland[48] Fishers, or the Hollanders, Cape-blanke, or Newfound land, who must be at much more charge then you) may easily be conjectured by this example.

Two thousand will fit out a ship of 200. tunnes, and one of 100. tuns, if of the dry fish they both make fraught, that of 200. and goe for Spaine, sell it but at ten shillings a quintall, but commonly it gives fifteene or twenty, especially when it commeth first, which amounts to 3. or 4000. pound, but say but ten, which is the lowest, allowing the rest for waste, it amounts at that rate to 2000. which is the whole charge of your two ships and the equipage, then the returne of the mony and the fraught of the ship for the vintage or any other voyage is cleere gaine, with your ship of one hundred tunnes of traine Oile and Cor-fish, besides the Bevers and other commodities, and that you may have at home within six moneths if God please to send but an ordinary passage; then saving halfe this charge by the not staying of your ships, your victuall, overplus of men and wages, with her fraught thither with necessaries for the Planters, the Salt being there made, as also may the nets and lines within a short time;[49] if nothing may be expected but this, it might in time equalize your Hollanders gaines, if not exceede them, having their fraughts alwaies ready against the arrivall of the ships, this would so increase our shipping and sailers, and so incourage and imploy a great part of our Idlers and others that want imployment fitting their qualities at home, where they shame to doe that they would doe abroad, that could they but once taste the sweet fruits of their owne labours, doubtlesse many thousands would be advised by good discipline to take more pleasure in honest industry, then in their humors of dissolute idlenesse.

But to returne a little more to the particulars of this Countrey, which I intermingle thus with my projects and reasons, not being so sufficiently yet acquainted in those parts, to write fully the estate of the Sea, the Aire, the Land, the Fruits, the Rocks, the People, the Government, Religion, Territories, Limitations, Friends and Foes: But as I gathered from their niggardly relations in a broken language, during

48. *Iland* may refer to Iceland.
49. Smith's program hinged on having a colony in existence to prepare for the ships' arrival.

the time I ranged those Countries, etc. the most Northerne part I was at, was the Bay of Pennobscot, which is East and West, North and South, more then ten leagues: but such were my occasions, I was constrained to be satisfied of them I found in the Bay, that the River ranne farre up into the Land, and was well inhabited with many people, but they were from their habitations, either fishing amongst the Iles, or hunting the Lakes and Woods for Deere and Bevers: the Bay is full of great Iles of one, two, six or eight miles in length, which divides it into many faire and excellent good Harbours. On the East of it are the Tarrentines, their mortall enemies, where inhabit the French, as they report, that live with those people as one Nation or Family: And Northwest of Pennobscot is Mecaddacut, at the foot of a high Mountaine, a kinde of fortresse against the Tarrentines, adjoyning to the high Mountaines of Pennobscot, against whose feet doth beat the Sea; but over all the Land, Iles, or other impediments, you may well see them foureteene or eighteene leagues from their situation. Segocket is the next, then Nuskoncus, Pemmaquid, and Sagadahock: up this River, where was the Westerne Plantation, are Aumoughcawgen, Kinnebeke, and divers others, where are planted some Corne fields. Along this River thirtie or fortie miles, I saw nothing but great high clifts of barren Rocks overgrowne with Wood, but where the Salvages dwell there the ground is excellent fat, and fertill. Westward of this River is the Country of Aucocisco, in the bottome of a large deepe Bay, full of many great Iles, which divides it into many good Harbours. Sawocotuck is the next, in the edge of a large Sandy Bay, which hath many Rockes and Iles, but few good Harbours, but for Barkes I yet know; but all this Coast to Pennobscot, and as farre as I could see Eastward of it is nothing, but such high craggy clifty Rockes and stony Iles, that I wonder such great Trees could grow upon so hard foundations. It is a Countrey rather to affright then delight one, and how to describe a more plaine spectacle of desolation, or more barren, I know not, yet are those rocky Iles so furnished with good Woods, Springs, Fruits, Fish and Fowle, and the Sea the strangest Fish-pond I ever saw, that it makes me thinke, though the coast be rocky and thus affrightable, the Vallies and Plaines and interior parts may well notwithstanding be very fertill. But there is no Country so fertill hath not some part barren, and New-England is great enough to make many Kingdomes and Countries, were it all inhabited. As you passe the coast still westward, Accominticus and Passataquack are two convenient Harbours for small Barkes; and a good Country within their craggy clifts. Augoan is the next: this place might content a right curious judgement, but there are many sands at the entrance of the Harbour, and the worst is, it is imbayed too farre from the deepe Sea; here are many rising hils, and on their tops and descents are many corne fields and delightfull groves: On the East is an Ile of two or three leagues in length, the one halfe plaine marish ground, fit for pasture or salt Ponds, with many faire high groves of Mulbery trees and Gardens; there is also Okes, Pines, Walnuts, and other wood to make this place an excellent habitation, being a good and safe Harbour.

Naiemkeck, though it be more rocky ground, for Augoan is sandy, not much inferiour neither for the harbour, nor any thing I could perceive but the multitude of people: from hence doth stretch into the Sea the faire headland Tragabigzanda, now called Cape An, fronted with the three Iles wee called the three Turkes heads; to the north of this doth enter a great Bay, where we found some habitations and Corne fields, they report a faire River and at least 30. habitations doth possesse this Country. But because the French had got their trade, I had no leisure to discover it: the Iles of Mattahunts are on the west side of this Bay, where are many Iles and some Rocks that appeare a great height above the water like the Pyramides in Ægypt, and amongst them many good Harbours, and then the country of the Massachusits, which is the Paradice of all those parts, for here are many Iles planted with Corne, Groves, Mulberies, salvage Gardens and good Harbours, the Coast is for the most part high clayie sandy clifts, the sea Coast as you passe shewes you all along large Corne fields, and great troupes of well proportioned people: but the French having remained here neere six weekes, left nothing for us to take occasion to examine the Inhabitants relations, viz. if there be three thousand people upon those Iles, and that the River doth pierce many daies journey the entrailes of that Country: we found the people in those parts very kinde, but in their fury no lesse valiant, for upon a quarrell we fought with forty or fifty of them, till they had spent all their Arrowes, and then we tooke six or seven of their Canowes, which towards the evening they ransomed for Bever skinnes, and at Quonahasit falling out there but with one of them, he with three others crossed the Harbour in a Canow to certaine rockes whereby wee must passe, and there let flie their Arrowes for our shot, till we were out of danger, yet one of them was slaine, and another shot through his thigh.

Then come you to Accomacke an excellent good Harbour, good

land, and no want of any thing but industrious people: after much kindnesse, wee fought also with them, though some were hurt, some slaine, yet within an houre after they became friends. Cape Cod is the next presents it selfe, which is onely a headland of high hils, over-growne with shrubby Pines, hurts and such trash, but an excellent harbour for all weathers. This Cape is made by the maine Sea on the one side, and a great Bay on the other in forme of a Sickell, on it doth inhabit the people of Pawmet, and in the bottome of the Bay them of Chawum: towards the South and South-west of this Cape, is found a long and dangerous shoule of rocks and sand, but so farre as I in-cercled it, I found thirty fathome water and a strong currant, which makes mee thinke there is a chanell about this Shoule, where is the best and greatest fish to be had winter and summer in all the Country; but the Salvages say there is no Chanell, but that the Shoales beginne from the maine at Pawmet to the Ile of Nawset, and so extends beyond their knowledge into the Sea. The next to this is Capawucke, and those abounding Countries of Copper, Corne, People and Mineralls, which I went to discover this last yeere, but because I miscarried by the way I will leave them till God please I have better acquaintance with them.

The Massachusets they report sometimes have warres with the Bashabes of Pennobscot, and are not alwaies friends with them of Chawum and their alliance; but now they are all friends, and have each trade with other so farre as they have society on each others frontiers, for they make no such voyages as from Pennobscot to Cape Cod, seldome to Massachuset. In the North as I have said they have begun to plant Corne, whereof the south part hath such plenty as they have what they will from them of the North, and in the Winter much more plenty of fish and fowle, but both Winter and Summer hath it in one part or other all the yeere, being the meane and most indifferent tem-per betwixt heat and cold, of all the Regions betwixt the Line and the Pole, but the Furs Northward are much better, and in much more plenty then Southward.

The remarkablest Iles and Mountaines for land Markes are these: the highest Ile is Sorico in the Bay of Pennobscot, but the three Iles, and the Iles of Matinack are much further in the Sea: Metynacus is also three plaine Iles, but many great Rocks: Monahigan is a round high Ile, and close by it Monanis, betwixt which is a small Harbour where we rid; in Damerils Iles is such another, Sagadahocke is knowne by Satquin, and foure or five Iles in their mouth. Smiths Iles are a heape together, none neere them against Accomintycus: the three Turkes heads, are three Iles, seene farre to Sea-ward in regard of the Head-land. The chiefe Head-lands, are onely Cape Tragabigzanda, and Cape Cod, now called Cape James, and Cape Anne.

The chiefe Mountaines, them of Pennobscot, the twinkling Moun-taine of Acocisco, the great Mountaine of Sassanow, and the high Mountaine of Massachuset. Each of which you shall finde in the Map, their places, forme, and altitudes. The waters are most pure, proceed-ing from the intrailes of rocky Mountaines: the Herbs and Fruits are of many sorts and kinds, as Alkermes, Currans, Mulberies, Vines, Respises, Gooseberies, Plums, Wall-nuts, Chesse-nuts, Small-nuts, Pumpions, Gourds, Strawberies, Beanes, Pease, and Maize; a kinde or two of Flax, wherewith they make Nets, Lines, and Ropes, both small and great, very strong for their quantities.

Oake is the chiefe wood, of which there is great difference, in regard of the soyle where it groweth, Firre, Pine, Wall-nut, Chesse-nut, Birtch, Ash, Elme, Cipris, Cedar, Mulbery, Plum tree, Hazell, Saxe-fras, and many other sorts.

Eagles, Grips, divers sorts of Hawkes, Craines, Geese, Brants, Cor-morants, Ducks, Cranes, Swannes, Sheldrakes, Teale, Meawes, Gulls, Turkies, Dive-doppers, and many other sorts whose names I know not.[50]

Whales, Grompus, Porkpisces, Turbut, Sturgion, Cod, Hake, Had-docke, Cole, Cuske or small Ling, Sharke, Mackarell, Herring, Mullit, Base, Pinnacks, Cunners, Pearch, Eeles, Crabs, Lobsters, Mustels, Wilks, Oisters, Clamps, Periwinkels, and divers others, etc.

Moos, a beast bigger than a Stag, Deare red and fallow, Bevers, Wolves, Foxes both blacke and other, Aroughcunds, wilde Cats, Beares, Otters, Martins, Fitches, Musquassus, and divers other sorts of Vermin whose names I know not: all these and divers other good things doe here for want of use still increase and decrease with little diminution, whereby they grow to that abundance, you shall scarce finde any bay, shallow shore or Cove of sand, where you may not take many clamps or Lobsters, or both at your pleasure, and in many places load your Boat if you please, nor Iles where you finde not Fruits, Birds, Crabs, and Mustels, or all of them; for taking at a low water. Cod, Cuske, Hollibut, Scate, Turbut, Mackarell, or such like are taken

50. A grip(e) is a vulture, a brant is a small goose, and meawes are probably seagulls, the name being related to the sound they make. A dive-dopper is simply a diving bird.

plentifully in divers sandy Bayes, store of Mullit, Bases, and divers
other sorts of such excellent fish as many as their Net can hold: no
River where there is not plenty of Sturgion, or Salmon, or both, all
which are to be had in abundance observing but their seasons: but if a
man will goe at Christmas to gather Cherries in Kent, though there be
plenty in Summer, he may be deceived; so here these plenties have
each their seasons, as I have expressed; we for the most part had little
but bread and Vinegar, and though the most part of July when the
fishing decayed, they wrought all day, lay abroad in the Iles all night,
and lived on what they found, yet were not sicke: But I would wish
none long put himselfe to such plunges, except necessity constraine it:
yet worthy is that person to starve that here cannot live if he have
sense, strength and health, for there is no such penury of these blessings in any place but that one hundred men may in two or three
houres make their provisions for a day, and he that hath experience to
manage these affaires, with forty or thirty honest industrious men,
might well undertake (if they dwell in these parts) to subject the Salvages, and feed daily two or three hundred men, with as good Corne,
Fish, and Flesh as the earth hath of those kinds, and yet make that
labour but their pleasure: provided that they have Engines that be
proper for their purposes.[51] [*Generall Historie:* II, 407–420]

51. *Engin*, meaning "native wit or ingenuity," was applied to mechanical contri-
vances that were seen as expressions of such wit.

PART FIVE

THE FUTURE OF

COLONIZATION

John Smith's conception of colonization changed over the years, and he presented his developing program forcefully through his writings. Jamestown was founded by a joint-stock company that sold shares. It was a money-making venture, though with royal support, and in the early years everyone in the colony worked for the company. Captain Smith saw the flaw in such a plan earlier than most. The Virginia Company made one change after another, attempting to shore up the experiment while maintaining its essential character as an investment for gentlemen and a recourse for the very poor.

Smith began to pitch his writings at another level altogether. He appealed to the merchants who were used to organizing large enterprises efficiently and to the middling sort who wanted to set up on their own with land and security denied them in England. The problem was that establishing colonies required a large initial investment, which though it would be repaid, had to be made in a disinterested way in the beginning. Also, every colonist had to be staked, so Smith hoped that fathers would send their sons and villages their poor. If the nation and its people were to benefit, those with money must part with some now to gain great rewards in future. The payoff would come in the form of a thriving commonwealth of smallholders all working hard because they worked for their own families. Through such commitment would come the wealth and security of England. John Smith, despite his admiration for the Spanish example, was the first to argue that the promise of America was a bourgeois society.

I

In his writings on New England, John Smith first began to work out his model for the colonies. He saw it as the culmination of long historical development.

WHO CAN DESIRE more content, that hath small meanes; or but only his merit to advance his fortune, then to tread, and plant that ground hee hath purchased by the hazard of his life? If he have but the taste of virtue, and magnanimitie,[1] what to such a minde can bee more pleasant, then planting and building a foundation for his Posteritie, gotte from the rude earth, by Gods blessing and his owne industrie, without prejudice to any?[2] If hee have any graine of faith or zeale in Religion, what can hee doe lesse hurtfull to any; or more agreeable to God, then to seeke to convert those poore Salvages to know Christ, and humanitie, whose labors with discretion will triple requite thy charge and paines? What so truely sutes with honour and honestie, as the discovering things unknowne? erecting Townes, peopling Countries, informing the ignorant, reforming things unjust, teaching virtue; and gaine to our Native mother-countrie a kingdom to attend her; finde imployment for those that are idle, because they know not what to doe: so farre from wronging any, as to cause Posteritie to remember thee; and remembring thee, ever honour that remembrance with praise? Consider: What were the beginnings and endings of the Monarkies of the Chaldeans, the Syrians, the Grecians,

---

1. *Magnanimity* here means "loftiness of purpose, noble spirit."
2. "Without prejudice to any": Large-scale English settlement would, of course, be very detrimental to Indian life, especially if combined with some form of servitude as Smith seems to envision here. Ironically, the establishment of peaceful agricultural communities, because they competed more thoroughly for land and resources, did more harm to the Indian way of life than military outposts such as Jamestown for all their swaggering demands to be fed. Smith implicitly argues that the gift of Christianity would compensate the Indians for any expropriation. Slavery as it later evolved was unknown in the English colonies at this time, so there is no reason to assume that that is what Smith intended for the Indians. Servitude was an intermediate state between childhood and adulthood through which virtually all English people passed, so Smith may have had some analogous progression in mind. It was generally expected that the Indians would eventually take up a European style of life.

and Romanes, but this one rule; What was it they would not doe, for the good of the commonwealth, or their Mother-citie? For example: Rome, What made her such a Monarchesse, but onely the adventures of her youth, not in riots at home; but in dangers abroade? and the justice and judgement out of their experience, when they grewe aged. What was their ruine and hurt, but this; The excesse of idlenesse, the fondnesse of Parents, the want of experience in Magistrates, the admiration of their undeserved honours, the contempt of true merit, their unjust jealosies, their politicke incredulities, their hypocriticall seeming goodnesse, and their deeds of secret lewdnesse? finally, in fine, growing onely formall temporists, all that their predecessors got in many years, they lost in few daies.[3] Those by their pains and vertues became Lords of the world; they by their ease and vices became slaves to their servants. This is the difference betwixt the use of Armes in the field, and on the monuments of stones; the golden age and the leaden age, prosperity and miserie, justice and corruption, substance and shadowes, words and deeds, experience and imagination, making Commonwealths and marring Commonwealths, the fruits of vertue and the conclusions of vice.

Then, who would live at home idly (or thinke in himselfe any worth to live) onely to eate, drink, and sleepe, and so die? Or by consuming that carelesly, his friends got worthily? Or by using that miserably, that maintained vertue honestly? Or, for being descended nobly, pine with the vaine vaunt of great kindred, in penurie? Or (to maintaine a silly shewe of bravery) toyle out thy heart, soule, and time, basely, by shifts, tricks, cards, and dice? Or by relating newes of others actions, sharke here or there for a dinner, or supper;[4] deceive thy friends, by faire promises, and dissimulation, in borrowing where thou never intendest to pay; offend the lawes, surfeit with excesse, burden thy Country, abuse thy selfe, despaire in want, and then couzen thy kindred, yea even thine owne brother, and wish thy parents death (I will not say damnation) to have their estates? though thou seest what honours, and rewards, the world yet hath for them will seeke them and worthily deserve them.

I would be sory to offend, or that any should mistake my honest

3. A temporist is a time server; *formal* refers to preoccupation with outward forms while ignoring the real substance.
4. Shifts are expedients; to shark is to sponge, to live as a parasite.

meaning: for I wish good to all, hurt to none. But rich men for the most part are growne to that dotage, through their pride in their wealth, as though there were no accident could end it, or their life. And what hellish care do such take to make it their owne miserie, and their Countries spoile, especially when there is most neede of their imployment? drawing by all manner of inventions, from the Prince and his honest subjects, even the vitall spirits of their powers and estates: as if their Bagges,[5] or Bragges, were so powerfull a defence, the malicious could not assault them; when they are the onely baite, to cause us not to be onely assaulted; but betrayed and murdered in our owne security, ere we well perceive it.

May not the miserable ruine of Constantinople, their impregnable walles, riches, and pleasures last taken by the Turke (which are but a bit, in comparison of their now mightines) remember us,[6] of the effects of private covetousness? at which time the good Emperour held himselfe rich enough, to have such rich subjects, so formall in all excesse of vanity, all kinde of delicacie, and prodigalitie. His povertie when the Turke besieged, the citizens (whose marchandizing thoughts were onely to get wealth, little conceiving the desperate resolution of a valiant expert enemy) left the Emperour so long to his conclusions,[7] having spent all he had to pay his young, raw, discontented Souldiers; that sodainly he, they, and their citie were all a prey to the devouring Turke. And what they would not spare for the maintenance of them who adventured their lives to defend them, did serve onely their enemies to torment them, their friends, and countrey, and all Christendome to this present day. Let this lamentable example remember you that are rich (seeing there are such great theeves in the world to robbe you) not grudge to lend some proportion, to breed them that have little, yet willing to learne how to defend you: for, it is too late when the deede is a-doing. The Romanes estate hath beene worse then this: for, the meere covetousnesse and extortion of a few of them, so mooved the rest, that not having any imployment, but contemplation; their great judgements grew to so great malice, as themselves were sufficient to destroy themselves by faction: Let this moove you to embrace imployment, for those whose educations, spirits, and judge-

5. Bags of money.
6. "Remember us": Remind us.
7. *Conclusions* means "results."

ments, want but your purses; not onely to prevent such accustomed dangers, but also to gaine more thereby then you have. And you fathers that are either so foolishly fond, or so miserably covetous, or so willfully ignorant, or so negligently carelesse, as that you will rather maintaine your children in idle wantonness, till they growe your masters; or become so basely unkinde, as they wish nothing but your deaths; so that both sorts growe dissolute: and although you would wish them any where to escape the gallowes, and ease your cares; though they spend you here one, two, or three hundred pound a yeer; you would grudge to give halfe so much in adventure with them, to obtaine an estate, which in a small time but with a little assistance of your providence, might bee better then your owne. But if an Angell should tell you, that any place yet unknowne can afford such fortunes; you would not beleeve him, no more then Columbus was beleeved there was any such Land as is now the well knowne abounding America; much lesse such large Regions as are yet unknowne, as well in America, as in Affrica, and Asia, and Terra incognita; where were courses for gentlemen (and them that would be so reputed) more suiting their qualities, then begging from their Princes generous disposition, the labours of his subjects, and the very marrow of his maintenance.

I have not beene so ill bred, but I have tasted of Plenty and Pleasure, as well as Want and Miserie: nor doth necessity yet, or occasion of discontent, force me to these endeavors: nor am I ignorant what small thanke I shall have for my paines; or that many would have the Worlde imagine them to be of great judgement, that can but blemish these my designes, by their witty objections and detractions: yet (I hope) my reasons with my deeds, will so prevaile with some, that I shall not want imployment in these affaires, to make the most blinde see his owne senselesnesse, and incredulity; Hoping that gaine will make them affect that, which Religion, Charity, and the Common good cannot. It were but a poore device in me, To deceive my selfe; much more the King, and State, my Friends, and Countrey, with these inducements: which, seeing his Majestie hath given permission, I wish all sorts of worthie, honest, industrious spirits, would understand: and if they desire any further satisfaction, I will doe my best to give it: Not to perswade them to goe onely; but goe with them: Not leave them there; but live with them there. I will not say, but by ill providing and undue managing, such courses may be taken, may make us miserable enough: But if I may have the execution of what I have projected; if they want to eate, let them eate or never digest Me.[8] If I performe what I say, I desire but that reward out of the gaines may sute my paines, quality, and condition. And if I abuse you with my tongue, take my head for satisfaction. If any dislike at the yeares end, defraying their charge, by my consent they should freely returne. I feare not want of companie sufficient, were it but knowne what I know of those Countries; and by the proofe of that wealth I hope yearely to returne, if God please to blesse me from such accidents, as are beyond my power in reason to prevent: For, I am not so simple, to thinke, that ever any other motive then wealth, will ever erect there a Common-weale; or draw companie from their ease and humours at home, to stay in New England to effect my purposes. And lest any should thinke the toile might be insupportable, though these things may be had by labour, and diligence: I assure my selfe there are who delight extreamly in vaine pleasure, that take much more paines in England, to enjoy it, then I should doe heere to gaine wealth sufficient: and yet I thinke they should not have halfe such sweet content: for, our pleasure here is still gaines; in England charges and losse. Heer nature and liberty affords us that freely, which in England we want, or it costeth us dearely. What pleasure can be more, then (being tired with any occasion a-shore) in planting Vines, Fruits, or Hearbs, in contriving their owne Grounds, to the pleasure of their owne mindes, their Fields, Gardens, Orchards, Buildings, Ships, and other works, etc. to recreate themselves before their owne doores, in their owne boates upon the Sea, where man woman and childe, with a small hooke and line, by angling, may take diverse sorts of excellent fish, at their pleasures? And is it not pretty sport, to pull up two pence, six pence, and twelve pence, as fast as you can hale and veare a line?[9] He is a very bad fisher, cannot kill in one day with his hooke and line, one, two, or three hundred Cods: which dressed and dryed, if they be sould there for ten shillings the hundred, though in England they will give more then twentie; may not both the servant, the master, and marchant, be well content with this gaine? If a man worke but three dayes in seaven, he may get more then hee can spend, unlesse he will be excessive. Now that Carpenter, Mason, Gardiner, Taylor, Smith, Sailer, Forgers, or

---

8. *Digest* means, in addition to the modern sense, "to consider, learn from, and to bear or put up with."
9. To haul and veer (hale and veare) is to make a line taut by alternately paying out and rewinding.

what other, may they not make this a pretty recreation though they fish but an houre in a day, to take more then they eate in a weeke: or if they will not eate it, because there is so much better choise; yet sell it, or change it, with the fisher men, or marchants, for any thing they want. And what sport doth yeeld a more pleasing content, and lesse hurt or charge then angling with a hooke, and crossing the sweete ayre from Ile to Ile, over the silent streames of a calme Sea? wherein the most curious may finde pleasure, profit, and content. Thus, though all men be not fishers: yet all men, whatsoever, may in other matters doe as well. For necessity doth in these cases so rule a Commonwealth, and each in their severall functions, as their labours in their qualities may be as profitable, because there is a necessary mutuall use of all.

For Gentlemen, what exercise should more delight them, then ranging dayly those unknowne parts, using fowling and fishing, for hunting and hauking? and yet you shall see the wilde haukes give you some pleasure, in seeing them stoope (six or seaven after one another) an houre or two together, at the skuls of fish in the faire harbours, as those a-shore at a foule; and never trouble nor torment your selves, with watching, mewing, feeding, and attending them:[10] nor kill horse and man with running and crying, See you not a hauk? For hunting also: the woods, lakes, and rivers, affoord not onely chase sufficient, for any that delights in that kinde of toyle, or pleasure; but such beasts to hunt, that besides the delicacy of their bodies for food, their skins are so rich, as may well recompence thy dayly labour, with a Captains pay.

For labourers, if those that sowe hemp, rape, turnups, parsnips, carrats, cabidge, and such like; give 20, 30, 40, 50 shillings yearely for an acre of ground, and meat drinke and wages to use it, and yet grow rich: when better, or at least as good ground, may be had and cost nothing but labour; it seemes strange to me, any such should there grow poore.

My purpose is not to perswade children from their parents; men from their wives; nor servants from their masters: onely, such as with free consent may be spared: But that each parish, or village, in Citie, or Countrey, that will but apparell their fatherlesse children, of thirteene or fourteene years of age, or young maried people, that have small wealth to live on; heere by their labour may live exceeding well: pro-

---

10. *Stoop* means "swoop" and skuls are schools of fish. *Mewing* refers to the molting of hawks, and also to caging birds, particularly at the time of molting.

vided alwaies that first there bee a sufficient power to command them, houses to receive them, meanes to defend them, and meet provisions for them; for, any place may bee overlain:[11] and it is most necessarie to have a fortresse (ere this grow to practice) and sufficient masters (as, Carpenters, Masons, Fishers, Fowlers, Gardiners, Husbandmen, Sawyers, Smiths, Spinsters, Taylors, Weavers, and such like) to take ten, twelve, or twentie, or as ther is occasion, for Apprentises. The Masters by this may quicklie growe rich; these may learne their trades themselves, to doe the like; to a generall and an incredible benefit, for King, and Countrey, Master, and Servant.

It would bee an historie of a large volume, to recite the adventures of the Spanyards, and Portugals, their affronts, and defeats, their dangers and miseries; which with such incomparable honour and constant resolution, so farre beyond beleefe, they have attempted and indured in their discoveries and plantations, as may well condemne us, of too much imbecillitie, sloth, and negligence: yet the Authors of those new inventions, were held as ridiculous, for a long time, as now are others, that doe but seek to imitate their unparalleled vertues. And though we see daily their mountaines of wealth (sprong from the plants of their generous indevours) yet is our sensualitie and untowardnesse such, and so great, that wee either ignorantly beleeve nothing; or so curiously contest, to prevent wee knowe not what future events;[12] that wee either so neglect, or opresse and discourage the present, as wee spoile all in the making, crop all in the blooming; and building upon faire sand, rather then rough rockes, judge that wee knowe not, governe that wee have not, feare that which is not; and for feare some should doe too well, force such against their willes to be idle or as ill. And who is he hath judgement, courage, and any industrie or qualitie with understanding, will leave his Countrie, his hopes at home, his certaine estate, his friends, pleasures, libertie, and the preferment sweete England doth afford to all degrees, were it not to advance his fortunes by injoying his deserts? whose prosperitie once appearing, will incourage others: but it must be cherished as a childe, till it be able to goe, and understand it selfe; and not corrected, nor oppressed above its strength, ere it knowe wherefore. A child can neither performe the

11. To overlay is to encumber with too many people, to suffocate.
12. *Curiously* here means "elaborately, intricately." Smith seems to be ridiculing those who, despite the evident wealth of Spain, spend their time spinning objections or dangers.

office, nor deedes of a man of strength, nor indure that affliction He is able; nor can an Apprentice at the first performe the part of a Maister. And if twentie yeeres bee required to make a child a man, seven yeares limited an apprentice for his trade: if scarce an age be sufficient to make a wise man a States man; and commonly, a man dies ere he hath learned to be discreet: If perfection be so hard to be obtained, as of necessitie there must bee practice, as well as theorick: Let no man much condemne this paradox opinion, to say, that halfe seaven yeeres is scarce sufficient, for a good capacitie, to learne in these affaires, how to carrie himselfe: and who ever shall trie in these remote places the erecting of a Colony, shall finde at the ende of seaven yeares occasion enough to use all his discretion: and, in the Interim all the content, rewards, gaines, and hopes will be necessarily required, to be given to the beginning, till it bee able to creepe, to stand, and goe, yet time enough to keepe it from running, for there is no feare it wil grow too fast, or ever to any thing; except libertie, profit, honor, and prosperitie there found, more binde the planters of those affaires, in devotion to effect it; then bondage, violence, tyranny, ingratitude, and such double dealing, as bindes free men to become slaves, and honest men turne knaves: which hath ever bin the ruine of the most popular common-weales; and is verie unlikelie ever well to begin in a new.

Who seeth not what is the greatest good of the Spanyard, but these new conclusions, in searching those unknowne parts of this unknowne world? By which meanes hee dives even into the verie secrets of all his Neighbours, and the most part of the world: and when the Portugale and Spanyard had found the East and West Indies; how many did condemn themselves, that did not accept of that honest offer of Noble Columbus?[13] who, upon our neglect, brought them to it, perswading our selves the world had no such places as they had found: and yet ever since wee finde, they still (from time to time) have found new Lands, new Nations, and trades, and still daily dooe finde both in Asia, Africa, Terra incognita, and America; so that there is neither Soldier nor

---

13. In 1489 Bartholomew Columbus, brother of Christopher, was in England in search of backing for a voyage to the East by way of the West. Henry VII, who was at first receptive, rejected the notion after a committee had studied it. English experts knew that Asia was 10,000 or even 12,000 miles away. Those who urged the colonization of North America often pointed to the wealth Spain had derived from its American possessions and lamented the supposed shortsightedness of the English.

Mechanick, from the Lord to the begger, but those parts afforde them all imploiment; and discharge their Native soile, of so many thousands of all sorts, that else, by their sloth, pride, and imperfections, would long ere this have troubled their neighbours, or have eaten the pride of Spaine it selfe.

Now he knowes little, that knowes not England may well spare many more people then Spaine, and is as well able to furnish them with all manner of necessaries. And seeing, for all they have, they cease not still to search for that they have not, and know not; It is strange we should be so dull, as not maintaine that which wee have, and pursue that wee knowe. Surely I am sure many would taste it ill, to bee abridged of the titles and honours of their predecessors: when if but truely they would judge themselves; looke how inferior they are to their noble vertues, so much they are unworthy of their honours and livings: which never were ordained for showes and shadowes, to maintaine idlenesse and vice; but to make them more able to abound in honor, by heroycall deeds of action, judgement, pietie, and vertue. What was it, They would not doe both in purse and person, for the good of the Commonwealth? which might move them presently to set out their spare kindred in these generous designes. Religion, above all things, should move us (especially the Clergie) if wee were religious, to shewe our faith by our workes; in converting those poore salvages, to the knowledge of God, seeing what paines the Spanyards take to bring them to their adulterated faith.[14] Honor might move the Gentrie, the valiant, and industrious; and the hope and assurance of wealth, all; if wee were that we would seeme, and be accounted. Or be we so far inferior to other nations, or our spirits so far dejected, from our auncient predecessors, or our mindes so upon spoile, piracie, and such villany, as to serve the Portugall, Spanyard, Dutch, French, or Turke (as to the cost of Europe, too many dooe) rather then our God, our King, our Country, and our selves? excusing our idlenesse, and our base complaints, by want of imploiment; when heere is such choise of all sorts, and for all degrees, in the planting and discovering these North parts of America. [*Description of New England:* I, 343–350]

14. England saw its Protestant religion as a return to a purer form of Christianity, whereas Roman Catholicism had been "adulterated" by accretions throughout the Middle Ages.

In the course of his Description of New England, *Captain Smith returned to a subject that burned within him: his unique qualifications to write on colonization. The hardest part was to get his readers to see that not all "expertise" was equal; he particularly wanted to distinguish between experience in the field and learning that came from academic exercises.*

A ND T H O U G H I know my selfe the meanest of many thousands, whose apprehensive inspection can pearce beyond the boundes of my habilities, into the hidden things of Nature, Art, and Reason:[15] yet I intreate such give me leave to excuse my selfe of so much imbecillitie, as to say, that in these eight yeares which I have been conversant with these affairs, I have not learned there is a great difference, betwixt the directions and judgement of experimentall knowledge, and the superficiall conjecture of variable relation: wherein rumor, humor, or misprision have such power, that oft times one is enough to beguile twentie, but twentie not sufficient to keep one from being deceived.[16] Therefore I know no reason but to beleeve my own eies, before any mans imagination, that is but wrested from the conceits of my owne projects, and indeavours. But I honor, with all affection, the counsell and instructions of judiciall directions, or any other honest advertisement; so farre to observe, as they tie mee not to the crueltie of unknowne events. [*Description of New England:* I, 351–352]

II

Despite the eloquence of Smith's appeal, the fact remained that at the time he wrote no colonial investor had seen a return on that investment except through subsidiary activities such as privateering. If merchants were to invest and ordinary men and women were to put their lives into these ventures, then Smith must have something more solid than promises and hopes to show them. Because he could not get solid backing, Smith was unable to go to

15. *Apprehensive* refers to quickness of comprehension. *Habilities* may be simply an early spelling of *abilities*, but it also may carry with it overtones of competence specifically to *do*, to *act*.
16. *Misprision* means "misunderstanding," particularly the failure to recognize something as valuable and important.

America and build the kind of industries there that he knew were possible,
but he did what he could do: he answered each of the criticisms squarely and
fully. As time passed, he was more forthright about placing the blame for
past failures.

One reason for the backwardness of the English colonies, Smith argued,
was the primitive nature of the land when they arrived.

I T WA S the Spanyards good hap to happen in those parts where
were infinite numbers of people, who had manured the ground
with that providence, it affoorded victualls at all times.[17] And time had
brought them to that perfection, they had the use of gold and silver,
and the most of such commodities as those Countries affoorded: so
that, what the Spanyard got was chiefly the spoyle and pillage of
those Countrey people, and not the labours of their owne hands. But
had those fruitfull Countries beene as salvage, as barbarous, as ill peopled, as little planted, laboured, and manured, as Virginia: their
proper labours it is likely would have produced as small profit as ours.
But had Virginia beene peopled, planted, manured, and adorned with
such store of precious Jewels, and rich commodities as was the Indies:
then had we not gotten and done as much as by their examples might
be expected from us, the world might then have traduced us and our
merits, and have made shame and infamy our recompence and
reward.[18]

But we chanced in a Land even as God made it, where we found
onely an idle, improvident, scattered people, ignorant of the knowledge of gold or silver, or any commodities, and carelesse of any thing
but from hand to mouth, except bables of no worth;[19] nothing to
incourage us, but what accidentally we found Nature afforded. Which
ere we could bring to recompence our paines, defray our charges, and
satisfie our Adventurers; we were to discover the Countrey, subdue the
people, bring them to be tractable, civill, and industrious, and teach
them trades, that the fruits of their labours might make us some
recompence, or plant such Colonies of our owne, that must first make
provision how to live of themselves, ere they can bring to perfection

17. *Manured* simply means "cultivated."
18. *Traduced* means "slandered or blamed."
19. *Bables* for *baubles*. Smith here prefers to forget the hard bargaining with Powhatan in Virginia and the latter's care to conserve sufficient corn for his people.

the commodities of the Country: which doubtlesse will be as commodious for England as the west Indies for Spaine, if it be rightly mannaged: notwithstanding all our home-bred opinions, that will argue the contrary, as formerly some have done against the Spanyards and Portugalls. But to conclude, against all rumor of opinion, I onely say this, for those that the three first yeares began this Plantation; notwithstanding all their factions, mutinies, and miseries, so gently corrected, and well prevented: peruse the Spanish Decades; the Relations of Master Hackluit, and tell me how many ever with such small meanes as a Barge of 2 tuns, sometimes with seaven, eight, or nine, or but at most, twelve or sixteene men, did ever discover so many fayre and navigable Rivers, subject so many severall Kings, people, and Nations, to obedience, and contribution, with so little bloudshed.

And if in the search of those Countries we had hapned where wealth had beene, we had as surely had it as obedience and contribution, but if we have overskipped it, we will not envie them that shall find it: yet can we not but lament, it was our fortunes to end when we had but onely learned how to begin, and found the right course how to proceed. [*Generall Historie:* II, 206–207]

The Virginia Company was under investigation by a royal commission in 1624; the government was alarmed by the reported large number of deaths among colonists (approaching three out of every four colonists), by the Indian attack in 1622, and by the planters' absorption in tobacco cultivation even to the exclusion of subsistence crops. Tobacco was making some settlers rich, but it was hardly the kind of product that would make England great as Smith had promised. Captain Smith sent the commission a report setting the record straight on his time in the colony, and then answered its specific questions; he published his report and the questions and answers in his Generall Historie.

A briefe relation written by Captaine Smith to his Majesties Commissioners for the reformation of Virginia, concerning some aspersions against it.

HONOURABLE GENTLEMEN, for so many faire and Navigable Rivers so neere adjoyning, and piercing thorow so faire a naturall Land, free from any inundations, or large Fenny unwholsome Marshes, I have not seene, read, nor heard of: And for the building of Cities, Townes, and Wharfage, if they will use the meanes, where there is no more ebbe nor floud, Nature in few places affoords any so convenient. For salt Marshes or Quagmires, in this tract of James Towne River I know very few; some small Marshes and Swamps there are, but more profitable then hurtfull: and I thinke there is more low Marsh ground betwixt Eriffe and Chelsey, then Kecoughton and the Falls, which is about one hundred and eighty miles by the course of the River.

Being enjoyned by our Commission not to unplant nor wrong the Salvages, because the channell was so neere the shore, where now is James Towne, then a thicke grove of trees; wee cut them downe, where the Salvages pretending as much kindnesse as could bee, they hurt and slew one and twenty of us in two houres: At this time our diet was for most part water and bran, and three ounces of little better stuffe in bread for five men a meale, and thus we lived neere three moneths: our lodgings under boughes of trees, the Salvages being our enemies, whom we neither knew nor understood; occasions I thinke sufficient to make men sicke and die.

Necessity thus did inforce me with eight or nine, to try conclusions amongst the Salvages, that we got provision which recovered the rest being most sicke. Six weeks I was led captive by those Barbarians, though some of my men were slaine, and the rest fled, yet it pleased God to make their great Kings daughter the means to returne me safe to James towne, and releeve our wants, and then our Common-wealth was in all eight and thirty, the remainder of one hundred and five.

Being supplied with one hundred and twenty, with twelve men in a boat of three tuns, I spent foureteene weeks in those large waters;[20] the contents of the way of my boat protracted by the skale of propor-

20. "Being supplied with one hundred and twenty" refers to the new supply of settlers sent to the colony; Smith, as he says, took 12 with him exploring.

tion, was about three thousand miles,[21] besides the River we dwell upon, where no Christian knowne ever was, and our diet for the most part what we could finde, yet but one died.

The Salvages being acquainted, that by command from England we durst not hurt them, were much imboldned; that famine and their insolencies did force me to breake our Commission and instructions, cause Powhatan fly his Countrey, and take the King of Pamaunke Prisoner; and also to keepe the King of Paspahegh in shackels, and put his men to double taskes in chaines, till nine and thirty of their Kings paied us contribution, and the offending Salvages sent to James towne to punish at our owne discretions: in the two last yeares I staied there, I had not a man slaine.

All those conclusions being not able to prevent the bad events of pride and idlenesse,[22] having received another supply of seventie, we were about two hundred in all, but not twentie work-men: In following the strict directions from England to doe that was impossible at that time; So it hapned, that neither wee nor they had any thing to eat, but what the Countrey afforded naturally; yet of eightie who lived upon Oysters in June and July, with a pint of corne a week for a man lying under trees, and 120 for the most part living upon Sturgion, which was dried til we pounded it to powder for meale, yet in ten weeks but seven died.

It is true, we had of Tooles, Armes, and Munition sufficient, some Aquavitæ, Vineger, Meale, Pease, and Otemeale, but in two yeares and a halfe not sufficient for six moneths, though by the bils of loading the proportions sent us, would well have contented us,[23] notwithstanding we sent home ample proofes of Pitch, Tar, Sope Ashes, Wainskot, Clapboord, Silke grasse, Iron Ore, some Sturgion and Glasse, Saxefras, Cedar, Cypris, and blacke Walnut, crowned Powhaton, sought the Monacans Countrey, according to the instructions sent us, but they caused us neglect more necessary workes: they had better have given for Pitch and Sope ashes one hundred pound a tun in Denmarke: Wee also maintained five or six severall Plantations.

21. "The contents of the way of my boat . . . about three thousand miles": Smith refers to the total mileage of his exploring expeditions, but his measurements were off, causing him to exaggerate by one third to one half again.
22. *Events* means "consequences."
23. Smith's implication is that someone along the way cheated both the Virginia Company and the settlers, because the bill of lading did not match the supplies actually received.

James towne being burnt, wee rebuilt it and three Forts more, besides the Church and Store-house, we had about fortie or fiftie severall houses to keepe us warme and dry, invironed with a palizado of foureteene or fifteene foot, and each as much as three or foure men could carrie. We digged a faire Well of fresh water in the Fort, where wee had three Bulwarks, foure and twentie peece of Ordnance, of Culvering, Demiculvering, Sacar and Falcon, and most well mounted upon convenient plat-formes, planted one hundred acres of Corne. We had but six ships to transport and supply us, and but two hundred seventy seven men, boies, and women, by whose labours Virginia being brought to this kinde of perfection, the most difficulties past, and the foundation thus laid by this small meanes; yet because we had done no more, they called in our Commission, tooke a new in their owne names, and appointed us neere as many offices and Officers as I had Souldiers, that neither knew us nor wee them, without our consents or knowledge; since there have gone more then one hundred ships of other proportions, and eight or ten thousand people. Now if you please to compare what hath beene spent, sent, discovered and done this fifteene yeares, by that we did in the three first yeares, and every Governor that hath beene there since, give you but such an account as this, you may easily finde what hath beene the cause of those disasters in Virginia.

Then came in Captaine Argall, and Master Sedan, in a ship of Master Cornelius, to fish for Sturgion, who had such good provision, we contracted with them for it, whereby we were better furnished then ever.

Not long after came in seven ships, with about three hundred people; but rather to supplant us then supply us, their Admirall with their authoritie being cast away in the Bermudas, very angry they were we had made no better provision for them. Seven or eight weekes we withstood the inundations of these disorderly humors, till I was neere blowne to death with Gun-powder, which occasioned me to returne for England.

In the yeare 1609 about Michaelmas, I left the Countrey, as is formerly related, with three ships, seven Boats, Commodities to trade, harvest newly gathered, eight weeks provision of Corne and Meale, about five hundred persons, three hundred Muskets, shot, powder, and match, with armes for more men then we had. The Salvages their language and habitation, well knowne to two hundred expert Souldiers; Nets for fishing, tooles of all sorts, apparell to supply their wants: six Mares and a Horse, five or six hundred Swine, many more Powltry, what was brought or bred, but victuall there remained.

Having spent some five yeares, and more then five hundred pounds in procuring the Letters Patents and setting forward, and neere as much more about New England, etc. Thus these nineteene yeares I have here and there not spared any thing according to my abilitie, nor the best advice I could, to perswade how those strange miracles of misery might have beene prevented, which lamentable experience plainly taught me of necessity must insue, but few would beleeve me till now too deerely they have paid for it. Wherefore hitherto I have rather left all then undertake impossibilities, or any more such costly taskes at such chargeable rates: for in neither of those two Countries have I one foot of Land, nor the very house I builded, nor the ground I digged with my owne hands, nor ever any content or satisfaction at all, and though I see ordinarily those two Countries shared before me by them that neither have them nor knowes them, but by my descriptions: Yet that doth not so much trouble me, as to heare and see those contentions and divisions which will hazard if not ruine the prosperitie of Virginia, if present remedy bee not found, as they have hindred many hundreds, who would have beene there ere now, and makes them yet that are willing to stand in a demurre.

For the Books and Maps I have made, I will thanke him that will shew me so much for so little recompence, and beare with their errors till I have done better. For the materials in them I cannot deny, but am ready to affirme them both there and here, upon such grounds as I have propounded, which is to have but one hundred fifty men to subdue againe the Salvages, fortifie the Countrey, discover that yet unknowne, and both defend and feed their Colony, which I most humbly refer to his Majesties most judiciall judgement, and the most honourable Lords of his Privy Councell, you his trusty and well-beloved Commissioners, and the Honourable company of Planters and well-willers to Virginia, New-England and Sommer-Ilands.

Out of these Observations it pleased his Majesties Commissioners for the reformation of Virginia, to desire my answer to these seven Questions.

Question 1. What conceive you is the cause the Plantation hath prospered no better since you left it in so good a forwardnesse?

Answer. Idlenesse and carelesnesse brought all I did in three yeeres in six moneths to nothing, and of five hundred I left, scarce threescore remained, and had Sir Thomas Gates not got from the Bermudas, I thinke they had beene all dead before they could be supplied.

Question 2. What conceive you should be the cause, though the Country be good, there comes nothing but Tobacco?

Answer. The oft altering of Governours it seemes causes every man make use of his time, and because Corne was stinted at two shillings six pence the bushell,[24] and Tobacco at three shillings the pound, and they value a mans labour a yeere worth fifty or three-score pound, but in Corne not worth ten pound, presuming Tobacco will furnish them with all things; now make a mans labour in Corne worth threescore pound, and in Tobacco but ten pound a man, then shall they have Corne sufficient to entertaine all commers, and keepe their people in health to doe any thing, but till then, there will be little or nothing to any purpose.

Question 3. What conceive you to have beene the cause of the Massacre, and had the Salvages had the use of any peeces in your time, or when, or by whom they were taught?

Answer. The cause of the Massacre was the want of marshall discipline, and because they would have all the English had by destroying those they found so carelesly secure, that they were not provided to defend themselves against any enemy, being so dispersed as they were.[25] In my time, though Captaine Nuport furnished them with swords by truck, and many fugitives did the like, and some Peeces they got accidentally, yet I got the most of them againe, and it was death to him that should shew a Salvage the use of a Peece. Since I understand they became so good shot, they were imployed for Fowlers and Huntsmen by the English.

Question 4. What charge thinke you would have setled the government both for defence and planting when you left it?

Answer. Twenty thousand pound would have hyred good labourers and mechanicall men, and have furnished them with cattle and

24. *Stinted* means that the price of corn was restricted to 2s 6d.
25. Pieces are guns, *marshall* is for *martial*, and *carelessly secure* means "overconfident of their own safety."

all necessaries, and 100. of them would have done more then a thousand of those that went, though the Lord Laware, Sir Ferdinando Waynman, Sir Thomas Gates and Sir Thomas Dale were perswaded to the contrary, but when they had tried, they confessed their error.

Question 5. What conceive you would be the remedy and the charge?

Answer. The remedy is to send Souldiers and all sorts of labourers and necessaries for them, that they may be there by next Michaelmas,[26] the which to doe well will stand you in five thousand pound, but if his Majesty would please to lend two of his Ships to transport them, lesse would serve, besides the benefit of his grace to the action would encourage all men.

Question 6. What thinke you are the defects of the government both here and there?

Answer. The multiplicity of opinions here, and Officers there, makes such delaies by questions and formalitie, that as much time is spent in complement as in action;[27] besides, some are so desirous to imploy their ships, having six pounds for every Passenger, and three pounds for every tun of goods, at which rate a thousand ships may now better be procured then one at the first, when the common stocke defrayed all fraughts, wages, provisions and Magazines, whereby the Ships are so pestred, as occasions much sicknesse, diseases and mortality, for though all the Passengers die they are sure of their fraught;[28] and then all must be satisfied with Orations, disputations, excuses and hopes. As for the letters of advice from hence, and their answers thence, they are so well written, men would beleeve there were no great doubt of the performance, and that all things were wel, to which error here

26. Michaelmas was at the end of September. Those with experience of Virginia favored such a time for arrival because it was after the summer sickly season but with time for adjustment before winter. *Grace* here means that if the king was seen to favor renewed commitment to the colony, others would be encouraged.

27. "Complement": Smith means that time was wasted in ceremony and displays of courtesy.

28. "The Ships are so pestred": Because shipowners were paid by the passenger and ton of freight, they crowded as many people as possible on the ships, where disease took a heavy toll.

they have beene ever much subject; and there not to beleeve, or not to releeve the true and poore estate of that Colony, whose fruits were commonly spent before they were ripe, and this losse is nothing to them here, whose great estates are not sensible of the losse of their adventures, and so they thinke, or will not take notice;[29] but it is so with all men: but howsoever they thinke or dispose of all things at their pleasure, I am sure not my selfe onely, but a thousand others have not onely spent the most of their estates, but the most part have lost their lives and all, onely but to make way for the triall of more new conclusions, and he that now will adventure but twelve pounds ten shillings, shall have better respect and as much favour then he that sixteene yeere agoe adventured as much, except he have money as the other hath, but though he have adventured five hundred pound, and spent there never so much time, if hee have no more and not able to begin a family of himselfe, all is lost by order of Court.[30]

But in the beginning it was not so, all went then out of one purse, till those new devices have consumed both mony and purse; for at first there were but six Patentees, now more then a thousand, then but thirteene Counsailors, now not lesse then an hundred; I speake not of all, for there are some both honourable and honest, but of those Officers, which did they manage their owne estates no better then the affaires of Virginia, they would quickly fall to decay so well as it; but this is most evident, few Officers in England it hath caused to turne Banquerupts, nor for all their complaints would leave their places, neither yet any of their Officers there, nor few of the rest but they would be at home, but fewer Adventurers here will adventure any more till they see the businesse better established, although there be some so wilfully improvident they care for nothing but to get thither, and then if their friends be dead, or want themselves, they die or live but poorely for want of necessaries, and to thinke the old Planters can releeve them were too much simplicity; for who here

---

29. *Adventures* here means "investments."

30. In order to broaden its base of support, the Virginia Company had offered shares for sale at the relatively low rate of £12 10s. This amount was about equivalent to what it took to maintain one person in England for a year. Smith was angry that a new investor had more status than men like him who had given much more to the enterprise.

in England is so charitable to feed two or three strangers, have they never so much; much lesse in Virginia where they want for themselves. Now the generall complaint saith, that pride, covetousnesse, extortion and oppression in a few that ingrosses all, then sell all againe to the comminalty at what rate they please, yea even men, women and children for who will give most, occasions no small mischiefe amongst the Planters.[31]

As for the Company, or those that doe transport them, provided of necessaries, God forbid but they should receive their charges againe with advantage, or that masters there should not have the same privilege over their servants as here, but to sell him or her for forty, fifty, or threescore pounds, whom the Company hath sent over for eight or ten pounds at the most, without regard how they shall be maintained with apparell, meat, drinke and lodging, is odious, and their fruits sutable, therefore such merchants it were better they were made such merchandize themselves, then suffered any longer to use that trade, and those are defects sufficient to bring a well setled Common-wealth to misery, much more Virginia.

Question 7. How thinke you it may be rectified?

Answer. If his Majestie would please to intitle it to his Crowne,[32] and yearely that both the Governours here and there may give their accounts to you, or some that are not ingaged in the businesse, that the common stocke bee not spent in maintaining one hundred men for the Governour, one hundred for two Deputies, fifty for the Treasurer, five and twenty for the Secretary, and more for the Marshall and other Officers who were never there nor adventured any thing, but onely preferred by favour to be Lords over them that broke the ice and beat the path, and must teach them what to doe. If any thing happen well, it is their glory; if ill, the fault of the old directors, that in all dangers must endure the worst, yet not five hundred of them have so much as one of the

---

31. The royal commission heard complaints that a few of the "old Planters" took control of those sent over as servants and sold their time to other planters in the colony. Because the prices were bidden up, servants, it was alleged, were ruthlessly exploited and sometimes held beyond the terms for which they had signed.
32. "Intitle it to his Crowne": Smith suggests that Virginia be taken from the Virginia Company and made a royal colony, which was done in 1625.

others; also that there bee some present course taken to maintaine a Garrison to suppresse the Salvages, till they be able to subsist, and that his Majesty would please to remit his custome,[33] or it is to be feared they will lose custome and all, for this cannot be done by promises, hopes, counsels and countenances, but with sufficient workmen and meanes to maintaine them, not such delinquents as here cannot be ruled by all the lawes in England. Yet when the foundation is laid, as I have said, and a common-wealth established, then such there may better be constrained to labour then here: but to rectifie a common-wealth with debaushed people is impossible,[34] and no wise man would throw himselfe into such a society, that intends honestly, and knowes what he undertakes, for there is no Country to pillage as the Romans found: all you expect from thence must be by labour.

For the government I thinke there is as much adoe about it as the Kingdomes of Scotland and Ireland, men here conceiting Virginia as they are, erecting as many stately Offices as Officers with their attendants, as there are labourers in the Countrey, where a Constable were as good as twenty of their Captaines, and three hundred good Souldiers and labourers better then all the rest that goe onely to get the fruits of other mens labours by the title of an office. Thus they spent Michaelmas rent in Mid-summer Moone, and would gather their Harvest before they have planted their Corne.[35]

As for the maintenance of the Officers, the first that went never demanded any, but adventured good summes, and it seemes strange to me, the fruits of all their labours, besides the expence of an hundred and fifty thousand pounds, and such multitudes of people, those collaterall Officers could not maintaine themselves so well as the old did, and having now such liberty to doe to the Salvages what they will, the others had not.[36] I more then wonder

33. "His custome": The government imposed customs duties on goods brought in from the colonies. Smith suggests that these be suspended until the plantations are well established.
34. *Debaushed* for *debauched*. The argument is that you cannot build a new society with nothing but the refuse of England; "sufficient workmen" must be sent.
35. Michaelmas, at the end of the harvest, was a traditional time of reckoning up; rents were paid then and servants signed their annual contracts.
36. *Maintenance* here means "being supplied with the necessities of life, a salary." Smith asserts that the earliest officers did not ask for a salary.

they have not five hundred Salvages to worke for them towards
their generall maintenance, and as many more to returne some
content and satisfaction to the Adventurers, that for all their care,
charge and diligence, can heare nor see nothing but miserable
complaints; therefore under your correction to rectifie all, is with
all expedition to passe the authority to them who will releeve
them, lest all bee consumed ere the differences be determined.
And except his Majestie undertake it, or by Act of Parlament some
small tax may be granted throughout his Dominions, as a Penny
upon every Poll, called a head-penny; two pence upon every
Chimney,[37] or some such collection might be raised, and that
would be sufficient to give a good stocke, and many servants to
sufficient men of any facultie, and transport them freely for paying onely homage to the Crowne of England, and such duties to
the publike good as their estates increased reason should require.
Were this put in practice, how many people of what quality you
please, for all those disasters would yet gladly goe to spend their
lives there, and by this meanes more good might be done in one
yeere, then all those pety particular undertakings will effect in
twenty.

For the Patent the King may, if he please, rather take it from
them that have it, then from us who had it first, pretending to his
Majesty what great matters they would doe, and how little we
did, and for any thing I can conceive, had we remained still as at
first, it is not likely we could have done much worse;[38] but those
oft altering of governments are not without much charge, hazard
and losse. If I be too plaine, I humbly crave your pardon; but you
requested me, therefore I doe but my duty. For the Nobility, who
knowes not how freely both in their Purses and assistances many
of them have beene to advance it, committing the managing of
the businesse to inferiour persons, amongst whom questionlesse
also many have done their utmost best, sincerely and truly according to their conceit, opinion and understanding; yet grosse errors
have beene committed, but no man lives without his fault; for my

37. *Poll* means "head"; a poll tax was a tax on each person in a household. Chim-
neys were still something of a luxury, many cottages having nothing but a smoke-
hole in the center of the roof.
38. Smith's argument is that the king has more reason to take the patent from
those who now have it than in the earlier change of patent that had ousted Smith
from the presidency.

owne part, I have so much adoe to amend my owne, I have no leisure to looke into any mans particular, but those in generall I conceive to be true. And so I humbly rest

Yours to command, J. S.

[*Generall Historie:* II, 323–332]

In his writings on New England, Captain Smith faced a greater challenge in attempting to convince his readers that the country, if managed properly, would be a rich colony for England. His dedication of the Description of New England *to the merchants who could make the hope a reality set out his platform.*

TO THE RIGHT WORSHIPFULL
Adventurers for the Countrey of
New England, in the Cities of
London, Bristow, Exceter, Plimouth,
Dartmouth, Bastable, Totneys, etc.
and in all other Cities and Ports,
in the Kingdome of England.

IF THE LITTLE Ant, and the sillie Bee seek by their diligence the good of their Commonwealth;[39] much more ought Man. If they punish the drones and sting them steales their labour; then blame not Man. Little hony hath that hive, where there are more Drones then Bees: and miserable is that Land, where more are idle then well imployed. If the indeavours of those vermin be acceptable, I hope mine may be excuseable; Though I confesse it were more proper for mee, To be doing what I say, then writing what I knowe. Had I returned rich, I could not have erred: Now having onely such fish as came to my net, I must be taxed.[40] But, I would my taxers were as ready to adventure

---

39. *Silly* here means "simple, rustic." The ant and bee, who were supposed to organize their nests into true hierarchical commonwealths, provided a favorite metaphor for colonial promoters.
40. *Taxed* means "accused, censured."

their purses, as I, purse, life, and all I have: or as diligent to furnish the charge, as I know they are vigilant to crop the fruits of my labours. Then would I not doubt (did God please I might safely arrive in New England, and safely returne) but to performe somewhat more then I have promised, and approve my words by deeds, according to proportion.

I am not the first hath beene betrayed by Pirats:[41] And foure men of warre, provided as they were, had beene sufficient to have taken Sampson, Hercules, and Alexander the great, no other way furnisht then I was. I knowe not what assurance any have do passe the Seas, Not to bee subject to casualty as well as my selfe: but least this disaster may hinder my proceedings, or ill will (by rumour) the behoofefull worke I pretend;[42] I have writ this little: which I did thinke to have concealed from any publike use, till I had made my returnes speake as much, as my pen now doth.

But because I speake so much of fishing, if any take mee for such a devote fisher, as I dreame of nought else, they mistake mee.[43] I know a ring of golde from a graine of barley, aswell as a goldesmith: and nothing is there to bee had which fishing doth hinder, but furder us to obtaine. Now for that I have made knowne unto you a fit place for plantation, limited within the bounds of your Patent and Commission; having also received meanes, power, and authority by your directions, to plant there a Colony, and make further search, and discovery in those parts there yet unknowne: Considering, withall, first those of his Majesties Councell, then those Cities above named, and diverse others that have beene moved to lend their assistance to so great a worke, doe expect (especially the adventurers) the true relation or event of my proceedings which I heare are so abused; I am inforced for all these respects, rather to expose my imbecillitie to contempt, by the testimonie of these rude lines, then all should condemne me for so bad a Factor, as could neither give reason nor account of my actions and designes.[44]

Yours to command,
John Smith.

[Description of New England: I, 311–312]

41. Smith's last attempt to reach New England ended when his ship was seized by French pirates.
42. *Pretend* means "intend"; *behoveful* (behoofefull) means "useful, advantageous."
43. *Devote* means "devoted."
44. *Furder* for *further*, assist. *Event* means "outcome." A factor is an agent.

In that part of his Generall Historie *devoted to New England, Smith returned to the theme of the great opportunity that was being lost by ignoring the north. By then, the small Pilgrim enclave was established at Plymouth at the entrance to Cape Cod, so Smith felt greater pressure to encourage general development. To those who feared hazarding their money, Smith never tired of pointing out that his risk and contribution had been infinitely greater.*

N OW I KNOW the common question is, For all those miseries, where is the wealth they have got, or the Gold or Silver Mines? To such greedy unworthy minds I say once againe: The sea is better then the richest Mine knowne, and of all the fishing ships that went well provided, there is no complaint of losse nor misery, but rather an admiration of wealth, profit, and health. As for the land were it never so good, in two yeeres so few of such small experience living without supplies so well, and in health, it was an extraordinary blessing from God. But that with such small meanes they should subsist, and doe so much, to any understanding judgement is a wonder. Notwithstanding, the vaine expectation of present gaine in some, ambition in others, that to be great would have all else slaves, and the carelesnesse in providing supplies, hath caused those defailements in all those Plantations, and how ever some bad conditions will extoll the actions of any Nation but their owne: yet if we may give credit to the Spaniards, Portugals, and French writings, they indured as many miseries, and yet not in twenty yeeres effected so much, nay scarce in fortie.

Thus you may see plainly the yeerely successe from New England by Virginia, which hath beene so costly to this Kingdome, and so deare to me, which either to see perish, or but bleed; Pardon me though it passionate me beyond the bounds of modesty, to have beene sufficiently able to fore-see their miseries, and had neither power nor meanes to prevent it. By that acquaintance I have with them, I call them my children, for they have beene my Wife, my Hawks, Hounds, my Cards, my Dice, and in totall, my best content, as indifferent to my heart, as my left hand to my right. And notwithstanding, all those miracles of disasters have crossed both them and me, yet were there not an Englishman remaining, as God be thanked notwithstanding the massacre there are some thousands; I would yet begin againe with as small meanes as I did at first, not that I have any secret encouragement

(I protest) more then lamentable experience; for all their discoveries I have yet heard of, are but Pigs of my owne Sow, nor more strange to me, then to heare one tell me hee hath gone from Billingsgate and discovered Gravesend, Tilbury, Quinborow, Lee, and Margit, which to those did never heare of them, though they dwell in England, might bee made some rare secrets and great Countries unknowne, except some few Relations of Master Dirmer.[45] In England, some are held great travellers that have seene Venice, and Rome, Madrill, Toledo, Sivill, Algere, Prague, or Ragousa, Constantinople, or Jerusalem, and the Piramides of Egypt; that thinke it nothing to goe to Summer Iles, or Virginia, which is as far as any of them; and I hope in time will prove a more profitable and a more laudable journey: as for the danger, you see our Ladies and Gentlewomen account it nothing now to goe thither; and therefore I hope all good men will better apprehend it, and not suffer them to languish in despaire, whom God so wonderfully and oft hath preserved.

What here I have writ by Relation, if it be not right I humbly intreat your pardons, but I have not spared any diligence to learne the truth of them that have beene actors, or sharers in those voyages;[46] In some particulars they might deceive mee, but in the substance they could not: for few could tell me any thing, except where they fished. But seeing all those have lived there, doe confirme more then I have writ, I doubt not but all those testimonies with these new begun examples of Plantation, will move both Citie and Country, freely to adventure with me more then promises.

But because some Fortune-tellers say, I am unfortunate; had they spent their time as I have done, they would rather beleeve in God then their calculations, and peradventure have given as bad an account of their actions, and therefore I intreat leave to answer those objecters, that thinke it strange, if this be true, I have made no more use of it, rest so long without imploiment, nor have no more reward nor preferment: To which I say;

---

45. "Pigs of my owne Sow": The discoveries that were bragged of were all in places that Smith had already seen, except for some made by Thomas Dermer. Smith is saying that we might as well praise someone who travels through England and "discovers" its towns and villages.

46. "Writ by Relation": Smith apologizes for possible errors in the relations of others that he has used.

I thinke it more strange they should tax me, before they have tried as much as I have, both by land and sea, as well in Asia and Affrica, as Europe and America, where my Commanders were actors or spectators, they alwaies so freely rewarded me, I never needed bee importunate, or could I ever learne to beg:[47] What there I got, I have spent; yet in Virginia I staied, till I left five hundred behinde me better provided then ever I was, from which blessed Virgin (ere I returned) sprung the fortunate habitation of Summer Iles.

This Virgins Sister, now called New England, at my humble sute, by our most gracious Prince Charles, hath beene neere as chargeable to me and my friends: for all which, although I never got shilling but it cost mee a pound, yet I would thinke my selfe happy could I see their prosperities.

But if it yet trouble a multitude to proceed upon these certainties, what thinke you I undertooke when nothing was knowne but that there was a vast land? I never had power and meanes to doe any thing, though more hath beene spent in formall delaies then would have done the businesse, but in such a penurious and miserable manner, as if I had gone a begging to build an Universitie: where had men beene as forward to adventure their purses, and performe the conditions they promised mee, as to crop the fruits of my labours, thousands ere this had beene bettered by these designes. Thus betwixt the spur of desire and the bridle of reason, I am neere ridden to death in a ring of despaire; the reines are in your hands, therefore I intreat you ease me, and those that thinke I am either idle or unfortunate, may see the cause and know: unlesse I did see better dealing, I have had warning enough not to be so forward againe at every motion upon their promises, unlesse I intended nothing but to carie newes; for now they dare adventure a ship, that when I went first would not adventure a groat, so they may be at home againe by Michaelmas, which makes me remember and say with Master Hackluit; Oh incredulitie the wit of fooles, that slovingly doe spit at all things faire, a sluggards Cradle, a Cowards Castle, how easie it is to be an Infidell.[48] But to the matter: By this all men may perceive, the ordinary performance of this voyage in five or six moneths, the plentie of fish is most certainly approved;

---

47. *Importunate* means "pressing," probably for funds or support.
48. Richard Hakluyt was the first great compiler of accounts of distant voyages. *Slovingly* is for *slovenly.*

and it is certaine, from Cannada and New England, within these six
yeeres hath come neere twenty thousand Bever skinnes: Now had each
of these ships transported but some small quantitie of the most in-
creasing Beasts, Fowles, Fruits, Plants, and Seeds, as I projected; by
this time their increase might have beene sufficient for more then one
thousand men: But the desire of present gaine (in many) is so violent,
and the endevours of many undertakers so negligent, every one so
regarding their private gaine, that it is hard to effect any publike good,
and impossible to bring them into a body, rule, or order, unlesse both
honesty, as well as authoritie and money, assist experience. But your
home-bred ingrossing Projecters will at last finde, there is a great
difference betwixt saying and doing, or those that thinks their directions can be as soone and easily performed, as they can conceit them;[49]
or that their conceits are the fittest things to bee put in practise, or
their countenances maintaine Plantations. But to conclude, the fishing
will goe forward whether you plant it or no; whereby a Colony may be
then transported with no great charge, that in short time might provide such fraughts, to buy on us there dwelling, as I would hope no
ship should goe or come emptie from New England.[50]

The charge of this is onely Salt, Nets, Hookes, Lines, Knives, Irish-
rugges,[51] course cloth, Beads, Glasse, and such trash, onely for fishing
and trade with the Salvages, besides our owne necessarie provisions,
whose endevours would quickly defray all this charge, and the Salvages
did intreat me to inhabit where I would. Now all those ships till these
last two yeeres, have beene fishing within a square of two or three
leagues, and scarce any one yet will goe any further in the Port they
fish in, where questionlesse five hundred may have their fraught as
well as elsewhere, and be in the market ere others can have the fish in
their ships, because New Englands fishing begins in February, in Newfoundland not till the midst of May; the progression hereof tends
much to the advancement of Virginia and Summer Iles, whose empty

49. Projectors are people who spin projects; to engross is to get control of a
commodity or scheme so as to sell its products at monopoly prices. *Conceit* means
"conceive, think of."
50. Smith's point was that, as fishing ships were going to New England annually,
colonists and supplies could be transported at little extra cost. On the other hand,
the colonists could then produce commodities for the ships and help with the
fishing.
51. Irish rugs are coarse blankets or mantles.

ships may take in their fraughts there, and would be also in time of need a good friend to the Inhabitants of Newfoundland.

The returnes made by the Westerne men, are commonly divided in three parts;[52] one for the owner of the ship; another for the Master and his Company; the third for the victualers, which course being still permitted, will be no hinderance to the Plantation as yet goe there never so many, but a meanes of transporting that yeerely for little or nothing, which otherwise wil cost many hundreds of pounds. If a ship can gaine twenty, thirty, fifty in the hundred; nay three hundred for one hundred in seven or ten moneths, as you see they have done, spending twice so much time in comming and going as in staying there: were I there planted, seeing the variety of the fishings serve the most part of the yeere, and with a little labour we might make all the Salt we need use, as is formerly said, and can conceive no reason to distrust of good successe by Gods assistance; besides for the building of ships, no place hath more convenient Harbours, ebbe, nor floud, nor better timber; and no Commoditie in Europe doth more decay then wood. [*Generall Historie:* II, 462-466]

The final paragraph in the long Generall Historie *restated his themes and chided those who needed more assurance than he had given.*

IF ANY DESIRE to be further satisfied, what defect is found in this, they shall finde supplied in me, that thus freely have throwne my selfe with my mite into the Treasury of my Countries good, not doubting but God will stirre up some noble spirits to consider and examine if worthy Columbus could give the Spaniards any such certainties for his designe, when Queene Isabel of Spaine set him forth with 15. saile, and though I promise no Mines of gold, yet the warlike Hollanders let us imitate but not hate, whose wealth and strength are good testimonies of their treasury gotten by fishing; and New-England hath yeelded already by generall computation one hundred thousand pounds at the least. Therefore honourable and worthy Country men, let not the meannesse of the word fish distaste you, for

52. The "Westerne men" were from the West of England, where many of the fishing voyages originated.

it will afford as good gold as the Mines of Guiana or Potassie, with lesse hazard and charge, and more certainty and facility.[53]

J. S.

[*Generall Historie:* II, 474]

III

John Smith's most engaging book was his last, Advertisements for the Unexperienced Planters of New England, or Any Where. *This book, published in the last year of Smith's life, 1631, is his most reflective and most cogently argued. Gone are the bits and pieces pasted together with impassioned pleas. Here Smith presented his vision of England's future in America in a more philosophical way.*

The Advertisements *was addressed to the planters of the recently founded Massachusetts Bay colony. Because these puritans, unlike the Pilgrims, were not separatists and were from the "middling group" in English society, Smith felt their venture would be good for New England as well as old. Their emphasis on private property distributed with rough equality among all the settlers and their ethic of hard work meant that finally Smith's program for the colonies was about to be tried. He offered them his advice to bring their plans to fruition. First he described these colonial leaders for his readers.*

B UT OF THOSE which are gone within this eighteene moneths for Cape Anne, and the Bay of the Massachusets: those which are their chiefe Undertakers are Gentlemen of good estate, some of 500, some a thousand pound land a yeere, all which they say they will sell for the advancing this harmlesse and pious worke;[54] men of good credit and well-beloved in their Country, not such as flye for debt, or any scandall at home, and are good Catholike Protestants according to the reformed Church of England, if not, it is well they are gone:[55] the

53. Ralegh had sought gold in Guiana, but no one had found the supposed mines there. The Spanish mines at Potosí in Bolivia were extremely rich.

54.*Undertakers* refers to anyone who undertakes to do something; colonial promoters were often referred to as undertakers.

55. "Catholick Protestants": *Catholic* here means "universal." Even though it had broken with the Roman Catholic church, the Church of England insisted that it was the heir of the ancient universal church and continued to use the word *catholic.*

rest of them men of good meanes, or Arts, Occupations, and Qualities, much more fit for such a businesse, and better furnished of all necessaries if they arrive well, than was ever any Plantation went out of England: I will not say but some of them may be more precise than needs,[56] nor that they all be so good as they should be, for Christ had but twelve Apostles, and one was a traitor; and if there be no dissemblers among them, it is more than a wonder: therefore doe not condemne all for some; but however they have as good authority from his Majesty as they could desire, if they doe ill, the losse is but their owne; if well, a great glory and exceeding good to this Kingdome, to make good at last what all our former conclusions have disgraced. [*Advertisements:* III, 270]

T HUS IT LAY againe in a manner vast, till those noble Gentlemen thus voluntarily undertooke it, whom I intreat to take this as a memorandum of my love, to make your plantations so neere and great as you can;[57] for many hands make light worke, whereas yet your small parties can doe nothing availeable; nor stand too much upon the letting, setting, or selling those wild Countries, nor impose too much upon the commonalty either by your maggazines, which commonly eat out all poore mens labours, nor any other too hard imposition for present gaine;[58] but let every man so it bee by order allotted him, plant freely without limitation so much as hee can, bee it by the halfes or otherwayes:[59] And at the end of five or six yeares, or when you make a division, for every acre he hath planted, let him have twenty, thirty, forty, or an hundred; or as you finde hee hath extraordinarily deserved, by it selfe to him and his heires for ever; all his charges being defrayed to his lord or master, and publike good: In so doing, a servant that will

56. The puritans were often referred to as the "precise," meaning that they were known for being scrupulous and strict about points of religious observance that others might consider unimportant.

57. *Vast* means "waste, empty." Smith has just discussed the previous efforts to develop New England. *Neere and great* means "close together and large," so that planters can help each other.

58. *Magazines* refers to the stores of supplies that colonization companies sent to their settlers and sold, typically, at a 25% markup to defray expenses. Colonists always complained when the backers insisted they buy exclusively from the magazine.

59. "By the halfes": In order to repay the investors in London, in many colonies settlers were initially tenants at halves; they owed half their crops to the company.

labour, within foure or five yeares may live as well there as his master did here: for where there is so much land lie waste, it were a madnesse in a man at the first to buy, or hire, or pay any thing more than an acknowledgement to whom it shall be due; and hee is double mad that will leave his friends, meanes, and freedome in England, to be worse there than here. Therefore let all men have as much freedome in reason as may be, and true dealing, for it is the greatest comfort you can give them, where the very name of servitude will breed much ill bloud, and become odious to God and man; but mildly temper correction with mercy, for I know well you will have occasion enough to use both; and in thus doing, doubtlesse God will blesse you, and quickly triple and multiply your numbers, the which to my utmost I will doe my best indevour.

IN ALL those plantations, yea, of those that have done least, yet the most will say, we were the first; and so every next supply, still the next beginner: But seeing history is the memory of time, the life of the dead, and the happinesse of the living; because I have more plainly discovered, and described, and discoursed of those Countries than any as yet I know, I am the bolder to continue the story, and doe all men right so neere as I can in those new beginnings, which hereafter perhaps may bee in better request than a forest of nine dayes pamphlets.

In the yeare 1629. about March, six good ships are gone with 350. men, women, and children, people professing themselves of good ranke, zeale, meanes and quality: also 150. head of cattell, as horse, mares, and neat beasts; 41. goats, some conies, with all provision for houshold and apparell; six peeces of great Ordnance for a Fort, with Muskets, Pikes, Corslets, Drums and Colours, with all provisions necessary for the good of man.[60] They are seated about 42. degrees and 38. minutes, at a place called by the natives Naemkecke, by our Royall King Charles, Bastable; but now by the planters, Salem; where they arrived for most part exceeding well, their cattell and all things else prospering exceedingly, farre beyond their expectation.

At this place they found some reasonable good provision and houses built by some few of Dorchester, with whom they are joyned in society with two hundred men, an hundred and fifty more they have sent to the Massachusets, which they call Charlton, or Charles Towne: I tooke the fairest reach in this Bay for a river, whereupon I called it

---

60. Corslets are body armor, and colours are flags or insignia.

Charles river, after the name of our Royall King Charles; but they find that faire Channell to divide it selfe into so many faire branches as make forty or fifty pleasant Ilands within that excellent Bay, where the land is of divers and sundry sorts, in some places very blacke and fat, in others good clay, sand and gravell, the superficies neither too flat in plaines, nor too high in hils.[61] In the Iles you may keepe your hogs, horse, cattell, conies or poultry, and secure for little or nothing, and to command when you list, onely having a care of provision for some extraordinary cold winter. In those Iles, as in the maine, you may make your nurseries for fruits and plants where you put no cattell; in the maine[62] you may shape your Orchards, Vineyards, Pastures, Gardens, Walkes, Parkes, and Corne fields out of the whole peece as you please into such plots, one adjoyning to another, leaving every of them invironed with two, three, foure, or six, or so many rowes of well growne trees as you will, ready growne to your hands, to defend them from ill weather, which in a champion you could not in many ages;[63] and this at first you may doe with as much facility, as carelesly or ignorantly cut downe all before you, and then after better consideration make ditches, pales, plant young trees with an excessive charge and labour, seeing you may have so many great and small growing trees for your maineposts, to fix hedges, palisados, houses, rales, or what you will; which order in Virginia hath not beene so well observed as it might: where all the woods for many an hundred mile for the most part grow streight, like unto the high grove or tuft of trees, upon the high hill by the house of that worthy Knight Sir Humphrey Mildmay, so remarkable in Essex in the Parish of Danbery, where I writ this discourse,[64] but much taller and greater, neither grow they so thicke together by the halfe, and much good ground betweene them without shrubs, and the best is ever knowne by the greatnesse of the trees and the vesture it beareth. Now in New-England the trees are commonly lower, but much thicker and firmer wood, and more proper for shipping, of which I will speake a little, being the chiefe engine wee are to use in this worke,[65] and the rather for that within a square of

61. *Superficies* means "surface of the land."
62. The maine is the mainland.
63. *Champion* means "open country."
64. Here again Smith, for all his independence, shows his need for a patron.
65. Smith adapts the word *engine*, which refers to human ingenuity and the tools that it can create, to present shipbuilding as the engine that will enrich New England.

twenty leagues, you may have all, or most of the chiefe materials belonging to them, were they wrought to their perfection as in other places.

Of all fabricks a ship is the most excellent,[66] requiring more art in building, rigging, sayling, trimming, defending, and moaring, with such a number of severall termes and names in continuall motion, not understood of any landman, as none would thinke of, but some few that know them; for whose better instruction I writ my Sea-Grammar, a booke most necessary for those plantations, because there is scarce any thing belonging to a ship, but the Sea-termes, charge and duty of every officer is plainly expressed, and also any indifferent capacity may conceive how to direct an unskilfull Carpenter or Sailer to build Boats and Barkes sufficient to saile those coasts and rivers, and put a good workman in minde of many things in this businesse hee may easily mistake or forget. But to be excellent in this faculty is the master-peece of all the most necessary workmen in the world. The first rule or modell thereof being directed by God himselfe to Noah for his Arke, which he never did to any other building but his Temple, which is tossed and turned up and downe the world with the like dangers, miseries, and extremities as a ship, sometimes tasting the fury of the foure Elements, as well as shee, by unlimited tyrants in their cruelty for tortures, that it is hard to conceive whether those inhumanes exceed the beasts of the Forrest, the birds of the Aire, the fishes of the Sea, either in numbers, greatnesse, swiftnesse, fiercenesse or cruelty; whose actions and varieties, with such memorable observations as I have collected, you shall finde with admiration in my history of the Sea, if God be pleased I live to finish it.[67]

FOR THE building houses, townes, and fortresses, where shall a man finde the like conveniency, as stones of most sorts, as well lime stone, if I be not much deceived, as Iron stone, smooth stone, blew slate for covering houses, and great rockes we supposed Marble, so that one place is called the marble harbour: There is grasse plenty, though very long and thicke stalked, which being neither mowne nor eaten, is very ranke,[68] yet all their cattell like and prosper well therewith, but indeed it is weeds, herbs, and grasse growing together,

66. A fabric is anything manufactured, especially by skilled workmanship.
67. Smith's history of the sea was never published, nor does it exist in manuscript.
68. *Rank* means "of uncontrolled growth."

which although they be good and sweet in the Summer, they will deceive your cattell in winter; therefore be carefull in the Spring to mow the swamps, and the low Ilands of Auguan, where you may have harsh sheare-grasse enough to make hay of, till you can cleare ground to make pasture, which will beare as good grasse as can grow any where, as now it doth in Virginia;[69] and unlesse you make this provision, if there come an extraordinary winter, you will lose many of them and hazard the rest, especially if you bring them in the latter end of Summer, or before the grasse bee growne in the Spring, comming weake from Sea. All things they plant prosper exceedingly: but one man of 13. gallons of Indian corne, reaped that yeare 364. bushels London measure, as they confidently report, at which I much wonder having planted many bushels, but no such increase.[70]

The best way wee found in Virginia to spoile the woods, was first to cut a notch in the barke a hand broad round about the tree, which pill off and the tree will sprout no more, and all the small boughs in a yeare or two will decay, the greatest branches in the root they spoyle with fire, but you with more ease may cut them from the body and they will quickly rot: betwixt those trees they plant their corne, whose great bodies doe much defend it from extreme gusts, and heat of the Sunne, where that in the plaines, where the trees by time they have consumed, is subject to both; and this is the most easie way to have pasture and corne fields, which is much more fertile than the other: in Virginia they never manure their overworne fields, which is very few, the ground for most part is so fertile: but in New-England they doe, sticking at every plant of corne, a herring or two, which commeth in that season in such abundance, they may take more than they know what to doe with.[71]

---

69. "Deceive your cattell in winter": Native meadow grasses, when dried, did not make nourishing cattle feed. The ultimate solution for the colonists was to sow meadows with English grasses. The "low Ilands of Auguan" were near modern Ipswich, Massachusetts. Sheargrass is sharp-edged grass that cuts the mouths of grazing animals or the hands of harvesters.

70. Anxious though he was to promote the fertility of New England, Smith felt constrained to set the record straight and to challenge overstatements that could lead to false expectations.

71. To spoil the woods is to destroy the trees; Smith here borrows without acknowledgment from his description of Indian methods of clearing a field for planting. The New Englanders planted fish in their fields in order to avoid the labor of clearing new ones.

Some infirmed bodies, or tender educats, complaine of the piercing cold, especially in January and February, yet the French in Canada, the Russians, Swethlanders, Polanders, Germans, and our neighbour Hollanders, are much colder and farre more Northward, for all that, rich Countreyes and live well. Now they have wood enough if they will but cut it, at their doores to make fires, and traine oyle with the splinters of the roots of firre trees for candles, where in Holland they have little or none to build ships, houses, or any thing but what they fetch from forren Countries, yet they dwell but in the latitude of Yorkshire, and New-England is in the heighth of the North cape of Spaine, which is 10. degrees, 200. leagues, or 600. miles nearer the Sunne than wee, where upon the mountaines of Bisky I have felt as much cold, frost, and snow as in England, and of this I am sure, a good part of the best Countries and kingdomes of the world, both Northward and Southward of the line, lie in the same paralels of Virginia and New-England, as at large you may finde in the 201. page of the generall history.[72]

Thus you may see how prosperously thus farre they have proceeded, in which course by Gods grace they may continue; but great care would be had they pester not their ships too much with cattell nor passengers, and to make good conditions for your peoples diet, for therein is used much legerdemaine,[73] therefore in that you cannot be too carefull to keepe your men well, and in health at Sea: in this case some masters are very provident, but the most part so they can get fraught enough, care not much whether the passengers live or die, for a common sailer regards not a landman, especially a poore passenger, as I have seene too oft approved by lamentable experience, although we have victualled them all at our owne charges.

IT IS TRUE, that Master John Wynthrop, their now Governour, a worthy Gentleman both in estate and esteeme, went so well provided (for six or seven hundred people went with him) as could be devised, but at Sea, such an extraordinarie storme encountred his Fleet, continuing ten daies, that of two hundred Cattell which were so tossed and brused, threescore and ten died, many of their people fell sicke, and in this perplexed estate, after ten weekes, they arrived in

72. Swethland is Sweden. *Nearer the sun* means "nearer the equator." Smith had not been in New England in the winter; he was here arguing from the fallacious assumption that latitude was the chief determinant of climate.
73. *Legerdemaine* here means "deception."

New-England at severall times, where they found threescore of their people dead, the rest sicke, nothing done, but all complaining, and all things so contrary to their expectation, that now every monstrous humor began to shew it selfe. And to second this, neare as many more came after them, but so ill provided, with such multitudes of women and children, as redoubled their necessities.

This small triall of their patience, caused among them no small confusion, and put the Governour and his Councell to their utmost wits; some could not endure the name of a Bishop, others not the sight of a Crosse nor Surplesse, others by no meanes the booke of common Prayer. This absolute crue, only of the Elect, holding all (but such as themselves) reprobates and cast-awaies, now make more haste to returne to Babel, as they tearmed England, than stay to enjoy the land they called Canaan; somewhat they must say to excuse themselves.[74]

Those he found Brownists,[75] hee let goe for New-Plimoth, who are now betwixt foure or five hundred, and live well without want, some two hundred of the rest he was content to returne for England, whose clamors are as variable as their humours and Auditors;[76] some say they could see no timber of two foot diameter, some the Country is all

74. Smith's marginal note ("The fruits of counterfeits") may refer to his belief that the puritans only simulated great piety. A surplice is the long white linen robe worn over a cassock by ministers in the Church of England. The confusion Smith refers to stemmed from the puritans' desire to return to the purity of the early church as described in the New Testament. The dissension arose over the question of how far this should go; the puritans also wanted to continue to be thought of as loyal members of the Church of England. The New England meetinghouses were unadorned, and the congregations that met there were self-governing. These puritans therefore rejected the rule of bishops, vestments and representations such as crosses, and use of the Book of Common Prayer.

Many Protestants, including the puritans, rejected the Roman Catholic teaching that one can earn salvation; they taught instead that God chooses whom to save and to those he gives his grace. These chosen people, whose identity only God knows for sure, are called the Elect; Smith ridicules the puritans' belief that they could know they were of this body. Smith's sneering phrase *absolute crue* implies that the puritans are a gang that has cut itself off from all authority. He clearly did not believe that men such as John Winthrop fell into this category.

75. *Brownists* was a common name for separatists, the most extreme of the puritans who wanted to separate completely from the Church of England.

76. *Auditors* means "listeners." Smith accuses those sent back of changing their complaints by whim or depending on whom they were talking to.

Woods, others they drunke all the Springs and Ponds dry, yet like to famish for want of fresh water; some of the danger of the rattell Snake; and that others sold their provisions at what rates they pleased to them that wanted, and so returned to England great gainers out of others miseries; yet all that returned are not of those humors.

Notwithstanding all this, the noble Governour was no way disanimated, neither repents him of his enterprise for all those mistakes, but did order all things with that temperance and discretion, and so releeved those that wanted with his owne provision, that there is six or seven hundred remained with him, and more than 1600. English in all the Country, with three or foure hundred head of Cattell, as for Corne they are very ignorant:[77] If upon the coast of America, they doe not before the end of this October (for toies) furnish themselves with two or three thousand bushels of Indian Corne, which is better than ours, and in a short time cause the Salvages to doe them as good service as their owne men, as I did in Virginia, and yet neither use cruelty nor tyranny amongst them; a consequence well worth putting in practice: and till it be effected, they will hardly doe well. I know ignorance will say it is impossible, but this impossible taske, ever since the massacre in Virginia, I have beene a suter to have undertaken, but with 150. men, to have got Corne, fortified the Country, and discovered them more land than they all yet know or have demonstrated: but the Merchants common answer was, necessity in time would force the Planters doe it themselves, and rather thus husbandly to lose ten sheepe, than be at the charge of a halfe penny worth of Tarre.[78]

Who is it that knowes not what a small handfull of Spaniards in the West Indies, subdued millions of the inhabitants, so depopulating those Countries they conquered, that they are glad to buy Negroes in Affrica at a great rate, in Countries farre remote from them, which although they bee as idle and as devilish people as any in the world, yet they cause them quickly to bee their best servants; notwithstanding, there is for every foure or five naturall Spaniards, two or three hundred Indians and Negros, and in Virginia and New-England more English than Salvages, that can assemble themselves to assault or hurt them, and it is much better to helpe to plant a country than unplant it and then replant it: but there Indians were in such multitudes, the

---

77. "very ignorant": The sentence break was improperly placed here. It should have gone after "with three or foure hundred head of Cattell."

78. *Husbandly* means "thrifty"; this is ironic.

Spaniards had no other remedy; and ours such a few, and so dispersed, it were nothing in a short time to bring them to labour and obedience.

It is strange to me, that English men should not doe as much as any, but upon every sleight affront, in stead to amend it, we make it worse; notwithstanding the worst of all those rumours, the better sort there are constant in their resolutions, and so are the most of their best friends here; and making provision to supply them, many conceit they make a dearth here, which is nothing so; for they would spend more here than they transport thither. One Ship this Summer with twenty cattell, and forty or fifty passengers, arived all well, and the Ship at home againe in nine weekes: another for all this exclamation of want, is returned with 10000. Corfish, and fourescore Kegs of Sturgion, which they did take and save when the season was neare past, and in the very heat of Summer, yet as good as can be. Since another ship is gone from Bristow, and many more a providing to follow them with all speed.

Thus you may plainly see for all these rumours, they are in no such distresse as is supposed: as for their mischances, misprisions, or what accidents may befall them, I hope none is so malicious, as attribute the fault to the Country nor mee; yet if some blame us not both, it were more than a wonder; for I am not ignorant that ignorance and too curious spectators, make it a great part of their profession to censure (however) any mans actions, who having lost the path to vertue, will make most excellent shifts to mount up any way; such incomparable connivency is in the Devils most punctuall cheaters, they will hazard a joint, but where God hath his Church they wil have a Chapel;[79] a mischiefe so hard to be prevented, that I have thus plainly adventured to shew my affection, through the weaknesse of my abilitie, you may easily know them by their absolutenesse in opinions, holding experience but the mother of fooles, which indeed is the very ground of reason, and he that contemnes her in those actions, may finde occasion enough to use all the wit and wisdome hee hath to correct his owne folly, that thinkes to finde amongst those salvages such Churches, Palaces, Monuments, and Buildings as are in England. [*Advertisements*: III, 287–295]

---

79. *Punctual* means "punctilious, exact in every detail." An old meaning of *joint* is "portion." Smith seems to be saying that it is impossible to keep such undesirable people out of colonization ventures and that, once in, they devote themselves to causing trouble.

In his Advertisements *Smith returned yet again to his experiences in Virginia, what he had accomplished and the obstacles he had faced. He was still attempting to work out the magnitude of his own accomplishments and the degree to which he had been cheated of credit for them. Finally he turned to biting satire to ridicule those in London who thought they knew everything. He began in a characteristically abrupt way.*

I T   I S   T R U E, in the yeere of our Lord 1622. they were about seven or eight thousand[80] English indifferently well furnished with most necessaries, and many of them grew to that height of bravery, living in that plenty and excesse, that went thither not worth any thing, made the Company here thinke all the world was Oatmeale there,[81] and all this proceeded by surviving those that died, nor were they ignorant to use as curious tricks there as here, and out of the juice of Tabacco, which at first they sold at such good rates, they regarded nothing but Tabacco; a commodity then so vendable, it provided them all things: and the loving Salvages their kinde friends, they trained so well up to shoot in a Peece, to hunt and kill them fowle, they became more expert than our owne Country-men, whose labours were more profitable to their Masters in planting Tabacco, and other businesse.

This superfluity caused my poore beginnings scorned, or to be spoken of but with much derision, that never sent Ship from thence fraught, but onely some small quantities of Wainscot, Clap-board, Pitch, Tar, Rosin, Sope-ashes, Glasse, Cedar, Cypresse, Blacke Walnut, Knees for Ships,[82] Ash for Pikes, Iron Ore none better, some Silver Ore, but so poore it was not regarded; better there may be, for I was no Mineralist, some Sturgion, but it was too tart of the Vinegar, which was of my owne store, for little came from them which was good; and Wine of the Countries wilde Grapes, but it was too sowre, yet better than they sent us any: in two or three yeeres but one Hogshead of Claret. Onely spending my time to revenge my imprisonment upon the harmlesse innocent Salvages, who by my cruelty I forced to feed

80. Smith included a note at the end of this book admitting that the council in Virginia said there were no more than 2,200 people there then.
81. Bravery is ostentation or grandeur in dress. "All the world was Oatmeale" refers to a proverb that ridicules those who think something is easy to attain.
82. *Knees* refers to naturally bent wood used in building ships; despite the commas, this may be modified by the preceding list of woods.

me with their contribution, and to send any offended my idle humour to James towne to punish at mine owne discretion; or keepe their Kings and subjects in chaines, and make them worke. Things cleane contrary to my Commission; whilest I and my company tooke our needlesse pleasures in discovering the Countries about us, building of Forts, and such unnecessary fooleries, where an Egge-shell (as they writ) had beene sufficient against such enemies; neglecting to answer the Merchants expectations with profit, feeding the Company onely with Letters and tastes of such commodities as we writ the Country would afford in time by industry, as Silke, Wines, Oyles of Olives, Rape, and Linsed,[83] Rasons, Prunes, Flax, Hempe, and Iron, as for Tabacco, wee never then dreamt of it.

Now because I sent not their ships full fraught home with those commodities, they kindly writ to me, if we failed the next returne, they would leave us there as banished men,[84] as if houses and all those commodities did grow naturally, only for us to take at our pleasure, with such tedious Letters, directions, and instructions, and most contrary to that was fitting, we did admire how it was possible such wise men could so torment themselves and us with such strange absurdities and impossibilities, making Religion their colour, when all their aime was nothing but present profit, as most plainly appeared, by sending us so many Refiners, Gold-smiths, Jewellers, Lapidaries, Stone-cutters, Tabacco-pipe-makers, Imbroderers, Perfumers, Silkemen, with all their appurtenances, but materialls, and all those had great summes out of the common stocke: and so many spies and super-intendents over us, as if they supposed we would turne Rebels, all striving to suppresse and advance they knew not what: at last got a Commission in their owne names, promising the King custome within seven yeares, where we were free for one and twenty,[85] appointing the Lord De-la-ware for Governour, with as many great and stately officers, and offices under him, as doth belong to a great Kingdome, with good summes for their extraordinary expences; also privileges for Cities, Charters for Corporations, Universities, Free-schooles, and Glebe-land, putting all those in practice before there were either people,

83. Oil from olives, rapeseed, and linseed.
84. The colonists would have taken this threat seriously; the Roanoke colonists had been abandoned.
85. James I had originally granted the Virginia Company freedom from customs for twenty-one years, but under the new charter of 1609, the company agreed to begin paying in seven.

students, or schollers to build or use them, or provision and victuall to feed them were then there: and to amend this, most of the Tradesmen in London that would adventure but twelve pounds ten shillings, had the furnishing the Company of all such things as belonged to his trade, such jugling there was betwixt them, and such intruding Committies their associats, that all the trash they could get in London was sent us to Virginia, they being well payed for that was good. Much they blamed us for not converting the Salvages, when those they sent us were little better, if not worse, nor did they all convert any of those we sent them to England for that purpose. So doating of Mines of gold, and the South Sea, that all the world could not have devised better courses to bring us to ruine than they did themselves, with many more such like strange conceits; by this you may avoid the like inconveniences, and take heed by those examples, you have not too many irons in the fire at once, neither such change of Governours, nor such a multitude of Officers, neither more Masters, Gentlemen, Gentlewomen, and children, than you have men to worke, which idle charge you will finde very troublesome, and the effects dangerous, and one hundred good labourers better than a thousand such Gallants as were sent me, that could doe nothing but complaine, curse, and despaire, when they saw our miseries, and all things so cleane contrary to the report in England, yet must I provide as well for them as for my selfe.

T HIS THE Mariners and Saylers did ever all they could to conceale,[86] who had alwayes both good fare, and good pay for the most part, and part out of our owne purses, never caring how long they stayed upon their voyage, daily feasting before our faces, when wee lived upon a little corne and water, and not halfe enough of that, the most of which we had from amongst the Salvages. Now although there be Deere in the woods, Fish in the rivers, and Fowles in abundance in their seasons; yet the woods are so wide, the rivers so broad, and the beasts so wild, and wee so unskilfull to catch them, wee little troubled them nor they us: for all this our letters that still signified unto them the plaine truth, would not be beleeved, because they required such things as was most necessary: but their opinion was otherwayes, for they desired but to packe over so many as they could, saying

86. *This* must refer to the difficulties of the colony. The mariners who brought supplies and colonists would report back to the company.

necessity would make them get victuals for themselves, as for good labourers they were more usefull here in England: but they found it otherwayes; the charge was all one to send a workman as a roarer,[87] whose clamors to appease, we had much adoe to get fish and corne to maintaine them from one supply till another came with more loyterers without victuals still to make us worse and worse, for the most of them would rather starve than worke; yet had it not beene for some few that were Gentlemen, both by birth, industry, and discretion, we could not possibly have subsisted.

Many did urge I might have forced them to it, having authority that extended so farre as death: but I say, having neither meat, drinke, lodging, pay, nor hope of any thing, or preferment: and seeing the Merchants onely did what they listed with all they wrought for, I know not what punishment could be greater than that they indured; which miseries caused us alwaies to be in factions, the most part striving by any meanes to abandon the Country, and I with my party to prevent them and cause them stay. But indeed the cause of our factions was bred here in England, and grew to that maturity among themselves that spoyled all, as all the Kingdome and other Nations can too well testifie: Yet in the yeare 1622. there were about seven or eight thousand English, as hath beene said, so well trained, secure, and well furnished, as they reported and conceited. These simple Salvages their bosome friends, I so much oppressed, had laid their plot how to cut all their throats in a morning, and upon the 22. of March, so innocently attempted it, they slew three hundred forty seven, set their houses on fire, slew their cattell, and brought them to that distraction and confusion within lesse than a yeare, there were not many more than two thousand remaining: the which losse to repaire the company did what they could, till they had consumed all their stocke as is said; then they broke,[88] not making any account, nor giving satisfaction to the Lords, Planters, Adventurers, nor any, whose noble intents had referred the managing of this intricate businesse to a few that lost not by it; so that his Majesty recalled their Commission, and by more just cause: then they perswaded King James to call in ours, which were the first beginners without our knowledge or consent, disposing of us and all our indevours at their pleasures.

---

87. A roarer is a wild and noisy reveler.
88. To broke is to negotiate or bargain and carries a suggestion of distaste.

NOTWITHSTANDING SINCE they have beene left in a manner, as it were, to themselves, they have increased their numbers
to foure or five thousand, and neere as many cattell, with plenty of
Goats, abundance of Swine, Poultry and Corne, that as they report,
they have sufficient and to spare, to entertaine three or foure hundred
people, which is much better than to have many people more than
provision. Now having glutted the world with their too much over-
abounding Tabacco: Reason, or necessity, or both, will cause them, I
hope, learne in time better to fortifie themselves, and make better use
of the trials of their grosse commodities that I have propounded,[89] and
at the first sent over: and were it not a lamentable dishonour so goodly
a Countrey after so much cost, losse, and trouble, should now in this
estate not bee regarded and supplied. And to those of New-England
may it not be a great comfort to have so neare a neighbour of their
owne Nation, that may furnish them with their spare cattell, swine,
poultry, and other roots and fruits, much better than from England.
But I feare the seed of envy, and the rust of covetousnesse doth grow
too fast, for some would have all men advance Virginia to the ruine of
New-England; and others the losse of Virginia to sustaine New-England, which God of his mercy forbid. [*Advertisements:* III, 271–274]

---

*John Smith wrote little about abstract questions, including the justice of
colonization. When he did take up that subject, his approach was to see
English settlements in America as following a long line of such plantations
reaching back to biblical days. The English themselves had been colonized by
the Romans and had learned of Christianity from them. This passage ends
with a statement that sums up Smith's world view.*

MANY GOOD religious devout men have made it a great question, as a matter in conscience, by what warrant they might goe
to possesse those Countries, which are none of theirs, but the poore
Salvages. Which poore curiosity will answer it selfe; for God did make
the world to be inhabited with mankind, and to have his name knowne
to all Nations, and from generation to generation: as the people increased they dispersed themselves into such Countries as they found

89. *Gross* means "common, plain, obvious."

most convenient. And here in Florida, Virginia, New-England, and Cannada, is more land than all the people in Christendome can manure, and yet more to spare than all the natives of those Countries can use and culturate. And shall we here keepe such a coyle for land,[90] and at such great rents and rates, when there is so much of the world uninhabited, and as much more in other places, and as good, or rather better than any wee possesse, were it manured and used accordingly. If this be not a reason sufficient to such tender consciences; for a copper kettle and a few toyes, as beads and hatchets, they will sell you a whole Countrey; and for a small matter, their houses and the ground they dwell upon; but those of the Massachusets have resigned theirs freely.

Now the reasons for plantations are many; Adam and Eve did first begin this innocent worke to plant the earth to remaine to posterity, but not without labour, trouble, and industry: Noah and his family began againe the second plantation, and their seed as it still increased, hath still planted new Countries, and one Country another, and so the world to that estate it is; but not without much hazard, travell, mortalities, discontents, and many disasters:[91] had those worthy Fathers and their memorable off-spring not beene more diligent for us now in those ages, than wee are to plant that yet unplanted for after-livers. Had the seed of Abraham, our Saviour Christ Jesus and his Apostles, exposed themselves to no more dangers to plant the Gospell wee so much professe, than we, even we our selves had at this present beene as Salvages, and as miserable as the most barbarous Salvage, yet uncivilized. The Hebrewes, Lacedemonians, the Goths, Grecians, Romans, and the rest, what was it they would not undertake to inlarge their Territories, inrich their subjects, and resist their enemies. Those that were the founders of those great Monarchies and their vertues, were no silvered idle golden Pharisies, but industrious honest hearted Publicans, they regarded more provisions and necessaries for their people, than jewels, ease and delight for themselves; riches was their servants, not their masters; they ruled as fathers, not as tyrants; their people as children, not as slaves; there was no disaster could discourage them; and let none thinke they incountered not with all manner of incumbrances, and what hath ever beene the worke of the best great Princes of the world, but planting of Countries, and civilizing barbarous and

90. *Coil* means "turmoil, tumult."
91. *Travell* for *travail*, meaning "hard work."

inhumane Nations to civility and humanity, whose eternall actions fils our histories with more honour than those that have wasted and consumed them by warres.

Lastly, the Portugals and Spaniards that first began plantations in this unknowne world of America till within this 140. yeares, whose everlasting actions before our eyes, will testifie our idlenesse and ingratitude to all posterity, and neglect of our duty and religion wee owe our God, our King, and Countrey, and want of charity to those poore Salvages, whose Countries we challenge, use, and possesse, except wee be but made to marre what our forefathers made, or but only tell what they did, or esteeme our selves too good to take the like paines where there is so much reason, liberty, and action offers it selfe, having as much power and meanes as others: why should English men despaire and not doe so much as any? Was it vertue in those Heros to provide that doth maintaine us, and basenesse in us to doe the like for others to come? Surely no; then seeing wee are not borne for our selves but each to helpe other, and our abilities are much alike at the howre of our birth and minute of our death: seeing our good deeds or bad, by faith in Christs merits, is all wee have to carry our soules to heaven or hell: Seeing honour is our lives ambition, and our ambition after death, to have an honourable memory of our life: and seeing by no meanes wee would be abated of the dignitie and glorie of our predecessors, let us imitate their vertues to be worthily their successors, or at least not hinder, if not further them that would and doe their utmost and best endevour. [*Advertisements:* III, 276–277]

INDEX